POLITICS, ALLEG

ESCAPING THE
BEAST

MICHAEL BURNS

Escaping the Beast
Politics, Allegiance, and Kingdom
© 2020 by Michael Burns

ISBN: 978-1-948450-99-7. Printed in the United States.

Illumination Publishers cares deeply about the environment and uses recycled paper whenever possible.

All Scripture quotations, unless indicated, are taken from the Holy Bible, New International Version, (NIV), Copyright © 2011, 2015 by Biblica, Inc. Used by permission. All rights reserved.

Cover design by Roy Appalsamy of Toronto, Canada. Interior layout by Toney Mulhollan. Copy editing by Amy Morgan.

Illumination Publishers titles may be purchased in bulk for classroom instruction, business, fund-raising, or sales promotional use. For information please email paul.ipibooks@me.com.

About the author: Michael Burns serves as a teacher in the Minneapolis-St. Paul Church of Christ. He is a graduate of Wesley Seminary of Indiana Wesleyan University (MA). He taught high school history in the central city of Milwaukee for nearly ten years. He is a national and international biblical teacher at churches and workshops. He teaches at the Ministry Development and Training Academies centered in Chicago, Illinois, and serves as an instructor in the Ministry Training Academies in Africa. He is the author of the C.O.R.E. Curriculum series of books, as well as *Crossing the Line: Culture, Race, and Kingdom,* and *All Things to All People: The Power of Cultural Humility.* He married his wife, MyCresha, in 1997. They have two sons and reside in Roseville, Minnesota.

.LUMINATION **iP**
PUBLISHERS

www.ipibooks.com
6010 Pinecreek Ridge Court
Spring, Texas 77379-2513

CONTENTS

Foreword

There are few things more polarizing than politics. There are even fewer things more difficult to meaningfully discuss than our different views, opinions, and deeply held beliefs about politics. This topic strikes to the core of who we are and how we see the world around us. Often, the things we believe about the world have been formed by years of family or cultural tradition, significant trauma or loss, economic experiences, or powerful formative ideologies passed on to us through influential leaders, educators, and politicians. Political beliefs of all varieties most likely contain some truth. The problem is, the passion we feel about our political beliefs leads us to conclude that our particular expression of them is the entire truth itself. That misguided passion is probably why there is a widely held belief that the best way to kill the good vibes of a dinner party or family gathering is to bring up politics or religion!

Speaking of religion, if the polarization caused by political discourse is alarming, even more alarming is how few Christians truly understand what it means to live as citizens of God's kingdom. Do we understand the significance of inviting King Jesus to be the Lord of our entire life? Are we sure we realize the work involved in voluntarily opening our minds to the viewpoints of people we disagree with, or sincerely suspending judgment on people we believe to be completely wrong? Even more challenging, do we really grasp the ramifications of practical living here on earth while giving allegiance only and fully to the eternal kingdom of God, which won't be completely realized until our lives here are over? Further, are we willing to allow a kingdom view of the things we hold so dear prevail, causing us to seek peace, harmony, and mutual respect among the diverse body of Christ? These are the questions that need to be engaged if we are to glorify God and be a light to the nations.

I can't think of anyone better to start such a conversation than Michael Burns. His life experience, devotion to God's word, and ability to simply articulate topics this sensitive and complex make him uniquely qualified. We have a growing friendship that has been built through work together on various committees, and our personal conversations have allowed both of us to grow in our appreciation for a wide variety of opinions and perspectives. I can honestly say there is much we agree on, but as in any meaningful friendship, there are areas where we differ. Even though Michael and I don't see eye to eye on everything in this book, our common commitment to kingdom living and our desire to imitate the self-emptying stance toward relationships modeled by Jesus continue to guide our way in this kind of discourse. We're both hoping that can be an example for people to follow as we travel down this road together. We don't have to agree on politics, but we do have to agree to love each other deeply.

I live and lead in Seattle, Washington. That is my local context for now. As of 2019, it is the most educated large city in America, and because of the tremendous growth of many successful technology companies, it represents a dizzying array of religious and political worldviews. Finding complete agreement on these things in our city is not possible. I'm realizing that finding total consensus on politics in the church isn't possible either, but I'm also not convinced that should be the goal. As you read and process the concepts in this book, my prayer for everyone is twofold.

First, I encourage you to honestly assess where your allegiance lies and how the answer to that informs your instincts, impulses, and priorities. This is no easy task, and it might be necessary to read this book a bit slower than usual, augmenting the things you read with prayer and reflection. It requires a tremendous amount of humility to sincerely listen to alternative viewpoints and to consider changing your mind on something that may be firmly embedded in your DNA. However, isn't that precisely what true spiritual transformation is all about? Having said that, I would suggest that we lose the idea of changing each other's minds on these things. If that is the goal, we shouldn't enter into discussions on these topics. Rather, if each individual allows God to expose the areas in their life that are not fully devoted to the kingdom, and then has the courage to make necessary adjustments in their heart and mind, I believe a greater Christian unity will naturally emerge.

Second, I think we would do well to expand the way we think about political issues by making sure our thinking is undergirded by solid biblical principles. I am legitimately concerned today as I see many ideas entering the church through the gateway of the society around us. Sadly, Christians today can be more passionately activated by current events than by God's timeless truth. One changes constantly; the other never changes. Information these days comes at us at an alarming rate, and with everyone putting it out there, it can feel like it's the truth! If Christians grab hold of these ideas and discuss them with either/or thinking, debate and division aren't far behind. If ideas are disputable, perhaps we need to engage in more dialogue that is both/and, or amplified by nuance. I would encourage all of us to allow God's word to be absolute truth, and our opinions on things like politics to be open to change.

I want to thank Michael for having the courage and conviction to step into this important space, and I want to thank you for taking the time to read what he has written. It has never been easy for Christians to have fruitful dialogue about these things, but instead of avoiding it altogether and separating, we choose to let God's word influence us toward a better understanding of each other. That is who we are.

—Daren Overstreet
Seattle, Washington

In *Escaping the Beast,* Michael Burns writes about things that are by their very nature serious and complex topics. Trying to author a Cliff Notes version of such topics is not only impossible, it is dangerous. According to the Apostle Peter, Paul wrote about some difficult subjects that were hard to understand. Further, some assumedly Christ professors misunderstood and mistaught what he wrote, bringing about dire consequences. Since this is such serious spiritual business, let's have the exact biblical quote injected here: "He writes the same way in all his letters, speaking in them of these matters. His letters contain some things that are hard to understand, which ignorant and unstable people distort, as they do the other Scriptures, to their own destruction" (2 Peter 3:16).

When addressing biblically relevant topics, writers have at least two basic options. One, they can simply write about various general aspects of that topic without trying to be comprehensive in treating it. For example, one could write about gratitude or honesty with the purpose of simply inspiring more of those qualities in the readers. Two, the author can address topics that are both highly significant and highly complex, in which case the content cannot be general or briefly treated. Such topics demand an exhaustive, detailed approach. Michael's writing falls into this second category.

With that in mind, what should our expectations be as we begin reading this material? We should expect to read very deliberately and patiently. Please avoid making quick judgments about what you are reading. In the real estate world, it is said that the three most important things are location, location, and location. Similarly, in the Bible-reading world, inclusive of writings on biblical topics, the three most important things are context, context, and context. If I were to quote single sentences or paragraphs from this book, you could come to quick conclusions and assumptions that would be totally wrong without the contexts from which they were taken. Therefore, I urge you (even plead with you) to read carefully and thoroughly and delay judgment until you have finished the entire context of each chapter and, ultimately, of the whole book.

You are about to embark on a reading journey through a fantastic book! Make no mistake about that. This doesn't mean that you will end up agreeing with everything Michael has written, but it does mean that even if you disagree on some points, you will never view the subject in the same way again. You are now in for quite a treat and an adventure. Dig in!

—Gordon Ferguson,
Minister, Teacher, and Author
McKinney, Texas

Introduction

I began following Jesus as his disciple in January 1999. From that moment on I have done my best to proclaim him as my Lord and call others to do the same. Over the intervening decades I have talked to countless people about Jesus and shared with them from the Scriptures my convictions about becoming his disciple.

I have talked to people who were deeply interested and who readily and passionately became disciples themselves. I have sat with people who were intrigued by the idea of following Jesus but had one thing they couldn't let go in order to do so. I have interacted with others who were never willing to go beyond an intellectual exercise when considering Jesus. I met some who initially agreed to study more about Jesus but quickly broke off the studies after being stung by some of his more challenging commands. But then, much to my surprise, after wrestling with their heart on their own, they came back weeks or months later, humbled and expressing a desire to truly make Jesus Lord of their life. And I have spoken with many people who simply had no interest in learning more about Jesus or being challenged by his call on their life.

In all those conversations and interactions, there is one reaction that I can honestly say I have never heard. I have shared the good news of the gospel with people in the United States, Israel, Europe, Asia, and across the continent of Africa, yet not once have I heard this response or seen this specific reaction. I have seen passion, disdain, ambivalence, and everything in between, but still not one person has reacted this way.

So, what am I talking about? Before I answer that, we need to get in our time machine and travel back to the first century.

Trouble in Thessalonica

As was his custom, Paul's first stop in most cities was the Jewish synagogue, where he proclaimed Jesus as the Messiah. His trip to Thessalonica was no different. He demonstrated through the Scriptures that the true Messiah was different from what they had been expecting. He was not the mighty military leader they were hoping would unify them to throw off Roman oppression.

Jesus was different.

What proof did Paul have that Jesus was the promised Messiah? Well, that was interesting. Paul's evidence was that he willingly suffered and died on a Roman cross. Yes, he also declared that Jesus had resurrected from the dead. But he lost most Jews at the cross part. Most Gentiles thought that resurrection was so absurd that that's where he lost them.

In what was becoming an all-too-familiar response for Paul, Thessalonica broke out into enraged riots. The angry mobs, unable to find Paul, turned their wrath toward Jason, who had welcomed Paul and Silas into his home, and other new believers in the area.

The scene must have been chaotic. The angry and riotous crowd pressed in on these believers who were barely dried off from their baptisms, ready to pour all their wrath down on them. "These men…have caused trouble all over the world," they screeched (Acts 17:6), but that was not the heart of their complaint.

What crime had Paul and Silas committed? What had they done that had so agitated these Roman Jews? Romans were quite tolerant of other religions, so hearing another Messiah proclaimed should not have bothered them. Claiming that Jesus was the representative of God certainly would have angered Jews, but that doesn't seem to be their charge. Why were they so upset about a message that simply shared with people the good news that Jesus had died in their place for their sins, and because of that, if they would just believe it, they could have their sins forgiven and go to heaven to be with God for eternity?

The crowd's reasons for their angry response tell us much about the nature of the gospel that Paul was declaring. What was their response?

There Is Another King

It's time to get back in our time machine and return to the present day. What is the response that I have never heard?

I've never once heard of anyone getting angry after hearing about Jesus and declaring this message as treasonous. But that is precisely what the people of Thessalonica claimed.

"These men who have caused trouble all over the world have now come here, and Jason has welcomed them into his house" (Acts 17:6–7a). But here comes the real trouble. "They are all defying Caesar's decrees, saying that there is another king, one called Jesus" (Acts 17:7b).

Saying there is another king? Defying Caesar's decrees? This sounds like a revolution. But there was no army, no political organization, no rebellion. Wasn't this just a spiritual message about forgiveness of sin and receiving Jesus as one's personal savior? Couldn't they accept Jesus as the center of their new religious beliefs and then be free to support whatever governmental system or ruler they wanted? Wouldn't becoming a Christian make them a better citizen? Perhaps we have come to understand the gospel very differently from how our first-century brethren did.

⌐ In fact, if we fully understood the gospel message in a way that would cause us to think it was downright treasonous, might that change radically the way we think about and approach the topic of politics in the twenty-first century?

This is serious stuff. Few things in life can be as divisive and rouse our passions as can politics. I have seen disciples walk away from their fellowship over matters that were strictly political. I have seen disciples stop interacting or even speaking to one another because of their differences in political ideology.⌐

Some disciples of Jesus are deeply political and become extremely passionate about their beliefs, even to the point of creating divides within the body of Christ. Can this be what God wants for the people of his kingdom? On the other end of the spectrum are disciples who have turned their faith into an exercise of piety, spurning any involvement in politics whatsoever. This may sound spiritual, but can a faith that has nothing to say about the injustices and inequities of the world really be what Jesus had in mind with the kingdom of God?

These are questions that we must wrestle with. Should we embrace politics in the church? Doesn't that open us up to inherent divisions that will constantly separate us? Should we avoid politics completely? But can we be comfortable with a political approach that, were we living in the nineteenth century, would keep us out of the fray and comfortable with not commenting on or fighting against a political evil like slavery?

Who should we vote for in the next election? Should we vote at all? What if we live in a country that doesn't have legitimate elections? What then should be our approach?

Why This Book?

When I wrote *Crossing the Line: Culture, Race, and Kingdom* in 2017, it was not my intent to write a book on politics. To be honest, it wasn't on my radar in the least. What changed my mind? My wife and I gave over eighty Crossing the Line workshops across the US and internationally between 2017 and 2020, and a clear pattern began to show itself. We could not really engage on issues of race, culture, and unity in God's kingdom without the question of politics coming to the forefront. It almost always seems to be one of the first questions asked during Q&A times.

For me, it has become unavoidable.

But perhaps I should never have thought that it would be anything other than that. After all, a young man walking around Israel in the first century implying that he was the Messiah and proclaiming that the time of God's promised kingdom had arrived were deeply political claims. We tend to think that the Roman "empire" and the "kingdom" of God are entirely different entities from differing realms, but that's not really true. The word *basileia*, which is translated "kingdom" in the New Testament, was one of the words that was used to describe the Roman rule. It was the Roman Empire or the Roman Kingdom. It was the same concept in the first century.

That meant that to make claims about the kingdom of God was a deeply dangerous and political act. To declare Jesus as Lord was a direct affront to Caesar as Lord. And to refer to Jesus as the Son of God was to re-employ one of the phrases that the Caesars liked to use to describe themselves.

In many respects, the kingdom of God is political in nature. There is simply no way around it. But it is important to ensure that we are giving allegiance to the kingdom and acting politically in biblical ways rather than worldly ways.

And that gets to the heart of why I decided to write this book. One of the main things that spurred me on to begin the journey of writing *Crossing the Line* was my concern over how disciples of Jesus seemed to be approaching issues of race and culture in ways that were conditioned by the world around them rather than steeped in biblical thought that emanated from kingdom ethics. That is my same concern surrounding our approach to politics. I hear many opinions from Christians regarding politics, but precious few of them are deeply rooted in the kingdom worldview. To my surprise, few of the books about Christianity and politics are rooted in kingdom thinking. Instead, many of them focus on and are rooted in logical and pragmatic thinking rather than being guided by the radical world-flipping perspective of God's kingdom.

In This Book

In this book, I will seek to first lay out, in Section 1, a comprehensive examination of the scriptural worldview of the kingdom and how that calls us to approach our discipleship and our place in the world. In Section 2, I will consider the role of nations and the politics of the nations and where the kingdom of God stands in those domains. Finally, in Section 3, I will look at the more practical elements of how a Christian community should navigate through the murky waters of worldly politics and specific issues. We will work hard to ensure that Jesus is our guide throughout the journey.

The third section will take the identity that I have attempted to describe and show it lived out in the real world. The first section is like running on a paved trail. The footing is secure and stable. As we move into the second section, we move to a dirt trail cut through a forest. The route is a bit more winding and less sure than the pavement, but still quite secure and straightforward. By Section 3 we are running through a swamp. The path is not set and the ground is often unsure, but we move forward trying to find our way as best we can. Because the third section is an attempt to apply principles in concrete situations, there is more room to disagree. Each topic broached in Section 3 could be its own book. I have attempted to introduce an approach to each subject without being so brief that it is unhelpful or counterproductive. My goal in that section is not to provide the absolute answer but to show how we might work our way through difficult and thorny topics with a kingdom-minded approach.

At no time, however, do I want to give the impression that I have all the answers or even that we will be able to find clear and concise answers to every question that might arise. These are complex topics. The best that we can hope for is to find kingdom principles that will point us in certain directions, with the clear understanding that we may not always come to the same conclusions. I do not imagine that this book is the final word on the role of Christians in politics. It is intended to be part of an ongoing conversation. I am writing this book for today's environment. Were I writing in the next generation or to another time and context, I might need to rethink some of the specific applications of principles I will suggest. The benefit of principles is that they can be applied in any context. The challenge of principles is that we constantly need to rethink and discern how best to apply them in our context.

I do believe, however, that if we establish a clear and accurate vision of what Jesus meant when he talked about the kingdom of God, that this will demystify much for us and make the way much smoother. I am convinced that many of our political divisions find their roots in the fact that we tend to not have a solid understanding of God's kingdom. That is why we will start from there and move out to questions of politics and the world. If we can agree on the kingdom and have that as the most important element in our lives, I believe the fissures between us will become much, much smaller and easier to traverse.

The importance of followers of Jesus finding a common direction in our political engagement is difficult to overstate. My own context as an American illustrates this well. My country has entered a time that is significantly divided politically. That partisanship has spilled over into the church in ways that are unprecedented, in our lifetime at least. In many respects it has handcuffed the church, preventing it from filling one of the important roles that it should be playing in society.

I don't believe that the church was formed by Jesus to serve as ruler over the nations or as a power broker, taking over countries and societies and directing them through legislation, political might, or any other means available. We are to be the light. We are to be an alternative. We are to be a picture of what it looks like to represent God's character through community in the world. And we are to invite people to join us in that vocation.

That means that we will operate with the identity of an alternate way of being human, serving as a contrast to the world around us. But it also means that we must be able to serve in a prophetic function by pointing out when the cultures around us have strayed from the life-giving role of image bearers that God wants for all humans.

And herein lies the problem when followers of Jesus yoke themselves to partisan political agendas, philosophies, or parties. We no longer operate as a true alternative nor can we fulfill the prophetic function. If I were to stand up today and criticize the Republican Party, one of its politicians, or the conservative political ideology as straying from God's character in a particular situation, I would be roundly criticized and attacked by the half of the church that ascribes to that side of the aisle. The opposite is also true. Were I to criticize some aspect of liberal or democratic philosophy or individuals from that party, I would be attacked by Christians who have accepted that side of the aisle as their "team." In short, we cannot fulfill an important aspect of the church's role because we have yoked ourselves with things that are not of the kingdom of God.

That is not to imply that these issues are simple to discuss or resolve. They are not. This book is not intended to be "the answer." My intent is to initiate a conversation. Many will disagree with some of what I write here. I am okay with that. I write what I write out of love for God's kingdom and a desire for it to be all that it can be. There are some who love God's kingdom as much as I do, and we will still not agree on everything. That too is okay. Conversations in love can be highly productive.

When addressing the deep cultural differences among believers in Rome, Paul advises them that "whatever you believe about these things keep between yourself and God" (Romans 14:22). Before he says that, though, Paul has spent nearly fourteen chapters showing them how they need to transform their minds and embrace the fullness of the kingdom. If they have done that, then the gaps between them will be small enough and they will be able to process their differences so that simply keeping it to themselves would be a plausible solution. Without all the work that leads up to it, though, I don't believe it would be tenable or practical.

I also need to add that politics is a broad topic, and it varies widely from region to region, country to country, continent to continent. It would be virtually impossible to address this topic in a way that is considerate and fair to every possible political context, concern, and situation. Yet the body of Christ is present in nearly every nook and cranny of the globe. With that in mind, I will stick mostly with the context that I know best, that of the United States of America, but I will attempt to do so only to serve as illustration and not with the view that this is the only political situation that matters. My hope is to use our context as a jumping-off point to apply biblical principles that can then be utilized and adjusted to each political situation, as similar or dissimilar as your context may be to my own.

Preparing to Read

One of the keys to understanding the Christian relationship with politics is to understand the drastic difference between the kingdoms of the world and the kingdom of God. There can be no blending of the two. We may hold passports from nations of the world, but we are first and foremost citizens of the kingdom of heaven. Allegiance to God's kingdom must determine our values, daily choices, and the entire direction of our lives. There simply cannot be confusion about our citizenship in God's kingdom and loyalty to it.

Throughout this book I will seek to address the stark contrast between these two kingdoms. To help the reader find clarity, I will usually refer to the ruling authorities in the human realm as "nations" or "empire." When referring to the realm of the kingdom of God, I will exclusively use the term "kingdom." As I noted above, they are described using the same term in the New Testament, which clarifies that they vie for the same allegiance of heart. We must choose one or the other. All empires are based on human wisdom and thinking and therefore are destined to fall in time. The great empire of the New Testament, Rome, "sleeps in the dust of history," as my friend Gordon Ferguson expressed it to me. Your nation is destined to do the same. Such is the fate of every nation.

Only the kingdom of God can stand the test of time. If we are saved by the blood of Christ, we are already in his eternal kingdom and seated with Christ "in the heavenly realms," as Paul puts it, in both the present age and the age to come (Ephesians 2:6–7). In confessing Jesus as Lord, we were transferring our allegiance from one kingdom to another on a permanent and total basis. On this there can be no confusion or vacillation. We may be in this world, but we are decidedly not of it.

The early church was on a collision course with the Roman Empire. In all ages since, followers of Christ should have been on the same collision course. If we don't see that or experience it, something in our understanding of true Christianity is obviously missing. In our present setting, our views of politics are perhaps the acid test of how well we understand the differences in these two realms.

These are not topics that can be breezed through in a few Tweets or fast-moving YouTube videos. Please resist the temptation of trying to scan the material quickly to "get the point." I plead with you to take the time to read carefully. Even if you don't agree with everything I'm saying—and I doubt that anyone will agree with absolutely everything in this book—wrestle with the material and the scriptures cited and come to your own Scripture-based conclusions. Then, join the discussion as we seek to be the kingdom of God in a world that so desperately needs it.

I will take the position in this book that we are to be an alternative community that lives and approaches the world in a very different way than could be found anywhere else. Admittedly, it would be a much easier book to write if I took the position that we should just withdraw from politics and the world as much as possible. I will not do that. It would be easier to merely encourage us to get involved in politics full bore but keep it to ourselves. I will not do that. To be an alternative community that engages in the world as the kingdom but not through the means that the world typically uses is incredibly complex. I should warn you that you will struggle with my perspective in this book if you equate the idea of engagement with the word "politics." We can, I will argue, engage with the world, but should do so by involving ourselves in the political system only to the degree that is necessary, utilizing kingdom methods when doing so.

With much fear and trembling and much prayer, I will press forward and hope that this book helps begin the conversation about who we can be and should be as representatives of God's kingdom in the world.

Section 1

The Kingdom of the Lamb

Chapter 1

Created to Co-Rule

A few years back my wife and I decided to plant a garden in our backyard at our new house. We didn't wisely start with a garden box or two, by the way. Go big or go home, so we plotted out an area of about 350 square feet and got to work tilling and planting. We seeded several tomato and grape tomato plants, several types of squash, cucumbers, onions, carrots, beans, and a large host of various types of pepper plants. We put a fair amount of work into that plot, although I can't currently recall any of the reasons why we thought that would be a good idea.

For the first month and a half of the summer season things were going very well. I had made something of a ritual of going out each morning and praying while I slowly weeded the area or did some other work that needed to be done. Some people talk about gardening being relaxing. I tried to find it relaxing, but after giving it a fair shot, I'm not sure I could honestly report that I ever achieved that state.

The garden was coming along beautifully, though, thriving under all the careful attention it was receiving. But then things changed. We left for over a month on a ministry trip throughout the continent of Africa and left our older son, who was in his early twenties at the time, and another single brother from our church who was also in his twenties and who was living with us, to be in charge of the house while we were gone. They did a good job caring for the house with one exception, the garden. I had asked that it be watered each day, weeded when necessary, and harvested when ready. But none of that was done the way it needed to be. Suffice it to say, we returned to a mess of underwatered plants, weeds growing out of control, and a lot of harvestable produce lying in the dirt, slowly rotting. In our absence, they had not done our will, which had dire consequences for that little plot of land.

The Starting Point

Jesus came into a messed-up world not all that dissimilar from ours today. There was violence, crime, aggression, oppression, starvation, corruption, neglect, and much more. There are so many things that Jesus could have targeted in his mission and ministry. He could have become the real king of the world and not just some character in a movie, hanging over the bow of a ship screaming that he was king of the world to impress a girl. Surely, he could have solved many of the ills of the world if he had taken such an approach. He could have ruled over the nations in all wisdom.

Or he could have taken another angle altogether and come simply to forgive the sin of the world. He could have come and declared that everyone was in sin and thus separated from God, and he was going to die on their behalf so that they could receive forgiveness for those sins and personal salvation. And while forgiveness of sin and reconciliation with God was certainly part of the effect of Jesus' ministry, it was not the focus of his preaching or his ministry.

What Jesus did declare from the very beginning of his ministry was that "the kingdom of God has come near" (Mark 1:15). When Jesus began to preach that the time for God's kingdom had arrived, what did his original hearers think he meant? And how did Jesus think that this message was good news for a world so steeped in sin, oppression, injustice, and division?

To really consider those questions and the implications that they might have for a book about Christianity and politics, we need to go back to the beginning.

The Garden Is Planted

If you were to sit down this morning and crack your Bible open to the first page and read the book of the beginnings, Genesis, you wouldn't get farther than two verses in before discovering that when God set about to put his creation in order, we are told of something hovering above the waters. The Hebrew word used to describe that something can be understood as "life-force," "breath," "wind," or "spirit." The animating force and spirit of God moves into the realm of darkness and chaos and begins God's work of bringing about the conditions for life to exist and to flourish.

When Jesus spoke of the Spirit to his Jewish followers John 14,16, it was the life-giving and animating life-force of God from Genesis 1:2 that would have been at the forefront of his audience's minds. The Spirit's role in Genesis 1 was to bring order out of chaos and darkness.

By the sixth day of creation, of course, God tops off his grand creation project by singling out human beings to be in his image. "Image" comes from the Hebrew word *tselem*, and it carries the idea of being the representative of something. In the ancient world, the phrase "image of God" also carried connotations of kingship. It was kings who were images of the gods, meaning they were the direct representative of the gods' will and rule. The shocking revelation of Genesis 1 is that all humans were tasked with this privilege and responsibility, not just a few powerful kings. God created all humans to work together as his image bearers to co-rule with him and represent his character and will into the creation. That doesn't imply that we have the right to rule over other human beings. The task is to mediate God's rule, not our own, into his world and subdue it as he would have us do. The human vocation, in essence, is to co-rule with God over all creation.

But that's a huge job. Think about that for just a moment. I have heard popular biblical teacher Tim Mackie speak on this aspect of the Spirit, which inspires my next question. Would you have the necessary wisdom to rule over an entire nation? That would entail an awful lot, wouldn't it? You would need to know about economics, sociology, environmental science, political theory, ecology, urban planning, and much, much more. Even working collectively, ruling over a city, region, or nation has proven to be a very difficult task for humans. But what about ruling over the entire planet? Imagine what you would have to know to pull that off. Can you even fathom the wisdom that would be necessary to rule over the entire globe so that every part of it prospered and worked together with all the others in peace and harmony?

Yet that is the role for which humans were designed, as Psalm 8 confirms:

> When I look at your heavens, the work of your fingers,
> *the* moon and *the* stars which you set in place–
> what *is* a human being that you think of him?
> and a child of humankind that you care for him?
> And you made him a little lower than heavenly beings,
> and *with* glory and *with* majesty you crowned him.
> You make him over the works of your hands;
> all *things* you have placed under his feet:

> sheep and cattle, all of them,
> and also *the* wild animals of *the* field,
> *the* birds of *the* sky and the fish of *the* sea,
> *everything* that passes along the paths of seas.
> Yahweh, our Lord,
> how majestic *is* your name in all of the earth! (Psalm 8:2–9 LEB)

It is this vision of humanity that Paul refers to when rebuking the Corinthian church for failing to arbitrate trivial matters within the church without having to take matters to the Roman courts. "Do you not know," he asks in 1 Corinthians 6:2, "that the Lord's people will judge the world?" He is thinking here of judging in the sense of presiding and ruling over. In fact, he goes on and queries, "Do you not know that we will judge angels?" Paul assumes that if the role of created humanity was to rule over all creation, then the restored humanity in Christ who will one day be fully reinstated to that position and function should start accessing that wisdom to govern now. Are they going to access God's wisdom to do so or not?

That's really the question that hangs in the air of the biblical text from Genesis on. Given the role to co-rule over creation, what wisdom are we going to access to complete such a monumental calling? The ancient way of referring to that wisdom is the knowledge of good and evil. That's what hangs in the balance in Genesis 2 and 3 with the tree of the knowledge of good and evil. Are humans going to rely on God to give them the wisdom that they need or are they going to exercise their own, thinking they can get the job done without God's wisdom? Can we properly care for creation without representing God's will? Will we be able to flourish, thrive, and bring life as God designed us to do?

In a nutshell, the kingdom of God is God's human creation co-ruling with him over all creation by accessing his wisdom and reflecting his character and will as we fruitfully spread to every corner, creating the conditions for life to flourish. The kingdom brings life to the world.

Trouble in the Garden

The serpent figure in Genesis 3 makes a simple proposition to Adam and Eve. He lures them into exercising their own wisdom and will over God's. They don't need God's wisdom, he tries to convince them. They don't need to co-rule. They have everything they need to operate within themselves to fulfill their function. They buy into it. What could be the harm?

Their bad choice has devastating results. When a garden is not properly cared for, it quickly falls into chaos. There are developing, though still somewhat controversial, theories in certain academic circles that the area around the Amazon river was once a carefully planned agricultural center that fed a huge indigenous population in that area. According to this theory, the population died out, presumably due to disease, and the Amazon basin was left to its own devices. If this theory is correct, the wilds of the Amazon are one giant example of a garden without proper gardeners. It teems with life but is difficult, if not impossible, for humans to live in.

The impact of throwing off God's wisdom for that of the human variety was immediate both for humanity and for our environment. Humanity spirals. Genesis 4 depicts the very first human murder, and by chapter 6, we are told that humanity could be described with the term "great wickedness," and that the "human heart was only evil all the time." That doesn't sound like a group with the proper wisdom to rule over the earth and subdue it, does it?

Is there evidence that the entire creation has suffered because of the gardeners not properly caring for it? Have we perfectly balanced the environment, the economies, the relationships of the world over the past millennia? Paul puts it this way:

> For the creation waits in eager expectation for the children of God to be revealed. For the creation was subjected to frustration, not by its own choice, but by the will of the one who subjected it, in hope that the creation itself will be liberated from its bondage to decay and brought into the freedom and glory of the children of God.
> We know that the whole creation has been groaning as in the pains of childbirth right up to the present time. (Romans 8:19–22)

Why is the creation waiting for the children of God to be revealed? The original wording of this passage says, "sons of God" rather than "children of God," and the difference is important. "Sons of God" carries with it a strong connection to kingship and ruling. What Paul is saying here is that the creation is messed up, and it is waiting for co-rulers who will do their job. God gave us that responsibility, and he won't do it for us. The choice to access human wisdom rather than to operate completely by God's wisdom has had devastating effects on every aspect of the globe and will continue to until God's plan is complete to fully restore a people in his image who will rule wisely with him.

The earth has been fractured in virtually every manner possible because of our failure to live up to the calling of being image bearers. We have failed to consistently bring life and order to the world. And that's because human wisdom simply isn't up to the task of filling the earth and subduing it.

By its very nature, human wisdom is limited to the perspective of one person or perhaps a small group of people who attempt to pool their wisdom. Because human wisdom is limited in its scope, it will be divisive by its very nature. There will be competing strands of perspective. If we rely on human wisdom, we will be divided. The only way to avoid that is if humanity could somehow all access the same universal wisdom. It would have to be a wisdom that is big enough to guide us through the gargantuan mission of exercising dominion over every aspect of the creation. Clearly, only the wisdom of God could fulfill that requirement.

This will come into play as we think about the kingdom of God and secular politics. Because worldly politics are based on human wisdom, they can do some good and they can do great harm, but they will by nature divide human beings. Differing perspectives, varying history, and divergent circumstances will result in competing strains of wisdom. Those unique lines of thinking and belief will subsequently end in different political theories and beliefs. And more often than not, differing political beliefs cause division between groups, parties, and of course, nations.

What God Separates

If we return to the Genesis story, landing in chapter 11, we find that human wisdom continues to be preferred over God's and it is once again causing major problems. To head off some of the destruction of this rebellion, God decides to separate humanity into language groups and cultures. This is surely not his optimal will but a temporary measure.

Yet it is powerful. When preachers are about to introduce a newly married couple, they will often declare, "What God has joined together let no person tear asunder." The opposite is equally true, although we don't often think about it. What God has separated, no human will be able to put back together until God causes it to happen. God separated the nations, and humanity has tried many times throughout history to bring the nations back together using various methods, to no avail. We have tried through seemingly peaceful and positive means of diversity and love. Powerful men like Alexander the Great tried to bring the world together as one with varying degrees of force. But whatever the means, they all failed equally.

The very next chapter of Genesis depicts God coming to an insignificant man named Abram and promising that he would one day bless the nations and bring them back together somehow through his descendants (Genesis 12:1–3). This promise was returned to often in the pages of the Old Testament in passages like Isaiah 2:1–4; 42:4, 6; 49:6; 60:2–3; 66:18; Psalm 22:27; 67:1–2; Jeremiah 16:19–21; and Zechariah 2:11. God would one day gather the nations, doing what no group of humans could do in the power of their own wisdom.

Although occasionally humans have tried to bring the world together under one banner, most often their wisdom has led in the other direction, toward division and tribalism. This way of thinking became so entrenched that even many Jews before the coming of the Messiah thought that when the Messiah came, he would strike at the pagan nations and keep them separated. We can see this line of thought in the first-century-BC apocryphal book, the Psalms of Solomon.

> See, Lord, and raise up for them their king, the son of David,
> to rule over Israel, your servant, in the time which you chose, o God.
> Undergird him with the strength to destroy the unrighteous rulers,
> to cleanse Jerusalem from Gentiles who trample her to destruction;
> to drive out in wisdom and in righteousness the sinners from the inheritance;
> to crash the arrogance of sinners like a potter's jar;
> to smash all their substance with an iron rod;
> to destroy the lawless nations with the word of his mouth;
> to make the nations flee from his presence
> at his threat and to put sinners to shame by the word of their heart.
> (Psalms of Solomon 17:21–25)

The great hope of this psalm is that God would come one day through his Messiah and liberate Israel from their oppressors using politics and power. This is the hope of most nations. We have come to accept division as normal and even a good thing, as long as our tribe, group, or nation comes out on top and is free to do as we choose.

Humans were designed by God to mediate his perfect wisdom to every corner of his creation, but we have failed in that vocation. Our limited and fractured human wisdom has created an environment that is inequitable and uneven. It is beautiful for some and horrendous for others. It teems with overwhelming surplus for a few while many suffer crushing lack.

Why the Kingdom?

How could God possibly resolve the massive global problems humanity had created by accessing nothing more than various shades of its own wisdom? That's really the question. When Jesus came claiming to be God's long-awaited Messiah, how was he going to even begin to fix this massive catastrophe? His preaching centered on the kingdom of God, but how would that bring life and order to a world of "welter and waste"?[1]

Before we consider those questions, though, it will help us on our journey to look at the relationship between the nation of Israel and God and their connection to the political world of the other nations.

The Chapter in Review

- The Spirit brings life and order into places of darkness and chaos.

- Humans were created as God's image bearers for the purpose of reflecting his will into creation.

- Caring for creation as image bearers demands the encompassing wisdom of God.

- Our own wisdom is too small for the monumental task of creation care.

- Human beings have used our own wisdom and failed to bring life and order to the world.

- Humans, in our wisdom, have created an environment that is fractured, inequitable, and uneven.

The Big Idea

❖ Humans were created to co-rule God's realm utilizing his wisdom.

DISCUSSION QUESTIONS

1. If the role of the Spirit in Genesis 1 was to bring light and life to darkness and chaos, and humans are to mimic the work of bringing the order and life of God's wisdom to chaotic situations, what does that mean for the role of the church in the world today?

2. What are some areas in which even the church, and individual Christians, seem to utilize man's wisdom rather than God's?

3. What are some of the major problems that the world faces today due to utilizing human wisdom as the ruling standard?

Chapter 2

The Prophetic Community

In 1999, the supernatural drama, *Sixth Sense*, written and directed by M. Night Shyamalan, was released in theaters. The movie starred Bruce Willis as patient and insightful child psychologist Malcolm Crowe, who works with a frightened young boy, Cole Sear, played by Haley Joel Osment. Cole appears to be a deeply disturbed youngster who has trouble fitting in with children his age. Even his loving mother is deeply distressed by him and has apparently reached out to Crowe for help. As Crowe earns Cole's trust, the boy finally opens up with his therapist about his real problem. He is not mentally disturbed or ill, it's just that he sees ghosts constantly. They come to him, says Cole, because he is one of the few people that is tuned in enough to see them. But these ghosts have passionate agendas. They are all the victims of injustice of some kind and reach out to Cole for help.

The film is an engaging piece that explores the relationship that the doctor and his young patient slowly develop as Malcolm comes to believe and then tries to help Cole resolve the tragic issues that the dead are coming to him for in desperation. Cole explains to Malcolm that the dead need help but one of their main problems is that they don't know they're dead.

Admittedly, the film is slow at points and seems to drag ever so slightly. Just as we think we understand what the movie is about, though, everything is turned upside down. Spoiler alert: In one of the most famous twists in Hollywood history, it is suddenly revealed near the end of the movie that Malcolm is himself one of the dead. He has latched onto Cole because Cole can see and hear him, but the doctor is unaware that he has been murdered and needs to resolve his own case of injustice. In an instant, the movie that we thought we were watching takes on an entirely new spin and nearly every scene is recast in meaning and purpose. Malcolm Crowe was dead the whole time and never realized it.

In similar fashion, it is easy to think that we know what being a Christian is all about. But then we come across a concept that has been there all along, yet we may have missed it or not grasped the significance of it. Suddenly, everything is shifted. I believe that twist for Christians will happen when we understand the concept of being the prophetic community and how it will guide our role as kingdom people in the world.

The Prophetic Revolution

Humanity had rejected God's wisdom and the results were disastrous. This world was made to operate with God at the helm, as King, so to speak. Without God's wisdom, without his kingdom, humanity devolved into division and chaos.

God didn't leave us to wallow in that, though. He came to Abraham and laid out his plan to become King once again. But he would not force us to bow to him as King. It always has been and always will be a choice. He would work through Abraham and his descendants to create a kingdom that would gather the splintered people groups back into one people again.

But it quickly became obvious that Israel could not be the ultimate fulfillment of those promises. Yes, they were chosen by God as his special people, but they were every bit as rebellious and prone to trust their own wisdom as any other nation or empire. Soon, Abraham's descendants found themselves in servitude in Egypt. They had no identity and could certainly not be claimed to be the kingdom of God in any special way. But he brought them out of Egypt and out of slavery. He would form them to be a people with a new way of being in the world. To accomplish this, he sent them Moses, a man with the voice of a prophet.

When we think of what a prophet is and what he does, we need to avoid some of our modern constructs that twist the role. Biblical scholar Walter Brueggemann says that liberal thinkers tend to reduce prophets to radical leftists who are almost exclusively concerned with social justice in the present. Conservative thinkers, says Brueggemann, tend to see the prophet as future teller and want only to escape the present and know about prophecies that allegedly point to when that will finally happen. In the meantime, they try to control and shape the present to bring about the expected future, while at the same time escaping its realities in every way possible and living solely for the future.

Moses came with a prophetic voice. He brought what Bruegge-mann labels the prophetic revolution.[2] The true calling of the proph-et is to offer people a new consciousness, a new way to think and to approach life. The prophet speaks of the future but not to predict it. For him, the future is a signpost that anchors our affections and imag-inations to what the world would look like if God were really King. He will be King in the age to come, so the prophet beckons people to em-brace that future reality in the present and to work out what it would look like to live that way while still mired in the current reality of a fallen age.

The prophet doesn't aim to solely fix the problems of the present age or to get people to simply hold on until the evacuation can take place. Prophets light the fires and fan the flames of a consciousness that embraces an alternative way of being human in the world. Those who accept the message become a community of imagination that dares dream what the world could be were God the king and then seeks to live that out, regardless of the cost.

A word of clarification here. The prophet does want justice for the people of their day, and they will acknowledge the need for people to repent and strive for justice in the here and now. It is normal and good to react to present-day problems with humble conviction toward the injustices that we or others face and to want to make them right. We will return to this concept in the third section of this book. The pro-phetic community does care about justice; however, justice in the present age does not become its chief concern that trumps all others.

Prophet don't critique the culture just to bash it or show it how messed up it is. They don't become obsessed with social justice, as though the primary concern is to achieve equity, fairness, and justice in the present age. They know that the only solution for the present age lies in the future of God's kingdom. They don't become preoccu-pied with escaping this age and wait for the future either. The prophet seeks to create an alternative society that is rooted in the reality and values of the future by dismantling the addictions that people have to the life of the present age and the empires of power and provision.

This was what Moses offered in the escape from Pharaoh's Egypt. Egypt, like all empires, offered stability, affluence, and security through control, power, and optimism about the present conditions and age. Led by the Spirit, Moses didn't seek to escape one empire only to create another. He offered the people the freedom of living under God's rule.

Through the prophetic voice of Moses, God gave the people a new way of living and being human in the imperial age. He gave them a law that would retrain their consciousness and way of approaching the world. He gave them new holidays, a new weekly routine, a new way of interacting; in short, he gave them an entirely new culture that was rooted in his kingdom of the future.

They would have no king except God and had access to his wisdom as their ruling guidelines. Moses rooted his revolution in critique of the power of his day, Egypt. Through the plagues, he demonstrated that the great empire could not come through on their promises of the good life. It was a mirage that gave affluence and comfort to some at the expense of a great many. Egypt, like all empires, rooted existence in the present alone. When they thought about the future, it was completely predicated on the present. For empires, the future doesn't inform the present. They would rather maintain and increase the power they have. That's the extent and value of the future for them.

For empires, the politics of justice and compassion give way to the pursuit of affluence and sovereignty to control and determine their own fate. Order eclipses the freedom to truly choose. Security surpasses justice. The present outweighs the future. God is no longer needed as their king. At best God or the gods are used to keep people in line and keep them happy so that the empire can maintain the status quo.

The prophetic voice of Moses showed all that to be a sham. He didn't just criticize the empire, he demonstrated that it was devoid of true life. Empires make people numb to injustice, true freedom, and death. They need a certain measure of those things to incite a need for security and to create prosperity for the rest.

Moses called people to the danger of the desert. Here they were free to imagine what the future would look like in the present. What would be possible if a group of people made the choice to live under God's kingly rule and trust him alone? But empire would be a constant temptation, whether it was going by the name of Egypt, the Canaanites, Babylon, or any other. They would have to constantly retrain and restrain their consciousness to the future hope and let it mold them into a radically alternative way of life in the present.

Moses had three tasks within his prophetic calling. The first was to critique the empire and draw the people's hearts away from it. The second was to ignite their passion and imagination toward an alternative society based on the hope of the future, which for them was initially the promised land, but slowly morphed into the hope of living fully in God's kingdom and presence one day. The third task was to persevere, create resilience, and maintain allegiance to living under God's reign.

And it worked, for nearly half a millennium. It worked imperfectly, to be sure. But this revolution stood out in the world until around 1,000 BC. For hundreds of years, the descendants of Abraham had no king except God alone, although their collective consciousness often drifted back toward the lust for empire. But there was no empire in Israel. There was only the prophetic imagination of a society living in the present that was informed by the hope of the future.

The Siren's Call of an Emperor

Contrary to popular belief, having a human king was always part of God's plan for Israel. But it would be his type of king: one who maintained the prophetic community and who was nothing like the monarchs and emperors of the world. According to Deuteronomy 17:14–20, Israel's king must: (1) be chosen by God; (2) not be a foreigner; (3) not build an army (many horses); (4) not amass multiple wives; and (5) not amass wealth. But even more importantly, (6) he would be rooted in God's word, carrying it with him and reading it daily. He would lead Israel in devotion to God's word. Thus, he would keep them focused on being the prophetic community. The mistake Israel made when they clamored for Saul to be king was that they wanted a king "such as all the other nations have" (1 Samuel 8:5) rather than the type of non-warrior king who would lead them in study of the Torah.

Israel lost the imagination of the prophetic community in their desire for the normality and security of empire. They wanted a king like the nations around them, and God conceded, giving them the quintessentially impressive king by human standards in Saul, all the while reminding them through the prophetic voice among them, Samuel, that it was really God whom they were rejecting as their ruler and source of wisdom by not choosing the type of king he had told them to select. He warned the people again, though, as he had done as far back as Deuteronomy, what investing in empire would cost them. And it would be a lot. Kings live for the present and so must amass wealth and power to secure it.

So, even when David became king, a tradeoff was made. David was a mixture between kingdom and empire. His heart belonged to God, but his feet were often rooted in the values of empire. His rule, then, was an overlap of the prophetic community and the coming monarchy. He was a man after God's own heart (1 Samuel 13:14), yet he was not to build God a temple because he was a warrior (1 Chronicles 28:3). It was as if God gave the people a time to see both realities. David's reign pointed both to God as King and to empire.

Solomon's reign was not ambiguous at all, at least not for long. He began with a desire for God's wisdom, but soon corrupted it by soaking it in a pure formula of empire. He became the monarch in every imperial sense of the word. He took what he needed to maintain and even expand his imperial rule, and the necessary numbness crept into the hearts of the people. He veered from every description of God's type of king in Deuteronomy 17, and the people became blind to injustice and inequity. Israel had the veneer of God, but they became an empire like any other.

So, once again, God sent the prophetic voice. This time it wasn't just through one man, but through many prophets over a long period. They offered the same revolution as Moses. Solomon's vision was contrary to that of Moses. The Mosaic revolution was rooted in future hope; the Solomonic kingdom no longer needed God as King. While trumpeting God as King, Solomon and his successors quietly removed God from his throne in Israel. Everything they needed they had in the opulence of Solomon's kingdom.

But the prophets offered another vision. Once again, they would critique the empire, but this time the empire had become God's own people. That doesn't mean that they were the dominant empire of their day but that they had embraced the imperial consciousness. We will briefly consider the roles of Jeremiah and Isaiah to represent the vocation of the prophet during the monarchy.

The Prophetic Critique

Jeremiah's ministry clearly characterizes the prophet's role of critic. He especially carried it out through grieving. Grieving is necessary for the new community that wishes to escape empire, because it must admit that the security of the imperial is a fraud. Despite giving all impressions to the contrary, the empire will end because they all do. Anything built on the present or the past is doomed to fail. Only the society constructed on God's future will endure. We must grieve the end of the empire. We must come to the reality that it is not the embodiment of good. It is not the best version of humanity that ever existed. Almost all empires tell themselves that story, but it is nothing more than a child's fairytale that we are as ready to believe as we once were in Santa Claus, because we want to believe it. We need to believe it. And when we finally have our eyes opened by the prophet, we must mourn.

> Oh, my anguish, my anguish!
>> I writhe in pain.
> Oh, the agony of my heart!
>> My heart pounds within me,
>> I cannot keep silent.
> For I have heard the sound of the trumpet;
>> I have heard the battle cry.
> Disaster follows disaster;
>> the whole land lies in ruins.
> In an instant my tents are destroyed,
>> my shelter in a moment.
> How long must I see the battle standard
>> and hear the sound of the trumpet? (Jeremiah 4:19–21)

Jeremiah writhes in emotional agony because his eyes are opened to the fact that what he has known and trusted in will fall. Israel is no longer the prophetic society, calling to the world's empires to come join her in a different way of life. They wanted to be like the other nations and have succeeded. No longer alternative to the beast of empire, they have become just another monster.

> "My people are fools;
>> they do not know me.
> They are senseless children;
>> they have no understanding.
> They are skilled in doing evil;
>> they know not how to do good." (Jeremiah 4:22)

God's own prophetic community has lost their imagination for the future. They are satisfied with the present. They think they possess wisdom, but they have only exchanged the truth for a lie.

> How can you say, "We are wise,
>   for we have the law of the LORD,"
> when actually the lying pen of the scribes
>   has handled it falsely?
> The wise will be put to shame;
>   they will be dismayed and trapped.
> Since they have rejected the word of the LORD,
>   what kind of wisdom do they have?
> Therefore I will give their wives to other men
>   and their fields to new owners.
> From the least to the greatest,
>   all are greedy for gain;
> prophets and priests alike,
>   all practice deceit.
> They dress the wound of my people
>   as though it were not serious.
> "Peace, peace," they say,
>   when there is no peace. (Jeremiah 8:8–11)

They cry peace, they trust prosperity, but the people have been fooled by the false prophets among them who sound wise but are only enticing them to trust in the wisdom and political empires of the world. It must end.

> Are they ashamed of their detestable conduct?
>   No, they have no shame at all;
>   they do not even know how to blush.
> So they will fall among the fallen;
>   they will be brought down when they are punished,
> says the LORD. (Jeremiah 8:12)

And so it will end. Jeremiah tried to call the people out of their numbness and blindness to once again be the prophetic community, but they would not listen. Such is often the plight of the prophet.

The Prophetic Call to Ignite

We will look at Isaiah to help us understand the renewed hope based on the future and aimed at countercultural living. It is not as though Jeremiah only grieved and never sought to energize the people to action or that Isaiah never engaged in critique or the necessary time of grief. Rather, we look at these two to represent the full message of all prophets and merely highlight what was the centerpiece or focus of the prophetic call of each.

Isaiah knew that the time of Israel as empire would end. It must and it would. It was not the imperial consciousness that held hope for the future. Hope lay only in God's kingdom. Isaiah understood that hope rooted in the present age will be co-opted by the powers of this age. His hope was on the coming King and his kingdom. He would be the one to go forward with the call to look to God's presence (Isaiah 6:8–13) and to a future kingdom (Isaiah 11:1–13) as the hope that would inform who they were in the present. Isaiah's hope was almost entirely future oriented in the coming of the kingdom. This hope is the proclamation that we do not have to be citizens of an empire. There is a different way. When their imagination was filled with the kingdom, they would live out that reality and distinguish themselves as a true alternative to the world's empires.

Isaiah called them to see the servant who would suffer for the benefit of others (Isaiah 53) but who would become a light to the nations in so doing (Isaiah 49:6, 12). And he consistently pointed to a time when God would become king over his people (Isaiah 24:23; 33:22; 52:7), as did other prophets (Zephaniah 3:15; Zechariah 14:9).

Prophetic Success?

The prophets, including Jeremiah and Isaiah, succeeded in their critique of the system of empire, oppression, and the folly of human wisdom set against God's wisdom. They were right in the response to constantly call the people of Israel to mourn. Israel had rebelled against God and failed to be resilient in maintaining allegiance to the prophetic revolution of Moses.

In the end, Israel didn't want to be free from Egypt or the other empires. They wanted to be their own version of imperial greatness and thus lost their grip on being a true alternative. The beginning of the Davidic and Solomonic reign seemed like the golden age for Israel, but it was really just the beginning of the end. They lost their vision as the renewed humanity. The world would have to wait for a solution.

In the period of the prophets, though, we see a pattern emerge that is important to our understanding of the role that followers of Jesus can have in the world today.

First, it is necessary for a prophetic community to wake from their slumber and shake off the numbness to power, inequity, and death that empire instills. We serve as a critique of the nations. It is not simply to slander the culture around us or to criticize just to distinguish between our group and the rest of the world. It is criticism rooted in waking people to the fraudulent claims of empires. It is to recognize that no empire or nation, however benevolent or wise they might seem, is the kingdom of God. The prophetic community creates a clear distinction between our identity and the world in which we live. We understand that while we may live in a certain country or nation, that is not our primary citizenship. We embrace the reality that the empires will end, that they must end. And we seriously wrestle with the question of who really is the king or kingdom on which we set our hope and loyalty.

Second, fueled by the consciousness of the critique and with our eyes opened to failure of the great empires, we reorient our hope. The present is not devoid of meaning, something only to be escaped. But neither is it the dwelling place of true hope and security. For the prophetic community, the future is where hope resides. We become energized not from political strategy or social engineering, but from the freedom that God gives to imagine an alternate society. We become a people invigorated to look to God's future to find what we are to value and how we are supposed to live, and then we have the courage to live that way now, despite the cost. The prophetic community must keep our values anchored in the future while fighting to demonstrate what that future looks like to the present, so that it will not be co-opted by the flash and lure of empire.

Third, we create the alternative society, which offers people a different vision of what life can and should look like and what the purpose is for the community. This prophetic community must avoid thinking like empire or once again becoming enamored with the power and success of the world, knowing that the world will constantly try to woo the alternative society back to a thinly veiled version of itself. Please don't hear at this point that I am advocating for complete withdrawal or an approach of simply being unconcerned with the affairs of the world. [I am not arguing that we care about "spiritual matters" only and let the world fend for itself. We must be involved in the world to show it a true alternative, but we must also be careful that the alternative doesn't slowly allow in the ways and means of the world and, in effect, become just another flavor of the world's system.]

Fourth, we must remain resilient. We must remain allegiant to God and his vision for the present that looks at the world through the lens of the future kingdom. The kingdom comes as we do God's will on earth as though we were already in the heavenly saturated future (Matthew 6:10). But the kingdom can be lost as well. We must continue to recognize the smell of empire and be wary about splitting our allegiance.

The Chapter in Review

- Moses introduced a prophetic revolution, offering a glimpse of what it would look like if God became King.

- The prophet calls the people to become an alternative community of imagination that, despite the costs, lives out what it might be like if God were King.

- The lure of empire with all its security and power is a constant temptation for the prophetic community.

- David's rule over Israel pointed both to the imperial system of the world and to God as King.

- After Solomon, the prophets began to criticize Israel as just another empire among the nations.

- Hope lies only in God's kingdom, not in the empires.

- Prophetic communities critique the nations and empires to demonstrate the differences between them and the kingdom of God.

- Prophetic communities work to demonstrate that true hope is found in God's rule and kingdom alone.

- Prophetic communities create an alternative society to offer a different vision of what life can be.

- Prophetic communities must work to maintain allegiance to God over the nations.

The Big Idea

❖ God administers his co-ruling with humans through an alternative community that serves to call people away from the life offered to them in the empires.

DISCUSSION QUESTIONS

1. How would it change the mission and identity of most churches if they were to see themselves as a prophetic community?

2. In what ways is your church community a prophetic community right now? In what ways does it demonstrate a life that is virtually indistinguishable from the nations?

3. What are the biggest temptations that pull at our allegiance to God's kingdom and being the prophetic community?

Chapter 3

The King Who Would Not Be King

By the reigns of Caesars Augustus and Tiberius, the prophetic community of Moses, Jeremiah, and Isaiah had all but disappeared. Judea was under the rule of the iron fist of the mighty Roman Empire, perhaps the greatest and most powerful empire in the world to that point. It was the empire of empires. Rome had set itself up as the great hope in the cosmos that would save the world and bring peace to humankind. The great eagle empire would fulfill the hope of humanity. The hope of the prophetic imagination, though, was like a flickering flame hanging on to the last thread of charred wick just before it is snuffed out for good.

By the dawn of the first century, the people of Israel had splintered into factions. The Herodians grabbed power in Judea by ingratiating themselves to the force of Rome and by exploiting the dearly held religious traditions of the people and giving pretense to respecting those values and traditions. Rather than critiquing empire, they were tightly intertwined with it.

The Sadducees were a powerful group that controlled the high priest position and much of the Sanhedrin, the ruling council of the Jewish people. They were staunch religious conservatives who believed only in the "founding documents" of the books of Moses and rejected any hope of a future resurrection or messianic age. They too embraced empire, because it was the source of their influence and power.

The Pharisees were a deeply religious group that had caught the imagination of the people. They held no formal power but were very influential and progressive in many respects. They believed deeply in the coming resurrection age as a time when God would end the present age and begin to rule the world as King through Israel. But sinful Israel was the obstacle that kept this from happening. God would not return as King, they believed, until all sin had been eradicated from Israel. So they held very tightly to the Law, claiming that if Israel would fully observe the Law, even for a day, that God would send his Messiah, defeat the Romans, and install his kingdom. Their hope was solely in the future. For them, empire was something to be endured until God would come and fix everything and they could finally escape.

The Zealots rejected empire, yet embraced it more tightly than any other group, all at the same time. They despised Rome's rule over them and plotted to throw it off through whatever political and military means were necessary. They wanted to escape empire through the very method and means of empire. They critiqued the current embodiment of empire, namely Rome, but not the idea of empire itself. They simply wanted a self-determined form that worked for their benefit.

Finally, there were the Essenes. They believed in the danger of empire and that it had tainted the whole world. So they escaped to the wilderness as the set-apart community that would protect themselves from outside influence. They gave up on society as being hopeless but in withdrawing gave up an opportunity to truly provide an alternative way of living to the world around them. In that, they failed to be a prophetic community because they were not visible or accessible to the average person. They were insulated and safe from the world and lived their lives in the present in a way that was entirely formed by the future. They critiqued empire by withdrawing and embraced the future hope but didn't serve as a light or open the eyes of the world to the emptiness of empire.

I have neatly packaged and oversimplified these groups and their beliefs for ease of understanding the general situation of the first century. As with our own day, these groups were not so easy to define and identify at the time, and not everyone fit neatly within the thought system of one group to the exclusion of all others.

Empire and Allegiance

The whole world was not ruled by Rome in the first century, but it sure could have easily seemed that way to many. The Roman Empire was king from modern-day England to Africa, and modern-day Syria to Spain. About one out of every four human beings on earth lived under Roman rule.

Rome had once been a thriving republic, but no more. By the dawning of what we recognize as the first century, the emperors ruled Rome. As the power of the great empire grew, so did the esteem for the emperor. As the first century wore on, the emperors were viewed increasingly as living gods on earth. They gave themselves nicknames or monikers such as "son of god," "lord," "the divine one," or "the august one." The methods were decidedly human and rooted in their incredible power, but the hope that the empire professed sounds almost biblical to our ears. Rome, under the guidance of the supreme ruler Caesar, would bring peace on earth and good will to humanity. They would bring the nations together in peace under one lord. And it seemed wonderful, as long as one didn't pick up the rug of this Roman peace and find stashed under it a rotting heap of violence, war, oppression, and subjugation of those who would not embrace empire.

Allegiance to Caesar was demanded and expected. Cities or nations that wavered in their allegiance would soon find themselves on the ground with the inescapable boot of Rome pressing down hard against their windpipe. Every knee would bow either willingly and appreciatively or at the business end of a sword.

There was one thing that was clear in the world of the Roman Empire: Caesar was lord. To question that was to put your life in great peril.

Another King

Jesus was not just a religious leader. He didn't come to offer a new philosophy or even present himself as just another god. If he had done that, Rome would not have minded much. They were quite tolerant of religions, even new or strange ones. If one paid proper respect to Roman power, they were quite happy to accommodate. And even if a group of people rejected the Roman gods, they might think them strange, they might not like them, they might even get into conflict from time to time, but they were mostly okay with even that, as long as there was no question about their allegiance to Rome. Have whatever gods you want, as long as your primary loyalty is to the empire itself.

One of the clear messages of the Gospels is that Jesus was a rival king to all others, especially Caesar. Matthew identifies him as the son of David (Matthew 1:1), a clear reference to kingship in Jewish thinking. He identifies Jesus as the king of the Jews, a rival king to Herod who is sought out by the Magi from the east (Matthew 2:2). Luke focuses on the newborn Jesus as a very different kind of rival to Caesar (Luke 2:1–3). During his last week, Jesus entered Jerusalem on a donkey, in a clear nod to the kingly prophecy of Zechariah 9:9. When asked directly if he was the king of the Jews, Jesus didn't deny the identification (Matthew 27:11), which prompted Pilate to have a sign hung over the cross that read, "This is Jesus, the king of the Jews" (v. 37).

The term "Christ" that we are so accustomed to that we sometimes act like it was Jesus' last name is the Greek form of the word "Messiah," which means "anointed one." This idea was so closely associated with being king in the Jewish thinking of the first century that some newer Bible translations have taken to rendering passages that speak of "Jesus Christ," as "King Jesus."

Paul used the term "Christ" or "king" to refer to Jesus more than any writer. In Romans 1:2–4, Paul introduces Jesus, and nearly every word is saturated with ties to kingship or rulers at the time, including "gospel," "descendant of David," "appointed the Son of God in power," and "Jesus Christ our Lord." Paul also presents Jesus in Colossians as the king over all creation (Colossians 1:15–20; 2:10; 3:15). Truly, he is the "King of kings and Lord of lords" (1 Timothy 6:15; Revelation 19:16).

From the moment of Jesus' birth, something happened that challenged empire to its core. God had installed his king (Psalm 2:6). The angels break into the present realm, unable to contain their exuberance. There was no glory to Caesar or the mighty empire. The glory was to God in the highest heaven (Luke 2:14). Brueggemann says, "The birth of the new king, the one Rome did not anticipate and Herod could not stop, beings another history, which carries in it the end of all old royal histories."[3]

This message of a new order began not with the powerful and privileged, but it was for the ears of shepherds, those who well new the oppression and inherent unfairness of the old order. This new king was one of them. He would be found in an animal feeding trough, indicating that he wasn't born to a wealthy or powerful family. He was ordinary.

This king had created a new category that would not fit into the standard category of empire. This would not be the sort of order in which power and authority exist to dominate and direct or even manipulate others for the benefit of a few (Matthew 20:25). Instead, the work of this king would be for the benefit of the world. He would bring light to the darkness. "The blind receive sight, the lame walk, those who have leprosy are cleansed, the deaf hear, the dead are raised, and the good news is proclaimed to the poor" (Luke 7:22).

Jesus and the Prophetic Community

Jesus was king here to inaugurate a rival kingdom to those of the world, but that kingdom was not like the others. It was not rooted in the power structures and values of the world. His kingdom was in this world and for this world but was not of the world (John 17:16), meaning that its origins and power were rooted in God's presence, not in the authority of any earthly ruler or empire.

This kingdom would stand in stark contrast to all others because it was the fulfillment of Moses' revolution. This would be the prophetic community.

When Jesus arrived in Nazareth near the beginning of his public ministry, he went to the synagogue on the Sabbath and was selected to read that day. The passage he read was from Isaiah 61.

> "...because he has anointed me
>   to proclaim good news to the poor.
> He has sent me to proclaim liberty to the captives
>   and recovering of sight to the blind,
> to set at liberty those who are oppressed,
>   to proclaim the year of the Lord's favor." (Luke 4:18-19 ESV)

What kind of kingdom is this? Obviously one that is different from any sort that had existed before. It was a kingdom of upheaval. It was a kingdom where the blinding forces of surplus and lack would be extinguished.

Empires are built to favor the rich, the well fed, the pleasure filled, and the beloved. But this kingdom would turn everything upside down. Its values critiqued everything about empire. Look at the revolution that Jesus unleashes in Luke 6:24-26:

Woe to you who are rich,
for
you have already received your comfort.

Woe to you who are well fed now,
for
you will go hungry.

Woe to you who laugh now,
for
you will mourn and weep.

Woe to you when everyone speaks well of you,
for
that is how their ancestors treated the false prophets.

Nothing that makes sense in empire makes sense in the kingdom community. If these sorts of people will not prosper in this revolutionary new kingdom, then who will? Jesus answers that question in the preceding verses, Luke 6:20–23:

Blessed are you who are poor,
for
yours is the kingdom of God.

Blessed are you who hunger now,
for
you will be satisfied.

Blessed are you who weep now,
for
you will laugh.

Blessed are you when people hate you,
when they exclude you and insult you
and reject your name as evil.
Rejoice in that day and leap for joy,
because great is your reward in heaven.

Does this mean that those who embrace this kingdom revolution will simply need to hang on through the terrible and bleak existence of their miserable lives and then all will be good one day in heaven? Or that people should seek poverty and pain? That is not Jesus' point at all. This is a revolution.

Your kingdom come,

your will be done,

on earth as it is in heaven.

The kingdom community is good news for those who have been shut out, marginalized, or oppressed, because in the kingdom those categories will be erased. The kingdom comes, says Jesus in Matthew 6:10, as we live out his will as though we were already in the future. There will be no empire in the age to come. And there is no room in empire for the kingdom. They will be constant rivals. Old wine sacs cannot hold new wine.

The Dark Places

The hope of empire, notes Brueggemann, is a "cross-free hope." Empire offers security, comfort, and the good life. There is never equality in empire. Despite the promises, equality never emerges. Empires thrive by selling the idea that excess for a few is good for everyone. But the kingdom is entirely different. It is built on the cross. Its central ethic is sacrifice for the benefit of others. It is good news for all. This is a kingdom where the king, though he was rich, became poor for the benefit of his people; and through his poverty, we all share in his wealth (2 Corinthians 8:9). But that also means that the kingdom cannot and will not offer security, comfort, and the "good life" from the vantage point of the present age. God does offer us the peace of his kingdom, but that is vastly different from what we often prefer in the immediate.

When Jesus wanted his disciples to completely understand who he was and what following him would really entail, he took them to Caesarea Philippi (Matthew 16:13–20; Mark 8:27–30). In the first century, there was a cave just outside Caesarea Philippi that was known as the gates of Hades. It was known for pagan worship of the gods, especially the goat god Pan, and the cave itself was believed to be the entrance to the underworld. It was a dark and evil place that most rabbis forbade to people or discouraged them from going to. But this is exactly where Jesus took his disciples when he inquired as to who they thought he was. In both Matthew's and Mark's accounts, as soon as Peter rightly declares Jesus to be the Messiah, the king, it says that for the first time, Jesus began to explain to them that the kingdom he was bringing would have suffering and sacrifice as its central characteristic (Matthew 16:21–27; Mark 8:31–38).

I think Jesus was intentional about having that conversation at Caesarea Philippi. Here's why I think that. They were standing near the gates of Hades when Jesus declared to them that on the rock of understanding him to be "the Messiah, the Son of the living God," (Matthew 16:16), they would go to places like the gates of Hades and declare him to be King. They would go to the places of the world that seemed off limits, that seemed evil, that seemed hopeless. When they went to those places and declared that Jesus was King and offered a community that lived under his rule, committed to a different approach to life, those gates of Hades would not stand a chance. The kingdom will conquer if we are willing to give up our lives, carry our cross, and follow the example of our King (Matthew 16:24–25; Mark 8:34–35).

The Critique of Empire

Everything about Jesus' life and ministry was a critique of empire. Let's summarize here just a bit. He was born in a backwater of the Roman Empire in a very nontraditional way, was laid in an animal feeding trough, and first worshiped by shepherds, those among the very lowest rungs of the social order. In reflecting on his birth, his mother praised God in song, declaring, "He has brought down the rulers from their thrones but has lifted up the humble. He has filled the hungry with good things but has sent the rich away empty" (Luke 1:52–53). In other words, empire has been upended and put on notice.

As Jesus began his ministry, he proclaimed that the kingdom of God would come and said that it would be good news for those on the bottom rungs, those who were the most likely to be crushed by empire. That doesn't mean that it's *only* for them, but it is the only kingdom that is *for* them. Throughout his ministry Jesus was constantly with the lowly and challenged the influential. He enjoyed table fellowship with the outcasts, much to the dismay of the powerful. He challenged the mighty and said that the kingdom of God was wiping away those distinctions. The greatest in his kingdom would not be the typical rich and powerful, but those who were servants, those who were willing to give all they had to the poor, those who would lay their lives down for others.

That is what Jesus' kingdom looked like.

And when he hung on the cross, about to die at the hands of one of those empires, he cried out, "Father, forgive them, for they do not know what they are doing" (Luke 23:34). The nations are not wise. They do not impress God. They are blind and numb to oppression, to the burden they put on the poor, to the shame they put on the undesirables, and certainly to death. Death is a necessary tool for empires to keep their grip on power.

And Jesus would defeat it all, not by embracing empire, and not by leading empire in the right direction. He defeated it by taking upon himself all that empire could dish out.

That is what Jesus' kingdom looks like.

What if Jesus Were Emperor?

Have you ever wondered what it would have been like if Jesus had come and overthrown Caesar and become emperor? What would it be like for you if Jesus became the president or leader of your country? Think of all the good that would result. No one has ever been wiser. Surely, he could solve issues like hunger and poverty. He would avoid war. He would solve issues of education and urban decay. He would, no doubt, be the greatest emperor ever.

So, why didn't he do that? It's not that he didn't have the chance. Before the onset of Jesus' ministry, he went into the wilderness to fast and prepare himself through the power of the Spirit. Thinking he was at his weakest, the satan[4] pounced and tempted him to create his own provision rather than trusting God to provide (Matthew 4:3), but Jesus refused, declaring that he needed nothing more than God's provision to survive (v. 4). Then the satan encouraged him to do something flashy that would get the attention of the people, be monumentally impressive, and make him famous (v. 6). Jesus refused to take the easy way out (v. 7).

Then the satan hit him with perhaps the biggest temptation he could muster. He would give Jesus "all the kingdoms of the world and their splendor" if Jesus would just acknowledge the satan's ability to do that (Matthew 4:8–9). If Jesus would worship the satan, he could be king over the whole world. Just think of that! This was why he came, and now he could seemingly have it all in an instant. He could become the supreme emperor and fix all the problems in the world.

Or could he? This wasn't the only time Jesus had the offer of becoming king. At the height of his ministry, the Jews also wanted to make him king. They recognized that there would never be a better individual to become their king and take down the Romans and any other empire that got in their way. They were willing to use force to make him the king.

[But Jesus simply walked away from the crowd. He was not interested in the political power of empire.]That was his message to the satan in the wilderness as well. He would worship and serve God alone (Matthew 4:10). He had no desire to become emperor. Perhaps the only way for him to have become an emperor among the nations would have been to bow down to the satan.

The implications of this are huge. Jesus believed that his kingdom of the upside down, his kingdom for the oppressed, his kingdom of sacrifice for the benefit of others, was better news for the world than if he became the leader of the empire. Empire was not and could never be the good news. It could never be the kingdom of God, even with Jesus leading it. Empires and the model of a politically driven nation could never be God's solution for the world. It could only come through the path of rejection, emptying, and suffering that Jesus took. No matter how good an empire might be, it will never be God's kingdom and could never be his plan for the world. We must wrap our heads around all this. God wants a kingdom with Jesus as King, not an empire, even with Jesus as emperor.

Jesus turned away from the offer of being the ruler of all the empires of the world at once. He could have done much good, but he knew that there was something better. Rather than choose the highest position that the satan could offer in the earthly realm, he chose the way of the cross. Jesus considered the way of sacrifice, the way of the kingdom, as being more powerful and effective than any empire.

That is what the kingdom of God will look like.

The Chapter in Review

- Rome had absolute power in the first century as the empire of empires.

- Jesus came as a direct challenge to the power of Rome, but in a way that was unexpected.

- Jesus was a rival king but in a kingdom that was completely different from the empires and nations.

- The kingdom will never promise or deliver security, comfort, or the good life.

- The kingdom requires sacrifice and a willingness to give up our lives in allegiance to Jesus and faith in him.

- Jesus was not trying to create a better version of empire. He was ushering in a complete alternative.

- Jesus refused to be emperor or king of the nations, opting instead to bring about the kingdom through his own death.

- The seemingly insignificant kingdom of God was better news for the world than if Jesus had become emperor of all the nations.

The Big Idea

- ❖ Jesus came to be King of his kingdom, the absolute alternative to the empires.

DISCUSSION QUESTIONS

1. In this chapter, the assertion is made that the kingdom of God was better news for the world than if Jesus had become an emperor or king of the nations and solved all the problems that plague societies. Do you agree or disagree with that? What are the implications of Jesus' refusal to be an earthly king?

2. What are the implications of recognizing that the empires/nations promise security and comfort, but the kingdom calls us to self-denial and sacrifice?

3. How can the way of the cross be more effective in the twenty-first century to bring about change in the world than the political solutions that the empires can muster?

Chapter 4

Citizens of the Kingdom

Just over an hour and a half to the Southeast of Montreal, Canada, there is a strange anomaly along the US-Canadian border. On the boundary between the state of Vermont and the province of Quebec are the American town Derby and the Canadian town Stanstead. They are one town, for all intents and purposes, but are seemingly haphazardly split into two by the international border. It seems that in the eighteenth century, the surveyors made a mistake, and the town was subsequently built right on the line between the two countries, as they thought the border was farther south. Now half of the town is in the United States and half in Canada.

Residents who were raised in the area say that the border was barely noticeable when they were growing up. It was more of a novelty than anything else. Since the tragic events of 9/11, however, things have changed dramatically. The border has been beefed up throughout the town, and residents can no longer move freely back and forth. Sometimes the border runs right down the middle of the road, while occasionally it cuts through buildings. One such place is the Haskell Free Library, where US citizens can enter on their side of the building and Canadian citizens enter on their side. Inside the library is one of the few places in town where citizens can go across the border without having to process their passport and go through border control. But movement in the little town is not so easy for residents in most areas. Many residents must go through security stations just to walk to the post office or go to a store if it is on the wrong side of the border.

All nations today have well-marked borders. Moving from one country to the other can be a bit of a process that involves going through security and showing your passport, at the very least. Some borders are relatively friendly and easy to cross other than the minor inconvenience of passport processing. There are stretches of the border in Derby and Stanstead that consist of a painted line or even a row of potted flowers. Some borders, however, are marked by walls or even a military presence that makes crossing a bit more difficult.

The phenomenon of national boundaries makes sense. Nations must define their borders so that they know where their territory starts and stops and what they must defend if need be. These borders are almost always clearly defined so that no one might wonder what country they are in and whose laws and expectations they must adhere to. That doesn't mean, however, that just because the nations define or defend their borders in a way that might make sense from the perspective of empire that this is something that a child of the kingdom should endorse. But let's not jump too far ahead of ourselves.

Empires have physical borders. Sometimes it's a friendly line. Sometimes it's barbed wire and people with weapons that are not so friendly.

A Kingdom without Borders

But the kingdom of God is different. It has no boundaries. One day while teaching, Jesus was asked by a group of Pharisees when the kingdom would come. Jesus' response is instructive.

> "The coming of the kingdom of God is not something that can be observed, nor will people say, 'Here it is,' or 'There it is,' because the kingdom of God is in your midst." (Luke 17:20–21)

Israel had borders clearly defined by God, and they never really sought to expand them. But Israel was not the kingdom of God. It was an early sample of it and as a prophetic community was supposed to be a light to the nations to show them what it could look like, but it was never the completeness of God's kingdom. It was how God worked within the system of empire.

But Jesus was bringing something new entirely. For this very reason, it is completely inappropriate for disciples of Jesus who are members of his kingdom to turn to the passages of the Old Testament to find instructions or models for political thought or behavior for the kingdom of God. They are two different animals entirely, and the old covenant can offer nothing more than a faint shadow of the behavior of the kingdom. That is not to imply that there is not much to learn about God from the Old Testament, but the nation of Israel does not provide a blueprint for the function of Jesus' kingdom.

In Luke 17, Jesus is talking about the arrival of the kingdom. It will not establish itself in the way that empires do. There will be no rev-olution, no base camp, no clearly defined military force. And once it comes, there will be no surveyors going out to establish its boundar-ies. There will be no national flag and no border patrol or outposts. No one will be able to travel to its capital or send emissaries to the throne room.

When Did the Kingdom Come?

This kingdom would not be like anything the world had seen be-fore. Asking questions about when it would come would not help. But it did come.

When Pilate wanted to understand what kind of kingdom this was and when Jesus envisioned establishing it, his answer was hopelessly puzzling for the Roman governor, who knew only empire. "My king-dom," said Jesus, "is not of this world. If it were, my servants would fight to prevent my arrest by the Jewish leaders. But now, my kingdom is from another place" (John 18:36). In that moment, Pilate would not understand this kingdom with no borders.

In their book, *The Kingdom of God, Volume 1,* Tom Jones and Steve Brown describe the coming of the kingdom of God in terms of waves that lap up against a shore. Some waves are bigger than others, but they keep coming. In one sense, the kingdom of God was on earth in the Garden of Eden, but it was forfeited. Aspects of the kingdom lapped ashore during the time of the nation of Israel. Yet it became painfully clear that Israel was not the rescue boat that the world need-ed, and it would not bring about the rule of God. Those tides receded.

When Jesus arrived, he couldn't stop talking about the kingdom. Most of his parables explain aspects of God's rule, and he even claimed that his miracles of driving out demons by the finger of God were clear evidence that the kingdom had arrived (Luke 11:19–20). When Je-sus declared that good news to the poor and oppressed had arrived (Luke 4:18–19), a wave rolled in. When Jesus performed miracles, more waves lapped onto the shore. When he carefully taught through what it would look like to live by the values of the kingdom of God in the present age, more waves poured onto the shore.

Jesus promised his followers that they would see the kingdom of God come in their lifetime in great power (Mark 9:1). Jesus submitting to death on a cross and being raised in the power of the Spirit were powerful markers of the kingdom of God being established on earth. And there is no question that when Peter stood before the mass of people on Pentecost and preached the gospel in Jerusalem before Jews from many nations, a more powerful wave of the kingdom rolled in than anyone could imagine. That quite possibly was even the moment Jesus alluded to in Mark 9:1.

The point is not to try to pinpoint the moment when the kingdom of God arrived on earth, because there is no one moment. At Pentecost, the kingdom became available and accessible to the nations. We could finally live under the rule of the king that God had chosen from the beginning of time (Psalm 2:6) and not one of the many poor human substitute kings or empires.

A Kingdom Like No Other

When Jesus stood before Pilate and asserted that his kingdom was not of this world, did he mean to claim that the kingdom of God was merely a spiritual truth or an inner feeling? Was he calming Pilate's fears and letting him know that this kingdom was not a real kingdom in the sense of being a rival to the kingdoms of the world? Was it more like a cellphone case that surrounds a phone and protects it while still allowing it to function the same as it always has? Or was it an entirely new way of communicating that would render the cellphone meaningless and unnecessary altogether?

The kingdom of God is unique in that it is built entirely on the wisdom and will of God. It is the rule of God in the lives of his people.

It is also unique in that it involves an anachronism. An anachronism is an event that takes places out of its proper time or sequence. The kingdom of God is eternal life, but that phrase in Scripture means something different from what we often suppose. Translated more directly, it would be "the life of the coming age." It's not just something that we go to when we die. In this case, time moves in the other direction. The future of God's ruling age, the time when the presence of heaven overlaps every part of the universe and fills it, has broken into the present age. God's reign can come now when we obey his will on earth as though we were already in heaven.

And it is unique because it is a real kingdom, but it has no borders. That may seem obvious, but it is vital that we break that down and understand it. According to David Bercot in *The Kingdom That Turned the World Upside Down,*[5] every kingdom consists of four basic components.

1. Every kingdom has a ruler.
2. Every kingdom has subjects or citizens.
3. Every kingdom has a domain or area of rulership.
4. Every kingdom has laws or a standard by which citizens live.

Every empire could easily fill in those four areas, and they would all look the same in that the answers would be cut from the same cloth. Regardless of how number 1 is configured, it would be a human or group of humans in some fashion that leads the country. Similarly, the remaining three categories would vary in form or function but not in category type.

The kingdom is entirely different. Jesus is Lord in the kingdom; that much is clear. That alone makes the kingdom very different. But does the fact that he is not physically accessible on earth mean that the kingdom of God is something spiritual and not a real kingdom in the terms of the empires? That is one of the most important questions that we can ask. If we get the answer wrong, we will head down what I believe is a very misguided path and create a version of the kingdom that bears little resemblance to the one that Jesus established.

Jesus Is Lord

The kingdom is very different, but it is very real. This is precisely where we can get lost in the woods. We imagine that the empires in which we live are real. They have the ruling authority over our lives, and our goal is to influence them spiritually to become more like the kingdom. From this perspective, nations can be judged on the degree to which they are or are not the kingdom of God. A nation can prostrate itself under God and become a Christian nation or the embodiment of the kingdom, or it can reject God and become an evil nation. But that quickly starts to sound like an approach of, "Here is the kingdom," or "There is the kingdom," something that Jesus said we would precisely not be able to do concerning its coming or at any other time.

The kingdom of God is not like any other, but it is a real kingdom that vies for our undivided loyalty. When the Pharisees claimed that Jesus' kingdom was the kind that had the satan at the helm, Jesus noted that he was driving out demons and fighting against satanic purposes in the world. His point? "Every kingdom divided against itself will be ruined" (Matthew 12:25). In other words, you can only be truly loyal to one king and one kingdom. Divided loyalty is no loyalty at all. You may have various commitments or relationships, but only one object of loyalty.

This is precisely why the early Christians declared at their baptism just where their loyalties lay.

> If you declare with your mouth, "Jesus is Lord," and believe in your heart that God raised him from the dead, you will be saved. For it is with your heart that you believe and are justified, and it is with your mouth that you profess your faith and are saved. As Scripture says, "Anyone who believes in him will never be put to shame." For there is no difference between Jew and Gentile—the same Lord is Lord of all and richly blesses all who call on him, for, "Everyone who calls on the name of the Lord will be saved." (Romans 10:9-13)

Who are the citizens of the kingdom? Those who have declared that Jesus is Lord, who have committed themselves in allegiance to the risen king, and who have died to themselves and entered the life of the King by calling on his name.

To declare Jesus as Lord was an act of exchanging loyalty. It was switching sides from empire to the kingdom. It was to publicly proclaim that Caesar was no longer the object of loyalty, that the Roman Empire was no longer the source of their trust. By believing that Jesus had resurrected from the dead, they were pledging their allegiance to him as King and entering the world of the new creation opened by his resurrection. To call on the name of the Lord was not some vague act of prayer. It was the act of being immersed into the death, burial, and resurrection of the king (see Acts 22:16; see also Romans 6:1-14). Baptism was a declaration that the person submitting to it was dying to themselves and living only the life that the King wanted them to.

The citizens of the kingdom are those who have made Jesus Lord. Declaring that to be so at one's baptism was a stark reminder that there could be no divided loyalty between the kingdom of God and the Roman Empire, their Jewish identity, or any other entities that would vie for their allegiance.

Paul was a Roman citizen (Acts 16:37–38; 22:26–29; 23:27) and would utilize that to the advantage of the kingdom of God, but at no point is there any sense that his loyalties were divided. Paul was a Roman citizen by happenstance, but a member of the kingdom by allegiance.

Paul never emphasized his Roman citizenship or showed any specific loyalty to Rome. He used it as a tool, but that was the extent of it. His citizenship in the kingdom of God was his identity and passion. He reminds his brothers and sisters in Philippi, a place that took great pride in their allegiance to Rome and the Roman way of living, that "our citizenship is in heaven" (Philippians 3:20). The idea in the Roman world was for citizens of Rome to spread out and show those in the far reaches of the empire what it looked like to live as a citizen of Rome and be loyal to the emperor. It is to this idea that Paul calls the Philippian Christians. He doesn't call them to be good Roman citizens. He doesn't blur the lines between a citizen of Rome and a citizen of the kingdom of heaven. They are distinct and separate. To give our complete loyalty to one is to denounce our allegiance to the other. Either Jesus is Lord or Caesar is. Period.

Similarly, Paul was Jewish in his identity, but never allowed that to supersede his citizenship in God's kingdom. He considered all the ethnic and national markers that should have brought him purpose, identity, and pride as a Jew: circumcised as a natural born Israelite; member of the tribe of Benjamin; Hebrew of Hebrews; zealous for the law (Philippians 3:4–6). But instead of allowing those things to bring him worth, he considered them worthless. They meant nothing compared to kingdom identity in Christ.

Paul wasn't alone in that. When Peter and John were brought before the Jewish ruling council, the Sanhedrin, including the high priest, they should have been quaking in their boots. Even though Jews were forcibly under the rule of Caesar and the Roman Empire, there was no greater authority on earth for the descendants of Abraham than this ruling body. But when the pair of disciples were ordered to stop proclaiming Jesus as King to the people of Jerusalem, they replied, "Which is right in God's eyes: to listen to you, or to him?" (Acts 4:19).

Whether it came to Caesar and Rome or their Jewish identity and heritage, the first Christians understood that their sole loyalty belonged to the kingdom of God. There was no such thing as divided or dual loyalty. When it came to their allegiance, they were citizens of the kingdom. They might be physical subjects of Rome or Israel, but there was no allegiance given to either of those empires.

Allegiance to the King

Author Matthew Bates, building on the work of other New Testament scholars such as Michael Gorman, N.T. Wright, John Barclay, and Richard Hays, makes a compelling case that the Greek word *pistis*, which is most often translated "faith" in English New Testaments, was understood differently than we tend to understand it today.[6] The modern reader often reduces that word to the concepts of trust or belief, but there was a bit more to it in the ancient world. Bates offers numerous examples of the use of *pistis* from a similar period in the Greco-Roman world and demonstrates that it was used quite often to carry the connotation of allegiance, especially when in connection to a king or empire. He examines a large number of New Testament passages where the translations "faith" or "faithfulness" represent *pistis*, shows how this understanding makes more sense of many important sections of Scripture, and asks the reader to consider how these passages become far deeper and richer if we include the concept of "believing allegiance" as the meaning of *pistis*.

Here are just a few examples, using Bates' suggested inclusion of "allegiance" rather than simply "faith":[7]

> What if some lack allegiance? Will their lack of allegiance nullify God's allegiance? (Romans 3:3).

> Yet we know that a person is not justified by the works of the law, but through allegiance to Jesus Christ, so we also have given allegiance to the Christ Jesus, in order to be justified by the allegiance to the Christ and not by the works of the law, because by works of the law no one will be justified (Galatians 2:16).

> It is no longer I who live, but the Christ who lives in me. And the life I now live in the flesh I live by allegiance to the Son of God, who loved me and gave himself for me (Galatians 2:20).

> Rather, I consider everything loss because of the surpassing greatness

of knowing the Christ, Jesus my Lord. On his account I have suffered the loss of all things and consider them as rubbish, in order that I may gain the Christ and be found in him, not having a righteousness by the law, but that which comes through allegiance to the Christ, the righteousness of God based upon allegiance–that I may know him and the power of his resurrection, and the fellowship of his sufferings, being conformed to his death, that by any means possible I may attain to the resurrection of the dead (Philippians 3:8–11).

For since, in the wisdom of God, the world did not know God through wisdom, God was pleased through the folly of the proclamation [of a crucified king] to save those who give allegiance (1 Corinthians 1:21)

If Bates is correct, and I believe that he is, as do a growing avalanche of scholars, this helps enrich passages like Ephesians 2:8, "For it is by grace you have been saved, through *allegiance*." We don't earn our gift of salvation, but we enter it through allegiance to our king.

Bates explains that understanding *pistis* as allegiance to a king helps makes sense of puzzling New Testament phrases such as "the obedience of faith" (Romans 1:5; 16:26 NASB) and "the law of Christ" (Galatians 6:2; 1 Corinthians 9:21; see also Romans 8:2; James 1:25; Romans 13:9). If the primary problem of following Christ is establishing our own righteousness through our own effort, works, and adherence to the law, then these phrases are indeed troublesome. But if faith in Christ is primarily allegiance to Jesus as King, then these are understandable expressions of what Bates calls "a posture of servant-minded loyalty."[8]

This concept of allegiance to Jesus as King rather than the satan or the empires of the world is perhaps nowhere clearer than in Jesus' words to the church in Pergamum:

"To the angel of the church in Pergamum write:
These are the words of him who has the sharp, double-edged sword. I know where you live–where Satan has his throne. Yet you remain true to my name. You did not renounce your faith (*pistis*) in me, not even in the days of Antipas, my faithful witness, who was put to death in your city– where Satan lives." (Revelation 2:12–13)

If we include this understanding of *pistis* as allegiance, the passage comes alive in new ways. Jesus is not commending them for continuing to give mental assent to who he is. He is praising them for remaining loyal to him as King and for not giving their allegiance to the satan and the empire. Jesus rebukes them in verses 14–16 for failing to discern false teachings about how he wanted them to live as kingdom citizens. But the commendation came because they had remained allegiant to their king and rejected the way of the empire.

Bates concludes that saving allegiance has three dimensions: *"mental affirmation* that the gospel is true, *professed fealty* to Jesus alone as the cosmic Lord, and *enacted loyalty* through obedience to Jesus as king."[9]

If Jesus is truly our Lord and King, then our allegiance is due him alone and his kingdom. There can be no other leader, nation, or empire to whom we would ever pledge our allegiance. Shared allegiance is no allegiance at all.

The Chapter in Review

- The kingdom of God is not like other nations and not even like Israel.

- It is a kingdom without borders.

- The kingdom arrived in many waves but became fully available to the nations at Pentecost.

- The kingdom of God is completely unique to any other system or rule in the history of the world.

- The kingdom is entirely different, but it is a very real kingdom that demands our complete allegiance.

- To be baptized is an act of dying to yourself and all previous loyalties and making Jesus alone your king.

- There is no such thing as divided loyalty for the citizen of the kingdom of God.

- Being a kingdom citizen requires absolute allegiance to Jesus alone.

- We can only pledge our allegiance to Jesus. Shared allegiance is no allegiance at all.

The Big Idea

❖ Our sole allegiance as Christians is to Jesus as King.

DISCUSSION QUESTIONS

1. How does it change our mindset and approach to politics if we understand the kingdom to be a real kingdom that requires our complete allegiance to it, its values, and its way of life, all of which are very different from the agendas of the nations?

2. Why is it necessary to die to self before entering this kingdom? What are the personal political implications of being part of a people who have died to themselves and dedicated to living for the benefit of others to show them the kingdom?

3. What are the implications of pledging our allegiance to Jesus and his kingdom alone?

Chapter 5

A Matter of Time

As my wife and I drove through Iowa on a trip from Wisconsin to Oklahoma, we realized that we needed to have some cash on hand, and we were just about out. So we pulled into a small Iowa town and drove up to a gas station. As I walked into the convenience store portion, I asked the cashier behind the counter if they had a time machine. She looked at me strangely, and paused as if to make sure that she had heard me correctly, before finally squeezing out a somewhat confused "N-o-o." I was a little surprised by that but climbed back into our car and drove down the street to another gas station. Once again, I left a befuddled employee wondering if this guy was seriously asking for a time machine. I was, and I left muttering about what kind of Podunk town has gas stations with no time machine. I tried a grocery store down the street; same story. We pulled into what seemed to be the last gas station in town and decided to make one last attempt.

I was losing hope but asked for a time machine anyway. Again, the clerk looked confused and then barked, "No, we don't have no time machine." Just as all seemed lost, a customer waiting at the counter snapped her head toward me and with a wry smile on her face, asked me, "Are you from Wisconsin?" A little shocked at what sort of witchery was this, I replied slowly, "Ye-es." She then turned to the clerk behind the counter and insightfully said, "He wants to know where your cash machine is." It was at that moment that I realized that growing up in Wisconsin, many of the ATMs were from the TYME company, and most people grew up calling all ATMs "time" machines by second nature. I thought I was asking for a cash machine in a very normal way, and these poor people thought some lunatic looking to time travel was on the loose in their town.

The true irony of that story is that I absolutely love the idea of time travel. Truth be told, I'm borderline obsessed with it. As a former history teacher and forever history nut, I have daydreamed more than I care to admit about being able to travel back in time and observe important historical moments. Traveling into the future is just as intriguing, although more difficult to daydream about because I have no idea what it will be like. From H.G. Wells' *Time Machine* to the 1980s TV show *Voyagers* to more current shows like *Travelers* or *Timeless,* if there is a book, movie, or television show about time travel, I'm in. And let's not forget about the timeless classic that is the *Back to the Future* trilogy.

While I love the idea of time travel, the thought of it can also be hopelessly frustrating because it is most likely impossible (I say most likely, because I need to hang on to a little bit of hope).

There is one way that we can experience time travel, though, believe it or not. How, you ask? Through the power of the gospel itself we can, in some respects, travel in time.

Traveling into the Future

The day that Moses was brought into the world, Israel was living under the grip of empire. As a people, they had experienced the good side of empire during the life of Joseph, but nearly 400 years later, they were living the life of the have-nots. They were the oppressed, those who exist merely for the good and prosperity of the empire. Empires always have casualties in some form or fashion. They are necessary to keep the peace, power, privilege, and prosperity flowing and to keep the illusion that everything is under control.

Just when there seemed to be no hope, God intervened. He had been preparing a deliverer, and when the time was right, he sent Moses to free his people from the shackles of the Egyptian empire. God used Moses to critique the empire and show that it never had the power it thought it had. And after a series of powerful demonstrations, Egypt was brought to her knees and released its grip on God's people, the descendants of Abraham. Now it was up to them to be the alternative to empire. But what does that really mean?

There is a little story tucked into the middle of the book of Numbers, in chapter 13, that demonstrates an important principle of being the prophetic community and understanding what the kingdom of God is all about.

God has brought Israel out of Egypt, through the Red Sea, and to the brink of the promised land. This is what they had been waiting for since the time of Abraham: a land that would be theirs. So Moses sends a group of men into the area of Canaan to explore and report back what they see. What they observed there both sparked their imagination and discouraged them at the same time.

The cities were impressive and intimidating. The people were even more so. The challenge of what lay ahead seemed so daunting that they were ready to return to the empire and enslavement.

But there were also wonderful things. The land that God had promised them was full of fruit and food and natural beauty like they had never seen. They took a single cluster of grapes that was so full and succulent that two men had to carry it on a pole. They also found pomegranates and figs the like of which they had never seen before. They brought this fruit from the promised land back to the wilderness where the people still resided.

We are not told explicitly that the people ate that fruit, but surely, they must have. Then they quickly lost sight of what was important. They began to fret about the empire they were facing, forgetting that God had just freed their bodies from the mightiest empire on earth at the time. Their bodies were free, but their hearts and souls were still enslaved and loyal to the belief that true power lay in empire and not in the God who had worked wonders before their very eyes.

They forgot about the fruit. There they were, in the wilderness, tasting the future. Enjoying the exquisite flavors of the promised land. They were experiencing the future even though they were still very much in their present situation. Had they embraced it and trusted God as their king, the future would have become their reality. Instead, only two of the spies were willing to do that. The other ten continued to believe in the power of empire, the power that they could see with their eyes.

The Message of the Bible

If we were to sit down and read through all four Gospels in one sitting for each gospel, we would find that Jesus' primary mission was to proclaim, demonstrate, and establish the kingdom of God. His was not a mission of personal salvation and spiritual growth. It was not a message of fixing the problems in society. It was not a mission of righting the wrongs and ending oppression. It was a message of God's kingdom.

God created humans to co-rule the creation through his wisdom, but we rejected that vocation repeatedly, choosing to attempt rule through our own wisdom and strength. God didn't just abandon his creation project, though; he chose Abraham and his descendants to start over and offer humanity the option of living under God's wisdom. One of those descendants, Moses, led the rest to the promised land where they could live as the prophetic community. They were not just to criticize the world but to be a light to the nations so that God could bring restoration to all peoples. But Israel soon gave in to the temptation to become empire and chose man's wisdom over God's.

Once again, God refused to give up and promised that he would one day come himself to bring his rule and healing to the nations. This was the kingdom of God. And it was this future reality and hope that the Jews from the time of exile up through the time of Jesus waited expectantly for. They longed for the day when God would cleanse the world of evil and rule as King. But it would have to wait until the Messiah came and announced that the present age was ending and that the future age had begun.

This was the good news message that Jesus preached and embodied. Jesus wasn't just offering some new sort of sage philosophy or a more correct religion or a just political system. He was inviting people to live in God's new world. And what would God's kingdom be like? There will be no disease, so Jesus healed. There will be no outcast, so he included all. There will no hate, so he loved even his enemies. There will be no poverty or oppression, so he lifted the marginalized.

This is the kingdom of God. It is at odds with the system of the world, and because of that it will not only serve as an alternative to empire; the empires of the world will also feel threatened by it.

In response to the threat, the story of the kingdom takes a terrible turn. The chosen king of God's kingdom should be conquering his enemies as he shows us how to live under God's rule, but instead he is crucified by them. But this was no accident. It, too, was a demonstration of the kingdom. Jesus suffered the rightful consequences of humanity's rebellion and in so doing showed us what the kingdom looks like. The power of God's kingdom comes through love and self-sacrifice.

When Jesus rolled back the stone and walked out of his grave three days after being murdered, something so much bigger happened than just one man cheating death. He took on the biggest weapon that empire has: death. Jesus' resurrection was the dawning of the kingdom of God. It had arrived on earth and when proclaimed, as it was at Pentecost in Acts 2, would become fully accessible to all who would accept Jesus as King.

From that moment on, the good news was proclaimed by Jesus' followers around the world. The new creation had finally arrived. There was a different way to live as a human. Humanity could finally live under the reign of this new king. But there was no powerful army that would impose its will on its enemies and oppress those that stood in its way. Instead, the most honored in this kingdom would be the oppressed and the outcasts. We live under God's reign by responding to enemies in love, caring for those most in need, and humbling ourselves to serve everyone.

This, of course, confused the Jews. They were expecting that God's kingdom, the future state of the world, would take place in the future. By definition, or so they thought, it couldn't happen in the present age, because when the kingdom came, this age would end and there would be no mistaking that the transition had occurred. This is precisely why John uses the phrase "eternal life" so often in his gospel. When the biblical writers use that phrase they are referring to the life of the age to come, and that's John's point. Jesus was the embodiment of the coming age. He was the future in the flesh. And now, through him, the age to come has broken into the present age and is available now. Now, that's what I call time travel!

In short, the kingdom of God was like eating the fruit of the promised land while standing in the wilderness. It offered a sample of the future. To live under God's rule means that we apply his wisdom and reign to life in the present, even though that will often make no sense.

Nowhere does Jesus make this clearer than in the Sermon on the Mount. What does it look like to live in the present as though we were already in God's future restored and renewed creation? That's what the Sermon on the Mount is all about.

Living the Future

Most biblical scholars agree that Matthew crafted his Gospel in a very intentional way to demonstrate that Jesus is a new and better Moses. Moses himself declared that God would one day raise up a prophet like him from among the Israelites (Deuteronomy 18:15), and God confirmed that he would do just that (v. 18). Matthew sets out to show that Jesus is that prophet.

Many biblical experts believe that Matthew constructed his book into five sections to mimic the five books of Moses. While that is possible but not certain, what is certain is that Matthew clearly depicts John the Baptist as an Old Testament prophet, but John himself is adamant that someone greater than he is on the way (Matthew 3:11–12). The mystery is solved immediately as Jesus arrives to be baptized and is declared to be God's beloved Son (vv. 13–17). He is the prophet greater than John, and it brings to mind Isaiah's prophecy:

> "Forget the former things;
> > do not dwell on the past.
> See, I am doing a new thing!
> > Now it springs up; do you not perceive it?
> I am making a way in the wilderness
> > and streams in the wasteland." (Isaiah 43:18–19)

We should not miss what Matthew is doing. As the last of the Old Testament prophets sees his ministry come to an end (Matthew 4:12), the new age begins to dawn (v. 17). The new prophet has come and begins to call his followers (vv. 18–22) and demonstrate that God's future age is breaking into the present (vv. 23–25). Then, just as Moses went up the mountain to receive the teaching for God's people that will show them how to live as his people, Jesus went up a mountainside and prepared to teach them (Matthew 5:1–2).

But we must be honest here. Moses' teaching made sense. It was practical, thorough, and comprehensive. We still deeply admire things like the Ten Commandments. Admittedly, there are parts of the Law that are puzzling for us, but those aspects made perfect sense in the context of ancient Israel, calling them to be separate from the pagan spiritual practices around them.

The Sermon on the Mount, though, is crazy. Take a few moments and read through Matthew 5–7.

It's absurd, isn't it? Blessed are the poor in spirit, those who mourn, the meek, and the persecuted? Really? You are the light of the world? Are you sure about that, Jesus? Turn the other cheek, love your enemies, pray for those who persecute you? That sounds downright dangerous and not a good formula to get very far in the real world. And on and on it goes. It doesn't sound realistic or particularly wise.

I will gladly admit that the Sermon on the Mount is ridiculous and makes no sense in the present age. It just doesn't. But I don't think it's meant to. It's not of the present age. This is straight from the coming age. This is when God sets things right in the world and those who love him will be with him in his presence for eternity (Revelation 21:1–5). In that age, there will no enemies or evil, for example, so there will be no hate. There will be no greed, so there will also be no surplus or lack. There will be no levels of superior and inferior, so there will be no oppressed or marginalized.

I hope this is starting to become clear. What Jesus is calling his people to is the kingdom. And what does the kingdom look like, how does it come? The kingdom comes when God's will is done on earth just as it is in heaven and will be done in the age to come (Matthew 6:10). Jesus wants us to live by the values of that age even though we are in the present age. That's our calling and our purpose.

We may want to do other things in life and accomplish different agendas with the time we have, but if we are going to follow Jesus and live under his rule in the kingdom of God, then this is life. We must give up any ideas of ownership of our lives to follow Jesus (Luke 14:25–27). This means our lives become about one thing: being the light. Displaying what the age to come will look like. That is the kingdom of God.

Don't get me wrong, it is monumentally difficult to live by the values of that age while surrounded by sin. It is not easy to live by the ethics of the kingdom while living in the time of the empires. It will seem strange. We will lose many of the benefits that the world has to offer. It will seem weak and ineffective. Surely there are better and more productive ways. But our purpose is not to gain power, influence, and success in the way that the world cherishes and strives for. We will be out of sync with the world. It will challenge their values and ideals if we live this way, and they will strike back. That is why Jesus promised us that we will have trouble in this world (John 16:33) and Paul confirmed that "everyone who wants to live a godly life in Christ Jesus will be persecuted" (2 Timothy 3:12).

For the kingdom people, the future is now. For this reason, I am convinced that kingdom Christians will never be anything more than an alternative society, distinct and apart from empire, though living in their midst. And the idea of a Christian nation becomes absurd.

A Matter of Time

How could a nation possibly live by the standards of the Sermon on the Mount? It wouldn't exist in the present age very long if it did. These are rules for radicals. This way of life is treacherous and only for those prepared to live in the margins as a prophetic alternative, determined to offer samples of what it looks like to live with Jesus as King and call people to that difficult life in the present age.

Absurd

The broad principles of Jesus' most complete sermon on record are ludicrous and otherworldly when we allow them to take top priority in our lives and doggedly avoid any temptation to water them down or make them more compatible with comfortable present-age living.

The kingdom people will find blessing in:

Recognizing that we can do nothing apart from God's wisdom and will (Matthew 5:3; 7:7-11)

Mourning over the seriousness of sin and the damage it does in the world, and then dealing with sin in ourselves first (Matthew 5:4; 7:1-6).

Controlling our passions and will and trusting in God's provision and rule (Matthew 5:5; 6:19-34).

Desiring and seeking only God's vision of justice for the world and doing right in God's eyes rather than in the world's eyes (Matthew 5:6; 6:1-18).

Showing mercy to all people groups, loving our enemies, and refusing to use violence as a means of response, no matter the cost (Matthew 5:7; 5:38-48).

Seeking only God's standard of purity and singular focus on living by the values of the age to come (Matthew 5:8; 5:26-37).

Taking active steps to make world peace and not just hoping for it, knowing that this is undertaken to show people what it looks like to live under God's rule (Matthew 5:9; 5:21-26).

Embracing the reality that this manner of living will result in being so out of sync with the rest of the world that persecution is sure to follow (Matthew 5:10; 5:11–20).

An Impossibility

Here's an important question to ponder. How can a nation-state embrace and live by the principles that Jesus puts forth in his sermon here? Jesus clearly rejects normal earthly power and forcing people to do things. That is the whole point of Matthew 5:38–43. When confronted by someone who wishes you harm, whether it is to assault and humiliate you, rip you off and cheat you, or racially subjugate and rule over you, Jesus rejects the typical human responses. He rules out the way of weakness and capitulation. But he also denies his followers the path of retaliation and fighting fire with fire.

If someone slaps you, don't run and don't hit them back. Stand there. Look them in the eye. Risk being hit again. We are showing them strength without violence, which might very well mean taking suffering onto ourselves. That is the way of the cross. It is risky, but our greatest concern is not to protect ourselves or our freedom or our safety. Our greatest concern is to show them the kingdom of God. It is to demonstrate the new way of being human in the present age that Jesus set loose when he made available the life of the age to come.

If a powerful enemy tries to take you to court and rip you off, says Jesus, you might not be able to win, but don't just give them the outer coat they are trying to take, give them your shirt as well. Again, no capitulation or self-protection here. The only thing on display is the kingdom ethic of acting in the best interest of the person and showing them what the kingdom looks like. We are willing to suffer to demonstrate God's will on earth as it is done in heaven (Matthew 6:10). I will say that it is important for us to find nuance in an example like this, because Jesus' point is not to let yourself get ripped off all the time. To walk around without a cloak was to bring shame on yourself. But to do this willingly would be a demonstration of the shame that the rich and powerful are trying to reduce others to. There may be times when defending yourself in court is okay, but it will take careful discernment to decide when and how to apply Jesus' words, remembering that they are likely to be far more challenging than we might care to admit.

What if a powerful empire like Rome had come in, taken over our country, ruled it with an iron fist, and allowed the soldiers to humiliate us, force us into labor for their benefit, and take away our freedom? Surely then we could fight back because God would want us to stand up for those in need, right? Jesus does want us to retaliate, but not in the way that we would expect. Again, the primary concern is demonstrating the kingdom. If they demand that we carry their pack one mile, do it. And then, according to your own free will, go another mile. Show them this new way of living and in so doing, you may suffer, but you may win them over.

Each of these examples shows God's version of victory over injustice and violence. I've seen many people try to make sense of some of the more challenging elements of the Sermon on the Mount. We want to water them down. We want to argue that they are only meant to be responses to religious persecutions. We want to believe that, yes, Jesus said love your enemies, but as early church leader Augustine argued in the fourth century, we can love our enemies and kill them at the same time. Try as we might, none of these arguments really stand up to scrutiny. For the first three centuries of the church, Christians held firm to Jesus' teaching in the Sermon on the Mount and really believed that he meant every word of it.

New Testament scholar N.T. Wright says, "These examples are only little sketches, like cartoons to give you the idea. Whatever situation you're in, you need to think it through for yourself. What would it mean to reflect God's generous love despite the pressure and provocation, despite your own anger and frustration?"[10] God's generous kingdom love is challenging, scandalous, and difficult.

We want his words to make sense in this age, but they're not designed to. Jesus' words seem crazy in the present age because they are. The values underlying his instructions are from the age to come. They are from the time when God's kingdom is fully and perfectly established and everyone in it has been transformed by God's own Spirit to be like Jesus. In that age, there will be no enemies, no sin, no hate, no murder or racism or wars. There will be only love as we all live and move in the presence of God. This is the challenge of Jesus' calling. He wants us to live on earth as though we were in heaven. This is the balance of the kingdom being here already but not yet fully.

No Place for Kingdom Life

If we take Jesus' words at face value and don't add to them, don't water them down, don't try to explain them away, they are incredibly radical. Yet, for the first three centuries of Christianity, his followers defined the Christian life as allegiance to just this way of living. For them, this is what it meant to seek the kingdom of God and his righteousness first (Matthew 6:33).

Let's return to the thought of a Christian nation embracing this lifestyle. How could a nation possibly follow the principles that Jesus lays out in this sermon? It is clear that many of his points, such as not lusting after another person, are only meant for individuals, but let's say that a country was determined to be a Christian nation and live by the Sermon on the Mount or expect all its citizens to. How could that work?

How could a nation turn the other cheek if aggression were displayed toward their borders? For how long could a nation allow itself to be ripped off by other countries and then give even more? How could a nation submit to subjugation and then go another mile to demonstrate that there is a new way of living?

In short, I see no way in which a sovereign nation could live according to the Sermon on the Mount. It's simply impossible. No nation has ever done it and no nation could.

My own nation, the United States of America, has long claimed to be one nation under God (at least since 1954 when that phrase was added to the Pledge of Allegiance), but even the biggest patriots would have a hard time claiming that the history of the United States is a reflection of loving enemies, turning the other cheek, and hungering and thirsting for righteousness alone.

It seems that Jesus had no intention of there being anything such as a Christian nation. The kingdom of God is meant to be an alternative to the kingdoms and nations of the world, not a partner. If a nation cannot live out the Sermon on the Mount, then it cannot be like Jesus. And if it cannot be like Jesus (1 John 2:6), then it cannot rightly call itself Christian.

This is not to imply that nations or their citizens that are not part of the kingdom of God are evil in every way or that everything they do is evil. But I do mean to imply that the aims between the nations and empires of the world and the kingdom should be so different that there is no way to reconcile the two or for them to be yoked together. We have a mission that will never jibe with the nations.

Even Old Testament Israel was rooted in the present age. It was to be different from the nations by adhering to the Law, but it still had only the solutions and options of the present age. The new covenant kingdom is so radically different because it is the future breaking into the present. The Sermon on the Mount can only be embodied by an alternative, prophetic community that understands that to be Christ-like we must live like Jesus (1 John 2:6). This means that a nation or group of people can only be a Christian nation or group to the degree that it looks and behaves like Jesus.

The Chapter in Review

- When Israel was physically freed from Egypt, they were not instantly freed in their minds, which were still enslaved to empire.

- The unifying theme of the entire Bible is the kingdom of God.

- The kingdom of God is the future of God's creation that has broken into the present age, enabling us to live in the present as though we were in the future.

- The Sermon on the Mount seems so unrealistic only because it is rooted in the values of the age to come. It is not designed as a manual for successful living in the present age, but it is absolutely meant to be lived out now.

- Nations cannot live by the standards of the Sermon on the Mount. Individuals who choose that life will always be out of sync with the world.

- The kingdom of God can never be embodied within the purpose and function of a nation as we know it.

- The kingdom is designed to be an alternative to the nations, not one of them.

The Big Idea

- ❖ The universal kingdom is the embodiment of God's future and cannot be employed or grafted in by any nation-state.

| 73

DISCUSSION QUESTIONS

1. Do you see any ways in which Christians in your country are still mentally enslaved to the power paradigm of the empires and don't fully trust in the methods of the kingdom?

2. What are the most challenging parts of the Sermon on the Mount?

3. If we understand that nations cannot be Christian nations, how might that change how we think about the involvement that Christians should have in the political sphere?

Chapter 6

The Kingdom of the Lamb

It was a rainy, late-summer day one August in Milwaukee, Wisconsin when my wife and I decided to take our sons to the zoo. We don't go to zoos anymore; this was a long time ago. It was a perfect day in many respects, highlighted by the muted crowds because of the precipitation, although it was only a light mist for most of the time that we wound through and around the streets of the zoo. The pinnacle of the day for me occurred when we went into the inside portion of the big cats exhibit and realized that we were the only humans in the entire building.

As I came around the corner, I saw the largest male lion of the pride leaning up against the thick display glass with his face pressed firmly on the glass. A waist-high railing had been installed about two feet from bottom of the glass enclosure, which angled out as it went up so that the top edge of the glass was almost directly above the railing. Feeling uninhibited by the fact that we were alone with these majestic creatures, I balanced myself and slowly leaned over the railing, getting closer and closer to the face of this beautiful animal. I remember being fascinated with the utter beauty of his eyes and marveling at the fact that my face was now a mere three to four inches away from his face. I was so lost in the splendor of looking directly into his eyes that I had forgotten something important. But I'll get to that in just a moment.

First, I have to make a confession. At the time, I was in my early thirties and had always believed that if I ever got into a situation in which I had to fight a lion with my bare hands and really had no other choice, I could take it. It wouldn't be easy, but I could do it. I was young, I felt strong and invincible, and lions are fierce, but if I had to...well, you get the idea.

Back to my mental lapse. As I peered deeper into his eyes and stretched to get just a little closer, I had neglected to think of the fact that in the animal kingdom, staring into the eyes of another is a challenge for dominance. The animal being stared at will either sense your dominance and look away or it will recognize its superior strength and attack. Guess which one this lion chose?

In a millisecond this creature went from lazily resting with his face leaning on the glass to attack mode. He rose up on his hind legs and batted the glass, attempting to smack me. His mouth opened and he gave a blood-curdling roar that reverberated through the empty building. Don't forget that the glass angled outward to almost above the railing, so it suddenly seemed like he was over me and about to pounce. I responded in the way that I think you might have too, so don't judge me. Rather than raising my hands to fight, I nearly crumpled underneath this monster and barely squeaked some sort of weak form of "Aaahhh." In that instant, I realized just how fast, how strong, and how mighty this beast was. Take him with my hands? That thought had shot out of my head faster than a speeding bullet. His strength, agility, power, and fierceness were like nothing I had ever seen. It was truly one of the most impressive things I had ever witnessed in my life.

The Scroll

The book of Revelation has been a mystery to interpret almost since it began making its way through the churches of the late first and early second centuries. It is full of images and symbols that seem strange to all but perhaps those who grew up immersed in the ancient Jewish cultural mix of the first-century world, when it was penned by a Christian named John. Chapter 4 depicts an overwhelming scene as the author is brought into view of the divine realm and sees the almighty God on his throne, surrounded by creatures who recognize and praise his greatness relentlessly. John witnesses the euphoric worship pulsating around the Great and Mighty and invites us on the journey.

John is amazed by what he sees; he leans forward over the railing, so to speak, to get a closer look. Just as he does that, it seems as though everything screeches to a halt. As chapter 5 begins, the one sitting on the throne, the Lord and God, is holding a strange scroll with writing on both sides, but the message is concealed because it is sealed with seven seals. The problem is that no one can break the seals to read this history-altering message. No one is worthy. Even a mighty angel acknowledges that he cannot open the seal, as he appeals for anyone who may be worthy to step forward, break open the scroll, and unleash its profound message upon the face of the earth.

But no one can. No one in any of the realms in the created order is worthy. Not a single creature in the divine realm can do it. No one on earth is able. Not even anyone in the realm depicted as being under the earth. No one. John's response is appropriate. He weeps uncontrollably. It would be like someone declaring that they have a document that contains the cures for every sickness and disease that strikes at human frailty and causes illness or death, only to proclaim that no one is able to open the document and release the cure. That would be a bitter pill to swallow indeed, knowing that the answers were so close but unattainable.

John weeps because no one can open the scroll or even look inside. The message will remain hidden, perhaps forever. And that's a big deal because what is in that scroll is everything. It is the solution to all the world's problems. But just as he comes to grips with the crushing reality that no one can reveal its contents, one of the elders who has been praising God tells him to stop crying. The time for lament is no more. There is one able to open the scroll. There is one magnificent and powerful enough to do what no one else could do.

What kind of majestic and powerful creature could do what no one else could even dream of doing? The description sounds appropriate: it is the Lion of the tribe of Judah. That makes sense. It would take someone so fierce and so bold as a lion to be able to accomplish what no one else ever could. They must be stronger, more powerful, and more deadly than anyone else. They must be…like a lion. Yes, the lion of the tribe of Judah. That sounds like a plausible descriptor of someone who could accomplish something so seemingly impossible.

Who is this lion and why would he be worthy to open the scroll?

I think a clue comes in the second descriptor of the Lion of Judah. He is also the Root of David. This is the key to unlocking the mystery. He is the promised heir to the throne of David. He is the Messiah. He is the one who would bring about the kingdom of God and the messianic age. The Root of David is the rightful ruler of the world.

The psalmist perfectly frames the role of the coming Messiah:

Why do the nations conspire
   and the peoples plot in vain?
The kings of the earth rise up

and the rulers band together
    against the LORD and against his anointed, saying,
"Let us break their chains
    and throw off their shackles."
The One enthroned in heaven laughs;
    the Lord scoffs at them.
He rebukes them in his anger
    and terrifies them in his wrath, saying,
"I have installed my king
    on Zion, my holy mountain."
I will proclaim the LORD's decree:
    He said to me, "You are my son;
        today I have become your father.
Ask me,
    and I will make the nations your inheritance,
    the ends of the earth your possession." (Psalm 2:1–8)

The kings of the earth will try to raise up and grab power. They will flail about seeking to become the one who can accomplish the impossible and bring all the nations together, ruling over them in peace. But each one has tried and failed. Some were more ambitious and came closer than others, but they have all failed. No one could open the scroll. No one could bring the blessing to the nations (Genesis 12:1–3). No one could crush the head of the serpent (Genesis 3:15). No one could gather the nations (Isaiah 66:18). No one.

But the kings of the earth were never intended to open the scroll. They never could have done it. They tried power and might. And one after the other failed. That is why God scoffs. It's like watching someone brag and taunt that they are about to open a lock when you know full well they have the wrong key. God had already installed his king. He knew who would open the scroll and bring about the kingdom that would gather the nations.

Plot Twist

John's anticipation must have been overwhelming in the moment. The elder has told him to look at the Lion of the tribe of Judah. That phrase was pregnant with its own messianic and kingdom overtones when a dying Jacob declared that his son Judah was like a lion, saying that "the scepter will not depart from" him. Not only that, but "the obedience of the nations shall be his" (Genesis 49:8–10). How impressive was this Lion of Judah going to be? What kind of mighty ruler could do what all the Pharaohs, Nebuchadnezzar, Cyrus, Xerxes, Alexander the Great, and even the mighty emperors of Rome failed to do? How powerful and mountainous must this man be? Yes, he must be a lion.

As John turned to look, though, he must have been confounded and bewildered. His eyes dancing with anticipation open wider as he sees…not a lion, but a lamb. And not just a lamb. A bloody lamb that has been slain. Doesn't that mean this lamb lost? A slain lamb is powerless, isn't it? What could be more disappointing? How would a slain lamb be up to a task that eluded the grasp of the greatest lions of history? Where is this mightiest of lions that was promised? Let's get him back in here.

But this Lamb embodies the spirit of God. Before John could probably even fully compute and come to grips with his disappointment, the Lamb plucks the scroll from the hand of the Almighty himself. Who could do that? Who could be so bold? God didn't give it to him. He took it. He was worthy. He could open the scroll. And the elders begin to sing in acknowledgement that he has done it. He has opened the seals and gathered the nations. God's promise to Abraham has finally been fulfilled. Like Arthur, who was the only one worthy of wresting Excalibur from its stone prison or Thor, who was worthy to wield *Mjolnir,* the Lamb is the only one who could bring together the scattered nations of Babel and finally craft them into the long-awaited kingdom of priests (Exodus 19:6).

All the kings had failed because they were not worthy, and they were using the wrong methods. Caesar certainly could not take this scroll, as powerful as he thought himself to be. Strength, power, military might, political acumen—by none of those things could rulers ever fulfill God's promises, try as they might. The Lamb was worthy because, according to the song of the elders, he was slain. He gathered the nations through self-sacrifice. That embodies the unexpected nature of the kingdom of God. Just when the powers of darkness thought they were gaining their most impressive victory yet, by slaying the Lamb they were sealing their own defeat. Had they understood, "they would not have crucified the Lord of glory" (1 Corinthians 2:8).

A New Song

The elders, who had been worshiping God on his throne, now turn their attention to praise the Lamb. Yes, he is worthy because of, not despite, being slain. He is the one that has received power, wealth, wisdom, and strength. This is a new song, because this is a new development. The Lamb has finally opened the scroll and ushered into the world the promised kingdom of God. There had previously been echoes and whispers and samples of the kingdom, but the Lamb has made it available. The nations will be blessed and gathered into God's people. The kingdom, at long last, has arrived.

Because of this stunning revelation, the Lamb is the one worthy of honor and praise. It's not just the elders, though. John hears "every creature in heaven and on earth and under the earth and on the sea, and all that is in them," (Revelations 5:13) praising not just the one who sits on the throne but praising the Lamb as well.

We will have to wrestle with this, because our hearts are not automatically oriented to desire and trust in a slain lamb. We want a lion. We want strength. The beast that will be introduced later in Revelation is far more impressive than a slain lamb. When he arrives, the inclination of the people is to worship the beast. "Who is like the beast?" they fawn, and "Who can wage war against it?" (Revelation 13:4). Even God's people who are being persecuted by this beast will be tempted to be so impressed that they will put their trust in it. That little lamb was killed, but death bounces off this beast like it's nothing (v. 12).

The beautiful scene of worship in Revelation 5 is so significant and challenging because it orients us toward the reality of the kingdom of God before we set off on the potentially winding path of politics and the role of Christians in a complicated world. There are five important truths that surface in Revelation 5 that will help us to navigate that route.

Kingdom Truth #1: It's All about Jesus

First and foremost is the reminder that the kingdom of God and our place in the world are all about Jesus. He is the Lamb that is worthy of all honor and glory and praise. He is our King, the one God chose before the foundations of the earth were laid. To give loyalty or allegiance to anyone or anything else is an exercise in futility.

I have seen many professing Christians become passionate and loyal to certain political ideologies or parties and never realize that they have become better ambassadors for their political affinities than for the kingdom of God. We can get so impassioned about these things, and so convinced that they reflect our Christian views, that we completely lose sight of the fact that our political positions and mantras have become more of a hindrance to others seeing the kingdom than a help. Others can no longer even see the kingdom in us because the view is blocked by our political and ideological opinions.

If the kingdom alone is not what we seek to reflect, then we have likely lost sight of the Lamb. For many, that doesn't bother them that much; they preferred the idea of the lion anyway.

The kingdom is all about Jesus.

Kingdom Truth #2: Victory Is through Self-Sacrifice

Second is the truth that the kingdom comes through self-sacrifice. The Lamb only becomes worthy to receive power and wealth and wisdom and strength after being slain. It is in giving away himself that he receives everything the kings and politicians of the world often seek to take.

The kingdom is not about power. It is not about imposing our way on others. It is about the way of the slain Lamb. This is why Jesus said that if we even want to think about following him, we must pick up the instrument of death and sacrifice (Luke 14:27). This is how the kingdom works. When we are truly carrying a cross, there is no room in our hands for anything else.

Jesus is a lion, but his methods are only those of the Lamb.

But this truth is often forgotten as soon as Christians being to wade into the political arena. Suddenly the lion is unleashed. It becomes about gaining ground and defeating our opponents. We need to get this law passed and that legislation introduced so that our position can become the most powerful. In short order, we have lost sight of the slain Lamb and can't really remember when was the last time we even saw him.

The kingdom is all about self-sacrifice.

Kingdom Truth #3: It Is Unexpected

The third truth is that the kingdom will be unexpected. That is true, at least from the perspective of the world. One key element of apocalyptic literature, which is the genre of the book of Revelation, is that it reveals spiritual truths that are not immediately obvious in the physical realm. That is because the spiritual truth of what is going on is so different from how most people perceive it.

The kingdom comes in unexpected and unlikely ways. Jesus seems to stress that again and again in several parables recorded in Matthew's Gospel. In the parable of the sower (Matthew 13:1–23), he imparts the truth that what matters with the gospel is the receptive nature of the heart to receive it. As explosive and important as the message is, it will not work through coercion or force. The gospel proclaimed will not produce fruit until it falls on humble ears and a soft heart. Another surprising fact is that the kingdom will not seek to conquer those who don't accept it and get them out of the way. That is the point of the parable of the weeds (vv. 24–30, 36–43). Rather, it will grow alongside the systems of the world, being barely distinguishable until the time of the harvest. Additionally, the kingdom is like the tiny mustard seed (vv. 31–35). It will look unimpressive and unable to bring about much change, but it will slowly and almost imperceptibly do its work among those who submit to Jesus as King.

This unexpected and unlikely nature of the kingdom carries on throughout the scenes of the Revelation. Upon arriving at the latter half of Revelation 19, we find that the beast and the kings of the earth have assembled to wage a final war with the rider of the white horse, who is none other than Jesus. The description of him is awe-inspiring. He is a blazing fire, with the power of many crowns. No one knows his name, meaning no one has power over him in any way. He has a sharp sword to strike down the nations and will rule with an iron scepter while treading the winepress of the fury of the wrath of God Almighty. He even has a robe dripped in blood. Finally! The Lion has shown up just in time for the final battle.

But a careful reading of the book and this scene in particular reveals something that we should have expected by this point, but that perhaps still catches us off guard. The sword is no sword at all. It is coming out of his mouth. The sharp double-edged sword that is coming from his mouth (Revelation 1:16; 2:16; 19:15, 21) is the word of God. And that robe dipped in blood? There has been no battle yet, so the blood must be that of the slain Lamb. And he will tread the winepress of wrath himself and take the judgment onto himself. Revelation 19 is not depicting a physical battle at some point in the future. It is demonstrating the truth of what Jesus' kingdom is all about. He will conquer his enemies with weapons that the world does not possess (2 Corinthians 10:3–4): the word of God and self-sacrifice. What a surprise! But that is the nature of the kingdom of God.

The kingdom is all about the unexpected and unlikely.

Kingdom Truth #4: The Nations Must Be Gathered

The fourth truth is that the kingdom of God includes the gathering of the nations. The new song that the elders sing in response to the opening of the scroll includes the recognition that the Lamb has not failed by shedding his blood. That was his very means of victory. And with that blood he has "purchased for God persons from every tribe and language and people and nation" (Revelation 5:9).

The original ideal of God having a kingdom of priests to reign with him comes from Exodus 19:6. It was the nation of Israel, just after being rescued from Egypt, who first heard those words. They would never live up to that ideal. But what they failed to do, the Lamb has accomplished.

The gathering of the nations is no small element of God's kingdom. It is one of the signs that it has come. God promised Abraham that he would bless the nations through his descendants (Genesis 12:1–3), and Isaiah prophesied about the time when the nations would be brought back together in God's kingdom (Isaiah 2:2–4; 66:18).

As Jesus gives his final instructions to his disciples in Matthew, he tells them to go and make disciples of all nations (Matthew 28:19). It is vital to note here that he did not just say, "Go and make disciples." That sentence is often cut in half, but simply saying, "Go and make disciples" robs Jesus' words of much of their connection to God's promises. The time to gather the nations has come. This inclusion of the nations is, Paul writes, the mystery of Christ (Ephesians 3:1–9; Romans 16:25; Colossians 1:26–27; 4:3) and the manifold wisdom of God on display to the powers of the world (Ephesians 3:10).

This is precisely why Paul was so adamant that divisions between the Jewish Christians and Gentile Christians must be resolved in every city and house church. The easier answer to their sharp cultural divides would have been to form two separate churches, but Paul knew that this would reflect nothing more than the divisions of the world rather than the gathering of the nations. So it is no small detail that perhaps the primary focus of the song of the elders is on the work of the Lamb finally bringing about the call of all nations to the kingdom of God.

The kingdom is all about the gathering of the nations.

Kingdom Truth #5: Jesus Is King

The fifth important truth in Revelation 5 is that Jesus is King. While it is never explicitly stated, we can easily infer such from this passage. He is the one who shares worship with God. He is the one who can sit on the Father's throne and subsequently allow others to do so (Revelation 3:21). If there is a kingdom, then there must be a king. Jesus is that king, and coming into his kingdom demands that we show him singular allegiance.

The kingdom is all about allegiance to the King.

Kingdom Truth #6: This Is a Real Kingdom

The sixth truth is that this is a real kingdom. We've already talked about this, but it is important enough to repeat here. The purpose and nature of apocalyptic literature was that it used signs and symbols to depict realities of the spiritual world as they were manifested in the physical realm. What was being depicted was real, but the true significance of it could easily be missed or marginalized. Apocalyptic writings helped to shed light on the reality of the situation.

That means that when Revelation speaks of a slain lamb that has inaugurated the kingdom of God that is now available to all people, it might not look like a typical kingdom of the world. It might easily be missed in the physical realm, but it is very real.

The kingdom is not simply a spiritual kingdom that makes no claims on or about the empires of the world. This is why the early Christians declared Jesus as Lord (Romans 10:9) before calling on his name in baptism (v. 13). This is why the early Christians decided to use a word like *metanoia*, repent, to describe what needed to take place as one entered the kingdom. *Metanoia* was used in the ancient world primarily as a word that meant to switch sides. If you were fighting for one army, the commander of the other side might offer *metanoia;* you either come over and join his side or face your fate if you refuse.

When we spiritualize the kingdom, we rob it of its power. We pretend that we can have dual allegiance to both the kingdom of God and some other nation, political system, or ideology. But the early Christians believed this to be a real kingdom with a real king that demanded the full loyalty of its citizens.

Why would the people of Thessalonica angrily charge Paul and his group with "saying that there is another king"? Because they were. That's exactly what they were saying. He wasn't a challenge to Caesar in the same way that another human king or ruler might be, but his kingdom was just as real, and allegiance could not be given to Jesus and Caesar at the same time. When one joined Jesus' kingdom, that became the sole object of their loyalty and fidelity. The kingdom requires that we live according to its standards and principles and leave behind those of the kingdoms of the world.

The kingdom is real and demands our allegiance.

The Chapter in Review

- The slaughtered lamb is not as impressive or desirous as the lion we hope for.

- The Lamb is not nearly as impressive or awe-inspiring as the beast.

- Our kingdom focus must be all about Jesus.

- Victory or lasting change will only come through self-sacrifice.

- The kingdom comes in unexpected and unlikely ways.

- The nations must be gathered.

- The kingdom is all about allegiance to King Jesus.

- The kingdom is real and demands our allegiance above all others.

The Big Idea

- ❖ The nature of the kingdom is rooted in self-sacrificial love for the world and not power or strength.

DISCUSSION QUESTIONS

1. When you want to see change in the world, do you tend to desire the strength of a lion or beast or the sacrifice of a lamb?

2. What is more difficult for you about trusting in the Lamb as opposed to a lion?

3. In what ways is the requirement of allegiance to Jesus' kingdom even more demanding than when the gospel is reduced to a message of personal repentance and forgiveness of sin?

Chapter 7

The Upheaval

One of the most popular forms of weight loss in our world today is through a medical procedure called bariatric surgery. The stomach is stapled and reduced in size, which cuts down on the ability to eat and process food, and will, in turn, result in dramatic weight loss for those who follow the protocols. The surgery is drastic but effective for most who receive it.

At least, for a time it works. Studies have demonstrated, however, that the people who return to their original weight or fairly close to it may be as high as 70 percent. Why would something so radical and so immediately effective end up failing, and those who experienced dramatic weight loss slowly slide back toward where they started?

While the answer isn't simple, it does often come down to lifestyle. The surgery forces people to reduce the amount of food they eat, but it cannot force them to change the way they eat. It cannot change their desires. And it cannot change their habits. Patients receive guidance and support to make all those changes, but often they lack the self-discipline to establish them as a permanent part of their life. Without those inner changes and adjustments in lifestyle, it is likely that the effects of the surgery will slowly wear off and the person will lose most of the progress that they have made.

In Romans 1:1–2, Paul says that he has been set apart for the good news proclamation of God, the gospel. In verses 3–4, he goes on in just about every way possible to make clear that this gospel proclamation is that God has fulfilled his kingdom promises through Jesus the King. He is the descendant of David, the Son of God in power, the Messiah, and the Lord. Each one of these concepts point to him being the promised king in a different way. And to top it off, he was resurrected from the dead, just as he said he would be, proving that he is the reigning king. That is the gospel in a nutshell. Jesus is King and his kingdom has arrived.

Paul then goes on to declare that he is not ashamed of this gospel, because "it is the power of God that brings salvation to everyone who believes" (Romans 1:16). Somewhere along the line, much of main-stream Christianity has gotten confused. We have reduced the gospel to the proclamation that Jesus is the divine member of the Trinity who died for our sins so that we could be forgiven, have a personal relationship with him, and go to heaven one day. Some form of that message has been proclaimed in almost every corner of the world in the past century or so, but there is just one problem. That message is not the gospel. This is some of the fruit of the gospel and important fruit, at that. But it is not the gospel message itself.

If we think that the gospel is a message of forgiveness of sin and personal relationship with Jesus, we can "accept it," and then go on about the rest of our lives, showing occasional gratitude to God to varying degrees. We can do all this without ever fully giving our allegiance to Jesus as our King and without becoming true submitting subjects in his kingdom.

But if we understand that the gospel message that we are to accept and share with others is that Jesus is King, his kingdom has arrived, and he offers us to lay down our lives, submit to his rule, and become ambassadors in his kingdom, then we will be saved. Or, as Paul puts it in Romans 10:9, if we declare that Jesus is Lord, we will be saved. Salvation and forgiveness are the fruit, but the gift is the kingdom. Trying to take the fruit without first committing to the gift is like engaging in sex without the commitment and boundary of marriage. What was once powerful and beautiful can became dangerous and destructive.

The kingdom of God is the way the created order *was* supposed to be. It is the way the created order *is* supposed to be. It is the way the created order *will* be one day. So when it breaks into the present realm, it will radically change those who submit to it. When we enter God's kingdom, we will be saved, because that's the fruit of being subject to Jesus as King. This is why Paul asserts in Romans 10:9 that when we confess Jesus as Lord, we will be saved. Submit to the gift and the fruit will come.

This is an important aspect of the kingdom to understand and will greatly influence how we approach a subject like politics. Changes cannot be forced upon people through laws, power, or any other shortcuts. They may, like bariatric surgery, be expedient, but by themselves, they will never bring about lasting change.

The Kingdom That Changed the World

From the opening sentence of Mark's gospel, he jumps right in and doesn't hold back any punches. Verse 1 of chapter 1 might look like an innocent opening to a spiritual book about Jesus, but that's only to our ears. Mark's words would have been a bit more explosive and confrontational to the ears of a first-century audience:

> The beginning of the good news about Jesus the Messiah, the Son of God. (Mark 1:1)

In just one verse, only fourteen words in this English translation, Mark lays out three separate, thinly veiled challenges to the kingdoms of the world, Rome being the chief among them at the time this was written. What Mark was writing was going to change everything.

His first challenge that would change the world comes in the term "good news." The English phrase "good news," often alternately translated "gospel," is the word *euaggelion* in Greek. In the first century, the primary use for that term was very specifically connected with kings and empires. It referred to a proclamation regarding a ruler. Everyone knew that, so when Mark opens with that word, there is little mistaking the claim he is making. This is a public proclamation about a new king.

The second challenge is in proclaiming Jesus as the Messiah. We often think of Messiah as another of those nice spiritual words that let us know that Jesus is our redeemer and savior. The Greek word for Messiah that Mark used was *Christos*, which has led many English versions of the Bible to transliterate it to "Christ" rather than using "Messiah." The term literally means anointed one. "Messiah" wasn't a safe word in the first century. The one declaring that identity was claiming to be king, and that was a challenge to Caesar and the empire of Rome. To be the Messiah, the king, was no small claim.

Mark's third indicator that the world is about to change is in saying that Jesus is also the Son of God. In the Old Testament, a son of God was someone who traced their roots directly back to God. But in the political world of the Ancient Near East, a son of God was nothing less than a king. The Caesars laid claim to that concept as well, and many claimed themselves to be a son of God.

Make no mistake, Mark is making huge political claims here for

Jesus. And this wasn't just his interpretation of Jesus. The first words Jesus speaks in Mark's Gospel are a declaration of the arrival of the kingdom. "The kingdom of God," he proclaimed, "has come near" (Mark 1:15).

Jesus is the Messiah, the true King come to establish his kingdom and change the world. This message is much bigger than a private spiritual experience or a conversion to a few important religious doctrines. The whole point of the kingdom of God is to change the world by offering a different way of being human. By making Jesus our King, we are restored to the way that humanity was supposed to function as God's image bearers.

It's easy to say Jesus is King, though. It's easy to declare him to be so but then keep him safely tucked away at church, and pull him out to praise and worship a little bit on Sunday morning and at our kitchen table for a few minutes early in the morning. But that Jesus is too small. Sunday morning and devotional Jesus is not the King. When Jesus is King it will challenge us to our very core. When Jesus is King it will change our world. When Jesus is King it will cause us to challenge everything around us that is not in submission to him. Nowhere is this clearer than in the tiny letter that Paul wrote to his friend Philemon.

How Onesimus Changes the World

As the early Christians slowly came to the realization of what the gathering of the nations would entail, they pushed the boundary markers of God's family deep into the Gentile nations. This brought with it all kinds of new challenges that they would not have had to face or think about had the church stayed in the safe confines of Israel, or not even to the same degree if the gospel had been kept just to diaspora Jews scattered throughout the Roman Empire. One of those challenges was slavery in the Roman Empire.

Slavery was a common part of life in the empire, except for Israel, where it was largely shunned. But just a few decades after Jesus ascended and sent his disciples to "the ends of the earth," there were many Christians who were enslaved. That might not have been so difficult to navigate, but it gets more complex when we realize that there were also slaveowners who had become disciples in Jesus' kingdom. It would seem that the gospel spread so fast that it included people who had submitted to Jesus but who had not fully worked out the complete implications of the kingdom of God. How were they going to handle these challenges?

This was a big question for the formative church. Should they issue a blanket statement outlawing slavery for anyone claiming to be a Christian? Would that risk making this a political cause like so many others? Would it even matter at a time when calling for the end of slavery would be as realistic as a contemporary church declaring that relying on fossil fuels is harmful for our environment and then calling for an immediate ban on all forms of nonrenewable electricity? These are great things to strive for, but they are such an interwoven part of the fabric of their societies that simply calling for them to be eliminated would be so close to unrealistic that it would have little to no effect. Plus, to ban something will usually involve coercion at some point. There must be a more effective way to attack slavery while keeping with the principles of the kingdom of God, which is never forced upon anyone.

If Paul were to simply write that slavery was a sin and wouldn't be allowed in the churches, what would that mean for the many who were slaves? Should they run away? Should they refuse to work and endure the beatings? Should they kill their masters or stage a slave rebellion?

What many modern readers want to know is why didn't Paul simply strike down slavery once and for all? Why didn't he say that it should be eradicated? Why didn't he denounce it?

Simply put, Paul had no interest in changing the Roman Empire. That would be like pulling up to the Titanic on a rescue boat and, rather than rescuing people from the doomed vessel, climbing aboard and spending all your time and energy in attempts to fix the massive gash in the side of the ship. Paul wanted to rescue people out of the dominions of darkness, not try to fix those empires. That reality will become increasingly important for us as we consider the role of the Christian in modern politics.

Look at something that Paul did write in the first century:

> You have taken off your old self with its practices and have put on the new self, which is being renewed in knowledge in the image of its Creator. Here there is no Gentile or Jew, circumcised or uncircumcised, barbarian, Scythian, slave or free, but Christ is all, and is in all. (Colossians 3:9–11)

The countercultural nature of what Paul has written in just a few words is cataclysmic. These disciples are being restored as image bearers. Those in the kingdom are to live the way human beings relying on God's wisdom were supposed to live. They are to be the gathering of the nations where the status, privilege, and power structures of the world have been thoroughly rejected. The gulf that separates Jew and Gentile? Gone. The barriers between the circumcised and the uncircumcised? Irrelevant. The absurd notion that either Jews or Greeks would welcome backward and uncivilized ruffians like the barbarian or Scythian? That's a normal day in God's kingdom. And a group that welcomes both the free people who have status and the enslaved who have none? This is exactly what the kingdom looks like.

The Little Letter with Big Impact

Imagine the little house church that sat in Philemon's house when Tychicus arrived, along with Onesimus and carrying a letter from Paul.[11] We can only imagine the intrigue that this would have caused among the other slaves in Philemon's household, some of whom may have been disciples themselves. But this would hold great interest to other slaves who were disciples in Philemon's house church, as well as the privileged free people in his group, and Philemon's entire family.

Onesimus had been Philemon's slave at one time and had run away for reasons unknown to us, likely stealing from Philemon in the process. We know that Paul was in prison when he wrote the letter, although it is unclear where he was imprisoned. But for some reason, Onesimus sought out Paul. Perhaps he knew that Paul was a fair man and held great influence in Philemon's life and could help him out in the present crisis. During his time with Paul, Onesimus had become a follower of Jesus and a most helpful companion to Paul. Paul would have liked to keep this young man with him, but he knew that there was a more important opportunity here, so he sent Onesimus back to Colosse, a very risky move if Philemon was like most other Roman slave owners.

You probably could have cut the tension with a knife before Tychicus began to recite Paul's short letter. What did the kingdom look like in this situation? Paul begins by sending warm greetings to his "fellow worker," Philemon, and quite probably his wife, Apphia, and son, Archippus, along with the rest of the house church. This was no private letter. It would be read publicly to the entire group, waiting as they were with great anticipation.

Verses 4–5 are a subtle but brilliant move. When Paul uses a phrase like "all his holy people," he's not just using that as a generic phrase for "everyone." It is a reference to the gathering of the nations and concepts like that of Colossians 3:11, a letter Philemon likely just heard read for the first time to his and the other groups in Colossae. Gentile, Jew, circumcised, uncircumcised, slave, free, barbarian, Scythian: they are all part of God's holy people and are to be fully embraced as equals. That's what the kingdom looks like.

Paul continues to remind Philemon how much their relationship means to him and then sets that next to how much his relationship with Onesimus is in that same vein. He is not a slave. He is Paul's son (v. 10). He is Paul's heart (v. 12). And Paul sends him back, hoping that Philemon will put the full implications on display in his own house.

Philemon from Another Perspective

If we read through the letter to Philemon from the perspective of one of his slaves or a disciple who was a slave, whether of Philemon or someone else, we can see the power of the kingdom that Paul unleashes. Think of how it felt to hear Onesimus, a runaway slave, being called "my son" and "my very heart" by Paul. How they would have marveled to hear that Paul could order such a man of privilege and power as Philemon to do what he "ought to do," but then refrain from doing so, instead appealing to Philemon to work out for himself the earth-shattering implications of the kingdom of God. Everything was different. Power, status, slave, free, important people, people who were nothing more than tools for the powerful—that was all gone in Christ. But so was coercion. Philemon, a man of power, had to see this for himself and work it out.

But the powerless also had to see it. Imagine their disbelief when they heard Paul declare that any debt Onesimus had incurred should be charged to Paul, knowing that Philemon would likely never hold this beloved apostle to a debt of any kind. Then to hear Paul urge him to welcome Onesimus, not as a slave, but as a brother. Don't sweep by that too fast. This would mean that he was part of Philemon's primary family and an equal. As a brother in the Lord, they were now siblings in a family that had no class distinctions of prestige and status.

Paul is so confident of the power of the gospel that he will simply leave it to Philemon to work this out but is sure that he will do even more than Paul is asking (v. 21). Many commentators read that statement to be implying that Paul thinks Philemon will grant his former slave his freedom. I don't think so. I think he has already implied that in the charge to welcome him as his brother. You don't enslave your brothers. Paul is asking him to go beyond even that.

It's important to take a step back here and consider some of the implications of this. The New Testament writers, and Paul specifically, are often criticized for not coming out with blanket dismissals of all Roman slavery. But it is vital to understand that the kingdom didn't come all at once, as though the minute everyone walked away from Pentecost, they fully understood all the implications of Jesus being the true king. Slavery was such a normal and accepted part of the ancient world that it may not even have occurred to anyone to challenge it until a situation like this presented itself. It took the early Christians time to recognize and come to grips with all the ways in which the kingdom would bring new life into their world and transform everything they thought they knew.

Okay Paul, Jesus is King, his kingdom has arrived, and that changes everything. That sounds nice. What does that mean for this runaway slave who has now become a member of God's household? It means there is no more slave or free. Oh, not in the sense that Paul can call for the end of slavery in the Roman Empire. To do that would send Christianity hurtling down a path of political power and coercion. No, the force of the kingdom is in choosing to love others and break down the barriers that the world constructs.

Paul's words to the Corinthians ring true here:

> I beg you that when I come I may not have to be as bold as I expect to be toward some people who think that we live by the standards of this world. For though we live in the world, we do not wage war as the world does. The weapons we fight with are not the weapons of the world. On the contrary, they have divine power to demolish strongholds. We demolish arguments and every pretension that sets itself up against the knowledge of God, and we take captive every thought to make it obedient to Christ. (2 Corinthians 10:2–5)

The kingdom had changed everything for those in Philemon's household and house church. Not through power but through love. That's what Paul was really urging Philemon to do: to love Onesimus. Paul had unleashed the new creation into this house through his letter, and life could not be the same.

Let's summarize the implications of the coming kingdom as it arrived in the household of a Colossian slaver owner who had pledged to make Jesus King.

The first is that Jesus is King. This is the very heart of the proclamation of the gospel and the truth on which everything else stands.

The second is that we must be allegiant to his way of life. That's what faith really is, allegiance. It is submitting to Jesus as King and trusting in the otherworldly way in which he has called us to live. Although we still reside in the present age, we are asked by our King to live by the values of the age to come. This is why Jesus directed us to strive for God's will on earth as though we were in heaven (Matthew 6:10).

The third implication is that everyone is equal in God's kingdom. What does it look like to live in a world where power and status over one another are soundly rejected? That is what we must work out. It will never be easy. We will never achieve it perfectly even in the church. But it must be the goal toward which we constantly strive.

The fourth truth is that the institutions of status, power, prestige, and privilege must hold no sway in the new creation. Not only do we turn away from being persons of status, we seek to eliminate the institutions of power over one another in God's kingdom. Again, that will take more work, but this is what allegiance to the king looks like. Paul called Philemon to recognize Onesimus as a brother and an equal rather than a subordinate person of no status. He then called him to do the math and figure out that the institution of slavery could have no place in the kingdom of God. This was going beyond just freeing one individual slave. Imagine what the other slaves present that day must have felt when they worked out the full implications of the kingdom arriving on earth.

The fifth implication can be the most puzzling to work out. The kingdom cannot come through power or coercion. It comes through people choosing to trust in Jesus as their King and then embracing the life of love that characterizes the kingdom. There will be constant temptations to bring about the values and life of the kingdom through means of power, but if we do that, it ceases to be the kingdom. That's the irony of it all. Where this gets especially challenging is that if we are really seeking the kingdom first, we will often be called to take up the cause of those who are powerless and oppressed, and the temptation to fight for them with whatever means necessary will be strong. Paul could have ordered Philemon to free Onesimus, but he knew that if he did that, it would no longer be the ground of the kingdom on which they were standing. That is the challenge of the new creation.

The final reality is that the true kingdom is powerful and eternal. Let's say that Paul focused all his energy on eliminating slavery from the Roman Empire. Let's say he succeeded. What does that amount to the moment the power of Rome ceases? The Roman Empire is long gone, but the power of the kingdom carries on precisely because it was not attached to Rome. By Paul not losing sight of what the kingdom was about and where its true power lay, it continues to impact every person who embraces the full implications of God's new world that he unleashed through the gospel.

The Chapter in Review

- The gospel message is the proclamation that Jesus is King and when we submit to that, then we receive the benefits of the kingdom.

- But if we think that the gospel message is that we can be forgiven if we just accept it, we risk ignoring submission to Jesus as King.

- The life of the kingdom cannot come about through laws, power, or coercion. It must be chosen.

- Paul called Philemon to view Onesimus as a member of his family, which changed everything about their relationship.

- Paul was balancing the kingdom characteristics that everyone is equal, but everyone must also be free to choose the life of the kingdom.

The Big Idea

❖ Embracing the kingdom fully will change every conceivable aspect of our lives.

DISCUSSION QUESTIONS

1. Why did Paul not simply say that slavery was not allowed in any way, shape, or form within the kingdom communities?

2. What impact might it have on our approach to political power to recognize that the kingdom of God must always be chosen, and people can never be coerced?

3. Are there any areas in the life of the church family in which you have yet to work out the full implications that the institutions or identities of power, prestige, and privilege hold no sway in the kingdom of God?

Chapter 8

For the Life of the World

I'm not sure there could be two songs that carry more divergent worldviews than "I Want It All" by Queen and the traditional hymn "This World Is Not My Home," written by JR Baxter but perhaps made most famous by country singer Jim Reeves.

The Queen song is an anthem for the dissatisfied who can see nothing beyond the present circumstances of this life. The narrating voice of the song is an "adventure seeker" who has "no time for doubt," and is desperate to find his future now with a willingness to move anyone out of his way who becomes an obstacle. He wants right now what he believes is his, and the only use for the future is to serve as a picture for what he plans to try to take right now. The chorus emphasizes his passion. "I want it all, and I want it now," he repeats over and over. This isn't just a side project in life, the narrator states. He has a one-track mind and has no room for compromise. He is going to live life to the full starting right now. He wants everything life has to offer because this is all there is.

JR Baxter's song depicts just the opposite perspective. The only thing that matters in this song is the future. "This world is not my home," says the narrator, "I'm just a-passing through." This life is temporary, and he knows it. His treasures are "somewhere beyond the blue," and he goes through life hearing the beckoning of angels to his future in heaven louder than any noise the world can offer. So much is he focused on this blissful future that he declares that he "can't feel at home in this world anymore." He thinks of how the Lord is far and away his best friend and how his mother waits for him in this utopian glory land. The saints are shouting victory and waiting for him, and he longs for the day when he can join them all in this eternal domain. The shine of the world grows fainter for him as the shouts and visions from heaven grow louder and more vibrant. Heaven has called, and he can't feel at home any longer in this dingy and pale world.

One narrator is singularly focused on this world in the present age and the other is uniquely concentrating on the future of heaven.

One will stop at nothing to grab everything the world has to offer by the throat and take what he wants and needs now. The other has developed a near disdain for the things of the world and wants nothing more than the future of heaven. One sees the things of the world as being of great importance and worth having, the other shares the vision of another beloved hymn, "and the things of earth will grow strangely dim in the light of his glory and grace."[12] One song sees no hope or value in anything beyond the present. The other sees no hope in the present and waits for evacuation.

These polar opposites capture the extremes that many Christians feel when it comes to our role in the world. Do we settle in and accept that our biggest concern is to bring justice, peace, and harmony right now because, after all, YOLO?[13] Or is the primary mission of Christians to warn the world that judgment is coming and they had better accept the salvation that Jesus has graciously offered and join those who are awaiting our eventual evacuation to the glorious bliss of sweet Beulah land, heaven? Do we accommodate to the culture and throw ourselves into it fully, investing our passion and hope, or do we separate from it completely, fervently waiting for our rescue from this cruel world?

In the Middle

Standing in between those two songs and worldviews is the perspective hinted at in the classic hymn, "This Is My Father's World," written by Maltbie Davenport Babcock in the late nineteenth century and put to music by Franklin L. Shepherd in the early twentieth century.

> This is my Father's world,
> And to my list'ning ears
> All nature sings, and round me rings
> The music of the spheres.
>
> This is my Father's world;
> I rest me in the thought
> Of rocks and trees, of skies and seas—
> His hand the wonders wrought.
>
> This is my Father's world;

The birds their carols raise,
The morning light, the lily white
Declare their Maker's praise.

This is my Father's world;
He shines in all that's fair;
In the rustling grass I hear him pass;
He speaks to me everywhere.

This is my Father's world;
Oh, let me ne'er forget
That though the wrong seems oft so strong,
God is the ruler yet.

This is my Father's world;
The battle is not done:
Jesus who died shall be satisfied,
And earth and heav'n be one.

The narrator of this song revels in the things of the world but in a much different way than the frustrated young man of "I Want It All." This person is not focused on themselves and the pleasure that they think should be theirs with no waiting. Rather, they marvel at the beauty and wonder of God's creation, seeing the good in it. They hear the melodies of the natural world and see them rightfully as wonders set forth by the hands of God. This is their Father's world.

But there is a stark realism in what they see as well. That the Father shines in all that is fair is a tacit admission that there is much in the world that is not fair. The battle remains unfinished. Unlike in "This World Is Not My Home," though, this narrator doesn't see the world as almost exclusively negative or a necessary inconvenience while waiting for heavenly glory. The world contains the wonders of God and much good. Some things are fair, and they see God in them. They pray that they will never forget that God is the ruler of this world, even though the wrong often seems so strong and dominant. In short, there is much work to be done for kingdom citizens.

"This Is My Father's World" shares the perspective of seeing good in the world but rejects the hedonism and "this is all there is" angst of "I Want It All." It finds common ground with "This World Is Not My Home," as it revels in God and his heavenly presence, but it rejects the mindset that this world is rotten and the only hope is escape. It ends with a powerful thought that comes straight from the language of Ephesians 1:10. The battle is not done, because Jesus' goal is that one day, heaven and earth will be brought back together as one.

Letters to the Exiles

In the biblical worldview, heaven and earth were supposed to be joined in one realm. Early Christians didn't see heaven so much as a location in the typical sense. It was the realm of the divine. Wherever God is, that is heaven. It is his presence. Before the Fall of humankind, the heavenly realm and the earthly realm freely overlapped, but sin put a necessary barrier between the human realm and the divine presence. They would now overlap at special times and places when God allowed it. It might be in a burning bush or the tabernacle, but wherever God's presence broke into the physical realm, that was the overlap of heaven and earth. In time, the temple of God became the place where heaven and earth were understood to overlap, almost exclusively. When the temple was destroyed, first in 586 BC and again in AD 70, it inaugurated a crisis for the people of God. Where could God's presence be found when there was no temple?

The first time the temple was destroyed, the people of Israel were carried off into captivity in the great empire of Babylon. They were defeated, the place where heaven and earth overlapped was no more, and they had little hope for the future. What were they to believe when the nations around them looked so much more powerful and effective than their God?

How were they to carry themselves during this time of exile? Should they follow the way of the turtle and try to protect themselves from this new culture around them at all costs? That would be fortification, and it certainly had its appeal. They could protect themselves and separate as best they could and wait it out. This could be accompanied by a private pietism, with their faith kept in private or in isolation, and would attempt to have little to no impact on the world around them.

Or, they could follow the way of the lion and attack. They could fight the culture around them and attempt to conquer it. This is the way of domination. That would be a tall task during the Babylonian exile, but they could try. They would be culture warriors, always on the prowl for a good fight and sensitive to any attacks or slights against their preferred way of living.

The prophet Jeremiah, though, seems to have called them in another direction altogether. Here is a portion of Jeremiah's letter to the exiles:

> This is what the LORD Almighty, the God of Israel, says to all those I carried into exile from Jerusalem to Babylon: "Build houses and settle down; plant gardens and eat what they produce. Marry and have sons and daughters; find wives for your sons and give your daughters in marriage, so that they too may have sons and daughters. Increase in number there; do not decrease. Also, seek the peace and prosperity of the city to which I have carried you into exile. Pray to the LORD for it, because if it prospers, you too will prosper." Yes, this is what the LORD Almighty, the God of Israel, says: "Do not let the prophets and diviners among you deceive you. Do not listen to the dreams you encourage them to have. They are prophesying lies to you in my name. I have not sent them," declares the LORD.
>
> This is what the LORD says: "When seventy years are completed for Babylon, I will come to you and fulfill my good promise to bring you back to this place. For I know the plans I have for you," declares the LORD, "plans to prosper you and not to harm you, plans to give you hope and a future. Then you will call on me and come and pray to me, and I will listen to you." (Jeremiah 29:4-12)

This is what it is going to look like to be a prophetic community given their situation in exile. It is significant and perhaps shocking to note that the first thing he tells them is that this is no surprise to God. He, not the Babylonians, led them into exile. The rest of the instructions are just as scandalous and point to neither domination nor fortification.

Instead, Jeremiah says to become part of life. Plant gardens, get married, increase in number. And not only that. They are to seek the peace and prosperity of the city in which they are in exile. They should pray relentlessly, because if the city prospers, they too will benefit.

Letters to the New Exiles

After the temple was destroyed and the people returned from Babylon to Judea, a second temple was eventually constructed. Yet many Jewish people would continue to embrace the identity of being in exile because they believed that the presence of God had not returned to the temple. It was no longer the overlap of heaven and earth. Some took the perspective of "I want it all, and I want it now," and lived accordingly. Others embraced more of a "this world is not my home" view of things and broke off from society, waiting for God to show up and institute his kingdom rule over the world and usher in the age to come.

One of the most shocking aspects of Jesus' message was that the kingdom was now arriving. Many of his hearers assumed that when he spoke of the kingdom, he meant God one day ruling the world through Israel in a new age where death, sin, evil, and the domination of the pagan nations were done away with. That's what they were hoping for. But they would soon find out that Jesus had something else in mind.

He spoke often about bringing eternal life for those who would follow him, but it is important to note that Jewish ears of the first century would hear that phrase differently than we tend to. He was announcing the *zōē aiōnios,* which can be translated as "eternal life," but, if you recall, more literally means "the life of the coming age." When Jesus spoke of bringing about eternal life, they didn't think it meant exclusively living forever; to them, it referred instead to the time of the age to come, when God's presence would fill the earth, he would establish his eternal kingdom, and heaven and earth would once again be one.

The twist of the Christian gospel for Jews was that Jesus did bring about the kingdom of God and his presence, but not in a way in which the present order of things was completely undone. The kingdom had come to earth, but not its fullness. In that time-travel sort of way, the age to come had broken into the present age. But it wasn't here completely. The time for that would wait. Suddenly the church found itself in an in-between time that they were not expecting. They realized that Jesus was the embodiment of the age to come, and they embraced that way of living and being human, but they were still living within the fallenness of the present age.

It slowly dawned on them that they were exiles. They were citizens of heaven living in the present age. Writing some thirty years after Jesus' death and resurrection, Peter recognizes this, addressing his letter to the "exiles scattered throughout the provinces" (1 Peter 1:1), and later goes on to say, "Dear friends, I urge you, as foreigners and exiles, to abstain from sinful desires, which wage war against your soul" (1 Peter 2:11).

Peter seems to have firmly embraced the identity of an exile and wanted the early Christians to do the same. Their homeland would be the full overlap of heaven and earth, and they were clearly not living in that time yet. In the meantime, they were to be the temple, the place of God's presence. They were the overlap. In other words, they were people of the coming age who were still living in the present age. They were, in all reality, exiles.

Living as Exiles

If the early Christians were exiles of a sort, and our situation is no different, that means we are exiles as well. Does that then mean that we can look to the lessons for the exiles of Jeremiah's day and carefully apply some of those principles to our own time? I think so, although there are some dramatic differences between our situation and theirs. If we consider Jeremiah's instructions in light of our own experience as exiles, what important principles can we discern?

First, they were to live as though this place was their home even though it wasn't (Jeremiah 29:5–6). Nowhere does God instruct the exiles to live in tents to remind themselves that this is not their real home. There are no directives to remember that Babylon is not their home and they're just a-passing through, so hang on tight and wait for the evacuation that is coming soon. In fact, we see the opposite. Even though the exile was a limited time, they are told to settle in and live lives that would look similar, in some respects, to those around them, at least in the areas of provision and existence. Jeremiah was instructing them to live as residents while keeping their identity as aliens.

Second, they were to demonstrate light and life to those around them (Jeremiah 29:5–6). What influence could they have if all they did was complain about how bad life was in Babylon and lived as though the only hope they had was to escape the exile and get back to Jerusalem? What would that really demonstrate about the power of their way of life? How would that impact those who were not inherently miserable living in Babylon? Their lives needed to display the power of the life-giver.

Third, they were to create the conditions for life to flourish and invite those around into that way of living (Jeremiah 29:7). If they prospered and flourished as a people, that would say something about their way of life. When they set up their communities, when they went to work, when they planted gardens, they should do so not just to subsist until evacuation or strictly for their own benefit, they were to act so that light and life would be demonstrated and offered to those around them.

Fourth, they were not to fool themselves; it would be challenging (Jeremiah 29:8–9). The people wanted false prophets who would constantly tell them everything would be okay, regardless of what lay ahead. Exile was not going to be easy. Even though they were to live lives that prospered and brought life, they would be different from the society around them, and that would bring challenges and heartache. There were some things that they could never embrace about where they lived. They were not to lose their identity, and that would bring about conflict and persecution as well. Yet they were to balance that struggle with flourishing life. This would be a tall order indeed.

Fifth, they were not to forget that this place was not their ultimate reality (Jeremiah 29:10). Their exile was a limited situation; they were to plan as though they would one day leave Babylon but still live like they would be there permanently. Yes, they were to live thriving and flourishing realities but never forget that they were exiles and had a greater reality ahead of them. Finding that balance would keep them on the mission of bringing life while avoiding the temptation to accommodate and lose themselves into the culture around them. Everything about the culture would seek to encourage them to give up their identity and embrace the power of Babylon, but they needed to resist and never forget that they were exiles.

Sixth, they were to know that God had put them in this period of exile to work toward his plan of redemption for the whole creation (Jeremiah 29:11). They might question why they had to go through this. Why wouldn't God just take them home now if that was his ultimate plan? They needed to understand that this was to prosper them in the long run. It was to bring life to them and the world. They should not just limit themselves to living life for themselves. They were there for the life of the world.

Living in the In-Between

So, how are Christians to live our lives now? We are foreigners and exiles, says Peter (1 Peter 2:11) and should live that way. We are waiting for the age to come, yet here we are in the present. Peter says to "live such good lives among the pagans that, though they accuse you of doing wrong, they may see your good deeds and glorify God on the day he visits us."

If we were to match up the six principles above, we see a remarkable correlation with what Peter instructs the exiles of the new covenant in 1 Peter 29–12.

Principles from Jeremiah 29	1 Peter 2:9–12
Settle into life	"Live such good lives among the pagans that…"
Demonstrate life	"…they may see your good deeds…"
Create the conditions for life to flourish	"… and glorify God…"
Embrace the challenge	"…though they accuse you of doing wrong."
Keep your eye on the ultimate reality	"…on the day he visits us."
Know that God has your good in mind	"Once you were not a people, but now you are the people of God; once you had not received mercy, but now you have received mercy."

The wording and order of principles, of course, is not identical, but the concepts are remarkably consistent. Embrace your life as a citizen of the kingdom, but that means that you live as an exile who strives to live a flourishing life that will create the conditions for life to thrive for those around you so that they will be drawn to God. It will not be easy, but God is using this for his plan, glory, and purpose.

The big twist between the life of an exile now and in Jeremiah's time is the coming of the kingdom. For Jeremiah, demonstrating a prosperous life was paramount, and it would not look all that different from the peoples' lives around them, save for their loyalty to the old covenant Law, whereas Peter goes on in verse 13–25 to show that the beautiful life to which they are now called is to follow the example of Christ, which includes suffering for doing good and not retaliating against enemies. They are bringing life to the world just as Jeremiah's exiles did, but now it is the life of the age to come, which will look even stranger than living by the Law did. The life that Jeremiah's exiles were to bring was still rooted in the present age, so it very much involved prosperity and blessing in the physical realm. While those do not become irrelevant for people of the age to come, spreading the life of the kingdom takes priority over temporary justice and abundance.

The Chapter in Review

- We can view life as something fleeting, with our only hope being to grab everything we can now, or something that is hopelessly negative and to be escaped as quickly as possible.

- Or we can embrace the alternative kingdom view that there is much that is both good and bad in the world and that we have been given the task of living for the life of the world.

- The people of the kingdom were to embrace identity as exiles, similar in some ways but also different in some important ways from the exiles who were taken to Babylon.

- The exiles were to settle in to their exile and live for the life of the people around them, while never losing their identity as exiles.

The Big Idea

❖ Kingdom people are exiles, living radically different lives than the world around but living for their benefit.

DISCUSSION QUESTIONS

1. What is similar between the situation in which Christians today find themselves in the world and what the exiles of Israel faced?

2. What does it mean to be in the world but not of the world?

3. In what specific ways does the world of the nations and politics seek to pull us away from our identity as kingdom exiles?

Chapter 9

The Dragon and the Beast

The prophet Daniel's dreams must have been terrifying. They were the sort of thing that would keep you from going to sleep at night. Early in Belshazzar's short reign, when he ruled as coregent with his father Nabonidus as king of Babylon, Daniel had a dream about four fearsome beasts that laid waste to anything that stood in their way. The first three were like a winged lion, a bear, and a leopard, and they were bad enough. But the fourth beast was so horrifying, Daniel couldn't even compare it to anything he had seen before. They were all beasts, but this one was like no other.

As John continues describing his own overwhelming vision that we know as the Revelation, he sees a beast that sounds much like Daniel's fourth beast, but it is even more monstrous than Daniel thought. It has combined the characteristics of the other beasts, yet is fiercer and more dangerous than one could imagine. We talked about this beast briefly in Chapter 6, but let's dive in a little further now.

The description in chapter 13 is the first we are hearing of this beast in Revelation, but the description sounds vaguely familiar. And not just because it resembles the beasts of Daniel's vision. This beast came out of the sea, the place of chaos and opposition to God in this type of symbolic literature, but he does not stand on his own authority. The real power behind the beast is the great dragon who stands approvingly on the shore, watching his monstrous creation arise. This beast is more terrifying and powerful than anything seen before. The dragon seems to be operating as the god of this realm and the beast is his anointed one. That's why this beast sounds recognizable; it bears the image of the great dragon.

Make no mistake, this beast is mighty, powerful, and impressive. The dragon has given him almost unlimited authority over the nations, something that he offered to Jesus in the wilderness but was rebuffed. He is adorned with crowns, which signify the great power and dominion that belong to him. Then the beast suffers a fatal wound, but he is so powerful and terrifying that not even a fatal wound can cause fatality. Don't forget how much more impressive this beast is than the Lamb, at least at first. The Lamb had been slain. But death has seemingly no effect on the beast. How terrifying.

The world, however, is not frightened by the beast; they are filled with wonder and they, in effect, worship the dragon, through their love for the beast. This is the most exceptional beast that has ever existed, praise the crowds. This beast can wage war like no other and will keep them safe. As we read on in Revelation, we find that the people love the beast because he also brings them economic security and booming prosperity. This beast is amazing. They should see it for what it is, but they don't.

If you don't see this beast as something of a reverse image of the Lamb, you should, because it is most likely that this is what John intends for his audience to do. The Lamb did not operate independently but was the anointed of the holy God on his throne. The expectation was a powerful and fierce lion, but when John looked, he got much less than he expected. He saw nothing but a lamb that had faced death and submitted to it.

Who is the real power in the world? That is the question of Revelation. The beast is not independent but is the anointed of the dragon, who, we have already been told, has his own counterfeit throne (Revelation 2:13). Rather than getting less than they expect, as when John turned to see the lion/lamb, the beast is more wildly impressive than expected economically, militarily, politically, and in every other way. It was given authority over every tribe, people, language, and nation, the very pool from which the worshipers of the Lamb come. This is clearly a competition of some sort. But when death came for the beast and it looked like it was about to topple, it shook it off and carried on through the sheer force of its own power. In every way, this beast looks like a clear favorite in any contest with a single lamb that was already slain.

The Great Roman Empire

Most biblical scholars agree that Daniel's four beasts are a vision of a succession of one manifestation of empire after another, culminating in the great Roman Empire. That is the magnificent and terrible beast of John's Revelation. The beast is then propped up by a second beast, which is likely the provinces, territories, and nations that feed at the table of the great beast and become accomplices in its quest for power and control.

The identity of the beast seems to be the Roman Empire. Yet John never states that directly, and I think that's intentional. The beast is Rome, but it is also any empire or country that embraces the way of worldly empires, which is seemingly most, if not all. John is exposing the true nature of the mighty Roman Empire, but he is also pulling the curtain back to expose empire in general.

It has become standard in the world of biblical interpretation to assume that Revelation was written to encourage first-century Christians who were hanging on for dear life during intense persecution under the reign of Domitian, or possibly an earlier emperor. But historians now tend to agree that there was a fierce persecution of Christians under the reign of Nero in the 60s AD that was limited to Rome. There is little evidence that there was widespread persecution under Domitian near the end of the first century.[14] Certainly, there were pockets of persecution, but much of that in the first century was at the hands of Jewish communities and not the Roman Empire itself. The more far-reaching and violent persecutions would come in the centuries to follow.

A look at the letters addressed to the seven churches in Asia Minor reveals a mixed bag. Two of the churches are commended for holding up under some level of persecution (it appears to have been a limited problem in Pergamum's past as well but not a persistent issue), but no mention is made of this being the case, or even a threat, for the others. They are dealing with the pressures of caving to false doctrines or drifting in their witness. And the church in Laodicea is directly challenged for being too comfortable in their material wealth and security.

New Testament scholar Craig Koester points out that:

> Revelation addresses the ordinary challenges facing Christians under Roman rule, rather than speaking only to those enduring a time of terror. Some of the readers were struggling, but others were affluent and complacent. The book's visions seek to alter the way they see the political, religious and economic dimensions of imperial life and to call them to renewed faithfulness to God and the Lamb.[15]

In other words, many Christians to whom this letter was addressed were quite comfortable. Life was good. They were apparently tempted to see the empire in which they lived as a pretty good thing. Perhaps they even viewed it as a blessing from the Lord. They were lucky to live in such a stable time and place where the "blessing" of economic boom was the reality and "peace" through the power of a mighty military machine allowed them to sleep serenely at night. They may have felt quite patriotic and proud. But Revelation is a wakeup call. Empires may seem benevolent and filled with blessings, but empire is a beast from the perspective of heaven's throne room. Nations have their role in the world, but we are not to fall in love with them. "Rather than speaking against an ominous change in imperial policy," Koester notes about the purpose of John's book, "Revelation challenges the dominant currents of imperial life."[16]

After Caesar Augustus united most of the known world, it was praised as the dawn of a new age of peace that they called the Pax Romana. The provincial councils of the cities of Asia Minor asked Caesar if they could construct temples to venerate him as a divine being.[17] Augustus was initially skeptical to go that far, but eventually allowed temples to be built in honor of Rome and even himself. His primary goal was to elicit political and national allegiance to the empire. The people were happy to do it and hailed Rome as the hope of humanity and the greatest nation in the history of the world. Looking through the rose-colored glasses of patriotism, Rome was a force for good and peace in the world. Its economic prosperity was a sign of blessing, and their fierce military machine was necessary for their safety and the peace of the world. Rome was a nation under the gods for the good of her people.

Through the course of the first century, political allegiance and veneration of the emperor became unfettered worship. In increasing measure, titles like the son of god and lord of the world were coupled with outright claims of divinity. Patriotism became religious devotion. And this would eventually bring kingdom people into conflict with Rome. Koester notes that:

> Rome did not demand exclusive allegiance to the emperor or to the gods. As long as Roman subjects showed due reverence for the gods and the emperors, they were free to also worship Jesus or almost any other deity. But most Christians did not permit such reciprocity within their ranks. For them there was "one Lord, one faith, one baptism, one God

and Father of all, who is above all and through all and in all" (Eph. 4:5–6). That radical exclusivity set the stage for a showdown with the empire.[18]

What Revelation Is

At the heart of Revelation is the looming question: Who really is king and lord of the world? Is it Rome or is it the Lamb? And before you answer too quickly, know that Rome is the beast, in league with the dragon. That is one of John's primary messages.

It is important to know that Revelation is a type of biblical literature that was well known in first-century Jewish culture. It's known as apocalyptic literature. Our modern imaginations often view this type of writing as though its main purpose is to tell about the end of the world. While it may often look ahead to the end of the age, the main function of apocalyptic literature is to reveal. It lets the readers know the spiritual realities behind the everyday events that are going on.

As John retells his vision of the events that will soon take place, he is exposing his readers to the realities of empire and of all societies then and in the future that exalt government as a type of civil religion or put their trust in it. Governments are necessary to keep peace and order, but they are a rival to the kingdom of God and always will be.

Revelation is meant to retrain our passions. It might be difficult for many of us to admit, but we like the idea of a beast in charge. Beasts keep us safe. They keep borders in check, the economy flowing, and our enemies at bay. The beast is the type of ruler that we want.

I am always amazed at how quickly we will compromise so much in exchange for the safety and comfort that a beast will provide, all the while convincing ourselves that the beast is good. And we seem quite willing to close our eyes to the fact that many of the behaviors of the beast might bring about this security that we crave but do so through methods that are much more consistent with the way of the dragon than with the way of the slain Lamb. We must ask ourselves: Which one imposes its will on others? Which one works through power over others rather than power under them? Which one will kill their enemies to keep safe rather than submitting to death at the hands of those enemies to show them that there is a different way to live and think that has broken into the world?

The way of the dragon is so fundamentally different from the way of the lamb that the two are hopelessly unreconcilable.

The dragon thrives in an atmosphere of fear. When people are afraid, they will give up more than they ever thought they might to find security once again. When terror strikes, the dragon promises comfort and beckons us to compromise.

The lamb calls us to take a longer view of reality. He calls us to beat our swords and instruments of war into instruments of peace. He calls us to treasure the way of heaven rather than storing up treasure on earth. He calls us to value the rule of God over and above temporary safety and security. He beckons us to understand the power of the slain Lamb. When we grasp that the Lamb was killed but conquered the world through that death, everything changes. It is this that caused the author of Hebrews to write,

> Since the children have flesh and blood, he too shared in their humanity so that by his death he might break the power of him who holds the power of death—that is, the devil—and free those who all their lives were held in slavery by their fear of death. (Hebrews 2:14–15)

The power of the kingdom lies in knowing that there is an entirely different reality at play than the one that empire lives by. This is why the true kingdom of God is such a threat. We must return to Matthew 6:10 for a moment to see how powerful this really is. Jesus' prayer was for the kingdom to come. But how does it come? By God's will being done on earth as it is in heaven.

That is a radical change of realities. And it demands an equally radical change in priorities. No longer is the agenda for a follower of Jesus about what will help us succeed in this present age. That cannot be what drives us. What becomes the only thing that matters is embracing God's will right now. That doesn't mean that in each moment in life there is some clear path that God wants us to take, and our lives are now reduced to uncovering the correct choice in every single instance. Make the wrong choice and God's will has been subverted. Which job do I take? Which person do I marry? Which city should I live in? What is God's will?

That's not what Jesus means when he speaks of God's will. I think Jesus has in mind something a little bigger and broader than that. It is about the direction we are heading. Are we going to live by the guiding values of the kingdom that he has been laying out in the Sermon on the Mount, or are we going to embrace the values of the present age and then try to be as godly as we can, given those presuppositions?

I must be honest here. If we have embraced the core values such as safety, security, and the good life now as the right ones, we will find the kingdom of God almost impossible to enter. It will be as difficult as a large camel walking through the eye of a needle.

The Stark Difference

John's vision demonstrates the difference between the way of the dragon and the way of the Lamb nowhere clearer than in Revelation 19. The conflict between the beast and the Lamb has reached its crescendo, and one of them must go. In one corner, we have the Lamb, who now appears riding on a white horse and is ready to wage war "with justice" (Revelation 19:11). In the other corner are the beast and the kings of the earth and all their armies (v. 19). This is going to be an epic battle, the war to end all wars.

But then in one of the most anticlimactic verses in the entire Bible, verse 20 simply says, "But the beast was captured." That's it? No great battle? No iconic back-and-forth struggle with the armies of the rider on the white horse finally winning? We might picture that some great battle like the one depicted in *Avengers: End Game* is coming, but we get nothing of the sort. How was this battle won so easily?

The careful reader of the Revelation will note that there, shockingly, is no battle. The Lamb is dressed in "a robe dipped in blood" (Revelation 19:13), and coming out of his mouth is "a sharp sword with which to strike down the nations. 'He will rule them with an iron scepter'" (v. 15). Those are all important symbols. If we hearken back to chapter 5, we recognize that the blood on his robe is most likely his own. It is lamb's blood. And his weapon is the word of God, which we are told not so subtly in verse 13 is the name of this rider. And the iron scepter? This is the promised king of Psalm 2. Yes, this slaughtered lamb of a king, says Michael Gorman, acts "on behalf of God to rid the world of evil, but he does so with only his own blood and a sword in his mouth...not with a sword in his hand to literally shed the blood of his enemies."[19]

This all means that the two weapons used to defeat the beast were nothing more than the Lamb's own blood and the word of God. The beast was amassing his armies, preparing for a battle because that is how he has always handled conflict. The one with the biggest army wins and gets to be the next empire, the biggest beast. But this time the beast is taken down without a single arrow being fired or a sword leaving its scabbard. Self-sacrifice and the proclamation of God's word; those are the only things that will take down the beast and turn our affections away from it.

Eventually, God will restore his creation; chapters 21 and 22 look ahead to that time. But for now, when one beast falls, another will move in to take its place. Each one will be a bit different. There will be beasts even more ferocious and violent than the Roman beast. Throughout history, there have been and will be kinder, gentler beasts that mean well. But a beast is a beast. The fundamental values of empire are so divergent from the fundamental values of the kingdom of God that the two can never truly mix. The kingdom can operate from within an empire and serve as an alternative way of life to those who would embrace it. This is the prophetic community, the wheat among the tares. But we must disabuse ourselves of the notion that any empire of the world can operate under the values of the kingdom of God. That is no more possible than this beast being a lamb.

Who Is Worthy to Open the Scroll?

What was in the scroll that was in the right hand of God back in Revelation 5? If we shorthand it and say that it contained the will of God, that makes something totally clear: only the Lamb was worthy to open that scroll. Don't ever forget that. The beast was just another in a long line of those that were unable and unworthy. The beast will try, but it will never be able to pluck that scroll from God's hand or open it. It will never be able to serve as an agent of God and reveal the contents of the scroll as the Lamb has done.

Only the one who can open the scroll is worthy of worship. Only the one who can open the scroll is worthy of allegiance and devotion.

So, Christian, it is time to ask. Is the Lamb in his kingdom the only recipient of your worship, your trust, your loyalty, your devotion, your allegiance?

The Chapter in Review

- The beast in Revelation is a reverse image of and rival to the Lamb. It represents Rome but also all empires in general.

- Revelation reveals that humans tend to crave and revere the security and comfort provided by the beast.

- Revelation reorients our affections away from loving the beast.

- Revelation exposes that we will put up with the methods of the beast, which are the complete opposite of the Lamb's, because we enjoy the benefits that the beast provides.

- The weapons that Jesus uses to defeat his enemies are nothing more than his own sacrificial blood and the word of God.

- The beast will never be able to open the scroll and reveal God's will to the world. Only the Lamb can do that.

- Only the Lamb is the proper recipient of our worship, only the kingdom the proper source of allegiance and devotion.

The Big Idea

❖ We must distinguish clearly in our hearts and minds between God's kingdom and the empires of the world.

DISCUSSION QUESTIONS

1. In what ways can Christians in the country in which you live be tempted to trust in their nation or national politics in similar ways to the temptations faced by the first-century Christians?

2. Do you see any evidence in your church family that people value security, comfort, and abundance more than they do self-sacrifice?

3. If John were to address our churches today, what might he have to say that is similar to his message in Revelation? What might be different?

Chapter 10

The Only Debt

> When in the course of human events, it becomes necessary for one people to dissolve the political bands which have connected them to another, and to assume among the powers of the earth, the separate and equal station to which the Laws of Nature and of Nature's God entitle them…they should declare the causes which impel them to the separation.[20]

So began the independent course of my country over two hundred years ago. The most influential men of the time had concluded that the interests of the thirteen colonies on the continent of North America no longer shared a common vision with the country to which they belonged. It was time, they believed, to cut ties with England and with her king, King George. There had already been several armed skirmishes between the colonists, who felt that they were being taxed oppressively with no real representation in England, and the soldiers of the king.

The excerpt above is from a document that is viewed as virtually a sacred text for Americans, known as the Declaration of Independence. It goes on to lay out the case for why separation from England was not only justified but was "self-evident" and based on the laws that the Creator himself has established. It ends with the assurance that they issued this declaration "with a firm reliance on the protection of Divine Providence." That's a strong statement, and they were fully convinced that they were doing what was right.

As an American myself, I was raised to revere the decision that these men made. We celebrate it joyously every year on the Fourth of July, shooting off fireworks, going to parades, honoring the founding fathers of the country, and spending time with friends and relatives reflecting on the blessings of our freedoms that we have in this country. Without question, these men were heroes and made the right decisions at the time, difficult as they may have been.

But I have a question. My question is not whether those decisions were right or wrong. My question is not whether their decisions were beneficial for what would become the United States of America. My question is not asked as an American at all. My question is asked as someone who stood before a cloud of witnesses in January 1999 in a room that used to be a kitchen on the third floor of an old convent and, just before I stepped into a large metal trough that would serve as a makeshift baptismal, pledged my allegiance to Jesus as my King.

My question is rather simple: Was the decision of the founding fathers to start a revolution a display of the kingdom of God?

That's a question that is difficult to ask but not nearly as challenging to answer. I'm not implying that they were evil for making the decisions that they did. I'm not necessarily commenting on what I think they might have done instead. But for a kingdom person, it should be obvious by now that this does not sound like the way of the Lamb.

The New Testament's Evaluation of Empire

In Warren Carter's book, *The Roman Empire and the New Testament: An Essential Guide,*[21] he gleans five principles from the New Testament that were intended to form a spectrum as to how Christians should view empire and, in their specific context, the Roman world around them. These principles, however, are not just limited to the first century. They continue to guide and direct God's people in any context as we evaluate our place in the world.

The first principle is that nations, human-run governments, and empires exist under the realm of the devil. It is the satan that the Gospels identify as controlling the world's empires (Matthew 4:8–9; Luke 4:6–7). From the perspective of the Gospel authors, God allows this situation to continue and uses it for his purposes, but that doesn't change the fact that the devil controls the world's empires and nations. In contrast to that, Jesus is bringing about God's one and only kingdom. I have carefully distinguished in this book between the empires of the world and the kingdom of God, but in the New Testament, the same Greek word stands behind both words. My purpose in using two different terms is to help us see the difference between these two realms. The New Testament writer's purpose in using the same term for the kingdom or empire of God that would be used in relation to Rome is to show the conflict between the two. The coming of God's kingdom was a direct confrontation and assault on the empires of the devil.

The second principle is that Rome, and all nations, are under the judgment of God. The New Testament asserts that Rome is under God's judgment and will eventually be shown for what it is. This stands in direct opposition to the Roman claims that Rome was the "eternal city" and an "empire without end."[22] The Gospel of John speaks repeatedly of "the ruler of this world" (ESV), who will be cast out (John 12:31), has no hold over Jesus (14:30), and has been condemned (16:11). Carter makes a compelling case by demonstrating that "ruler" here doesn't just refer to the devil but also to his representatives, the rulers in Jerusalem and Rome. It is these rulers who would not have put Jesus to death if they had understood that this apparent victory would instead be their undoing (1 Corinthians 2:8).

The nations are under judgment by the very existence of the kingdom of God in the present age. They are exposed and shown to be operating on a different plane. That doesn't mean that they will be literally destroyed, although each kingdom will fall in time (Hebrews 12:26–27). From one angle, the nations are being destroyed and judged by the coming of the kingdom. From another angle, they are being gathered into the kingdom as people from every tribe and nation submit to Jesus as King. We see the tension of these two angles described by the prophet Zephaniah.

"I have destroyed the nations; their strongholds are demolished," he declares in Zephaniah 3:6. And in verse 8 he says,

> "I have decided to assemble the nations,
>   to gather the kingdoms
> and to pour out my wrath on them—
>   all my fierce anger."

That sounds ominous. But then in the very next verses, God through the prophet proclaims,

> "Then I will purify the lips of the peoples,
>   that all of them may call on the name of the LORD
>   and serve him shoulder to shoulder.
> From beyond the rivers of Cush

my worshipers, my scattered people,
will bring me offerings." (vv. 9-10)

Through this passage in Zephaniah and the subsequent revelation of Scripture, it has become clear that the exiles that God gathers from the nations are not just Jews but the scattered of all nations (v. 20).

The third principle is that the world of the meantime needs transformation. The kingdom has not come just to provide personal salvation and evacuate people out of this world. Nor has it come to make people a little nicer to one another while leaving the world as it is. The kingdom is about transforming the world by making available a completely different realm of human possibility. When Jesus wanted to explain for the first time what his kingdom message was all about, he said that he was anointed by the Spirit,

"…to proclaim good news to the poor.
He has sent me to proclaim freedom for the prisoners
    and recovery of sight for the blind,
to set the oppressed free,
    to proclaim the year of the Lord's favor." (Luke 4:18-19)

We have already considered this passage and will unpack it further in the next chapter, but what is obvious is that the realm of the kingdom will be a transformed one like the world has not seen before.

The fourth principle is that kingdom communities will be alternative communities with alternative practices. These would be places that tore down social barriers. They would bring down the walls of ethnic and racial divide. They would empower women and give dignity to the marginalized. They would strive for economic sufficiency for all. They would reject schemes of worldly power over one another and they would live with love for others as their primary value. When Jesus is King, it looks like nothing the world has ever seen before.

But this doesn't come easily or naturally. To embody this will take great effort and submission. Paul urged those in Rome who were trying to embrace the kingdom life that they must "in view of God's mercy" offer their whole selves, meaning their bodies, "as a living sacrifice, holy and pleasing to God." This was their "true and proper worship." And they must remember that they would be a people who "do not conform to the pattern of this world," but were to "be transformed by the renewing" of their mind and consciousness. Only then would they be "able to test and approve what God's will is—his good, pleasing and perfect will" (Romans 12:1–2).

The fifth principle is the one I want to focus on now. It will take some development and analysis because, at first glance, it might seem out of place with the other four. It is simply this: in the meantime, we will submit to, pray for, and honor the emperor.

Pray for the Emperor

Let's start with this interesting aspect of the Christian's relationship with the ruling authorities. Paul says that we should pray for kings and emperors and be subject to them (1 Timothy 2:1–2; Titus 3:1–2). Peter implies a similar approach when he says, "fear God, honor the emperor" (1 Peter 2:17). In each of these directives, we should be careful not to miss the subtly subversive undertones. Give the respect and honor of holding an important position of power in the present age, say the apostles, but keep clear as to who the real authority is. It is God, if you were wondering.

There is even a quiet but strong subversive element to the command to pray for the king. In the first-century world it was expected that one would offer daily sacrifices to the emperor and say a quick prayer to him. Paul says to pray *for* him but not *to* him. This too is a recognition that the emperor is but a representative of the one true God and holds no true authority of his own.

But to what degree does the emperor or the governing authority function as the representative of God? And what does that mean for the relationship between the prophetic community and the political machine? To answer those questions, we turn to Romans 12 and 13.

Contrasting Realms

Reading Romans 12 and 13 in the same sitting can be a little confusing on the first pass. I would urge you to take a few moments and read those two chapters now.

They can almost feel a bit contradictory, can they not? Some interpreters have reasoned that Paul wrote Romans 13:1–7 to balance out some of the radical things that he penned in chapter 12. Others have proposed that Paul concedes that Christians are to take on one manner of living in their personal lives, avoiding retribution and violence while doing everything possible to live at peace with others. But then other options become appropriate for the public life and governing authority where violence, punishment, authority, and power are not just necessary but part of God's will. In their private life they are to hold to one standard, says this view, but in the public sector they can participate in and support a much different approach.

We will miss Paul's point in this passage by a country mile if we don't discern that he sees a marked distinction between ages. In the early Christian worldview, the world could be divided into two ages. There was the present age and the age to come (Matthew 12:32; Mark 10:30; Luke 18:30; 20:35; Ephesians 1:21; Galatians 1:4). The present age was the fallen world. It was characterized by sin, division, and violence. Evil is inevitable in the present age and can only be restrained by the methods of the present age.

This is the reality of the Old Testament period. God works in the world through the nation of Israel, utilizing the methods and avenues available in the present age, which sometimes included violence. Imperfect as she was, God worked through Israel to bring about the best possible outcomes given the situation that rebellious humanity had caused.

But there was always the promise of that future age when God would deal with sin and judge it, ushering in a time of sinlessness in which his will would be perfectly done. Students of the Scriptures assumed that when that age came it would be the absolute end of the present age and there would be no mistaking the transition from one era to the next. No one saw Jesus coming in the way that he did. He was the age to come in human embodiment. And through him the future age came crashing into the present in ways that we still don't fully understand or take hold of (1 Timothy 6:12).

It is this that makes all the difference. Having access to the eternal life now through Jesus changes absolutely everything. Those wishing to turn to the Bible for guidance in the biblical realm often make the mistake of failing to account for the arrival of the age to come. It is like comparing apples to oranges. No, check that, it is like comparing apples to a wedding day. There is just no comparison. It's not even close. Joseph is a wonderful and timeless example of a man of integrity and godliness in daunting circumstances. But there is no fruit for the disciple of Jesus in parsing the details of Joseph's life looking for principles of political engagement, because he had only the options of the present age available to him.

There is little value in scouring the pages of the Old Testament looking for pillars of how a Christian government might be structured, because we now have the kingdom of God, and it is virtually impossible to overstate how different the kingdom will look from even faithful Israel. Of course we can learn from the interactions between God and his people Israel, and there are limited times, such as the exile example from Chapter 8, that do hold some value, but for the most part, we must realize that there is very little in common between the political and societal function of God's people then and the new covenant people now. There is much in the Old Testament to guide us in our relationship with God, but not nearly as much that guides us in the world of politics.

The Alternative Community

The situation in the church in Rome had become contentious. Jewish Christians and Gentile Christians were clashing over matters of cultural and spiritual beliefs and practices, and Paul addresses those issues to avoid what could develop into a split in the church. In the first eleven chapters of Paul's letter to the Romans, he lays out why they must remain united in Christ and why they are a people unique from all others. They are kingdom people under the reign of the King, and that will mean ethnic and cultural diversity and unity, but it will also mean that they live their life together differently. That is what Paul addresses in chapters 12 and 13 before moving on to direct their necessary approach to maintain this uncommon unity and community life in chapters 14 and 15.

In view of God's mercy in bringing together all groups of people into the one family of the Messiah, Paul begins chapter 12 with a call to offer themselves as living sacrifices. This, he says, is the true act of worship. Worship is more than just a few moments of praise. It is a life devoted to the recognition of the proper status of someone or something. In this context, worship is giving every aspect of our lives in allegiance to Jesus as the king of all creation. This will not come naturally or easily, though. We must, urges the apostle, intentionally and constantly transform how we approach every aspect of life, or we will unwittingly be conformed to the patterns of the world. As we shall soon see, this includes our perspectives toward the political state and our connection to it.

Verses 3 to 8 are far more challenging than they might at first appear. In a nutshell, Paul's point is that the King's people must operate as one in the world. He's not just encouraging them to serve in one of the local ministries in the church. His point is that we no longer operate for our own benefit or individual agendas, but utilize our gifts and abilities to benefit and build up the common purpose of the body. There is a reason that Paul began this section with the call to be a living sacrifice and to transform our way of thinking. How do you think Jesus was able to have a group of twelve disciples that included a tax collector and a Zealot? These were enemies on the opposite ends of the political spectrum. It wasn't that they just kept their opinions to themselves. That would never work in the long run. They offered themselves as living sacrifices, transformed their minds, and then embraced the new kingdom way of approaching the world. It is to that way that Paul turns next.

Love and devotion to one another are the key ingredients for this radical way of living that he outlines in Romans 12:9–21. This way of life that Paul describes is very different from any that was typical within the world of the first-century Roman empire. He calls them to devotion and honoring others above themselves. That could hardly be more countercultural in a society that saw it as normal and good behavior to do everything in your power to get ahead and cause others to honor you.

They should also order their communities as places where there was no lack or surplus, but sufficiency as they shared with anyone who had need and put into practice this kind of world-altering and status-leveling hospitality.

But Paul is not done yet. They are to bless their persecutors rather than fight against them, he says in verse 14. This only makes sense if we keep in mind that their agenda is not comfort in life but to demonstrate what the kingdom of God looks like in the present age. They will serve the King, not their own security. To rejoice with those who rejoice and mourn with those who mourn is not simply a call to internal unity. He is calling them to be a community that can see the world from the perspective of the successful and the marginalized and can welcome them both. It is easy for some groups to so identify with the plight of the poor and oppressed that they become almost hostile to those who are doing well financially or in other ways. But it is also possible to become so amenable to what we would call the middle class and upper class that we become a church that ignores those on the bottom to the point that, from their perspective, the life of the community is unrealistic or unintentionally unfriendly to someone in their position. Paul calls them to be intentional about welcoming both, but he seems to sense that it will be more of a challenge to continue to welcome those of low position to the table, so he emphasizes that.

In verses 18–21, Paul sets out clear boundary markers for the alternative community. "Do not repay anyone evil for evil" (Romans 12:17). The early church of the first three centuries took that directive so seriously that they refused to take part in any government system or office that might involve them sending someone to prison or punishing them. They recognized that government had the right to such activities (more on that below), but they believed that it was not the role of their community to be involved in or yoked with those practices in any way.

What was their role as a community? To do everything in their power to live at peace with everyone, even their enemies. Fighting back and vengeance were off limits to them. That was the work of God alone. The only response they should have to an enemy of any kind was to feed them and give them drink. They were to focus on meeting the needs of their enemies rather than fighting them or trying to gain power for themselves.

In refusing revenge and retaliation, says Paul, they would "heap burning coals" on their enemies' head. This likely refers to a practice that took place if someone's fire went out. They would put a basket on their head and go to their neighbor to ask for burning coals so that they could return and restart their fire. Paul imagines a community that shows nothing but kindness to anyone, no matter how much they disagree with their life or have even been persecuted by them. This way of living may stir remorse or other feelings and bring to life the fire of the renewed humanity within them. This is how they will overcome evil with good. This is what will change the world. This is the way of the Lamb.

No Place for Us

In becoming the alternative community, did that mean that they were at such odds with the powers that be and the normal way of life that they could be left with no option other than rebelling against the governing authorities and removing them so that Jesus could really be King?

The problem, of course, is that if Jesus became king through such means then he wouldn't be king at all. Those who claim to follow him might take political power, but they would no longer be demonstrating or embracing the life of the kingdom.

To make sense of Romans 13:1–7, then, we must have the framework in mind that Paul has already laid out for what their lives will look like as the kingdom community. But how are they to interact with the empire or nation in which they live? The first step is to realize that God has allowed the governing authorities of the present age to engage in activities that limit and restrain evil, but those methods and options are simply not available to them as people of the coming age. There is simply no reconciliation between these patterns of life. What Paul is surely not doing is giving Christians an escape clause to ignore the very things, inspired by the Sermon on the Mount, that he wrote in chapter 12.

If we read these seven verses in isolation, it can easily seem like Paul is simply saying that governing authorities are a good force and that each one has been established by God to further his purposes in the world. But Paul seems to be speaking here of government in generic terms; and in the best-case scenario, God has ordained the institution of governments as an agent to restrain rampant evil and bring order.

When read in context, Paul's subversive intentions bubble to the surface. He admits that some will rebel against the government but doesn't elaborate on why anyone would if their intentions and actions are so pure. Paul is aware that governments, and certainly Rome, do not always act purely, but that makes no difference to the Christian community. He is describing a mythical perfect ruling system to make a point.

They are not to use their alternative society status as an excuse to stop paying taxes or become a movement of political rebellion when the system is not perfect. Even under the scenario of a perfect government in the present age, there is simply no way that the type of community Paul has just described in chapter 12 could be part of this type of ruling agency. Rulers hold terror for wrongdoers and enemies, but the kingdom people are to love their enemies and bless them. Rulers punish wrongdoers, but Paul has just instructed believers to "not repay anyone evil for evil" (Romans 12:17) and to "not take revenge" (v. 19). "Are we using Romans 13," asks author Brian Zahnd, "to help clarify how Christians should live as 'exiles' within an empire, or are we using Romans 13 to endorse the militarism of our favored empire?"[23]

Let me break this down. The kingdom community has its role in the world, and that is to throw off the pattern of the world and live in a completely different way to serve as a sample of what it will look like to live fully under God's reign one day.

The obvious question that arises is what about their response to evil? How would they deal with enemies and lawbreakers? Paul's answer is to the point. That is God's domain, not theirs, and he has assigned that work in the present age to ruling authorities, so leave them to do their work, even if they are not living up to the ideal for which their authority was granted. After all, Jesus didn't take away Pilate's authority when Pilate abused it. The governing authorities have been allowed by God, but that doesn't mean that they are not still under the rule of the god of this age, the dragon (2 Corinthians 4:4). To submit to these authorities does not mean that we yoke ourselves together with them and become part of the system. Their Lord is Caesar, or the beast, or the dragon, or their nation, or their idols, whatever they may be. Our Lord is Jesus.

I don't want to become guilty of painting in strictly black and white what can become quite gray at times in the real world. God can and will use the empires for his purposes. He used Babylon as his instrument on occasion. He used Cyrus to accomplish good. Nations have done good things. There may even be times when their actions seem so good and bring such justice that kingdom people may have a difficult time discerning whether they should partner in that activity or not. We will wrestle with some of these difficult decisions in Chapters 21–25, particularly Chapter 25. Admittedly, it would be nice if the separation between empire and kingdom were always neat and obvious. It will not be, and one of my primary purposes in this book is to help us navigate the times when it is not. What Paul presents here in Romans, though, are the norms for the Christian community. These should be the default positions from which we normally operate.

At the same time, we should note that Paul's instructions here are for a separate community to submit and operate in relation to the governing or ruling authorities. It is important to keep in mind that nowhere in the New Testament are Christians ever urged to actively take part in the political or ruling realm of the nations. Nowhere are we commanded to take up the sword or utilize violence for good. We are to be an alternative people.

The Only Debt

The ruling authorities are operating within the realm of the present age and use the weapons of that domain. Romans 12:9–21 rules out that this is a world in which Christians should participate. Let them do their job. If the governing authorities become the enemy, then bless and do not curse them as well. Pay taxes. They are to give respect and honor where they can, although Christians cannot engage in acts of submission that would call them to disobey God (Acts 4:18–20).

That is all they must do.

If they take on those simple acts of submission, they fulfill their obligations. They have no other debt, says Paul in Romans 13:8, than to love. Government's role is to enforce order in the present age. The Christian community's role is to enact the love of the coming age in the world of the present order.

Understanding the Present Time

Now that Paul has laid out the response to the realm of empire and nations, he returns in 13:8–10 to a summary of kingdom responsibility and caps off the task that lies ahead. "The hour has already come," he says, "for you to wake up from your slumber" (Romans 13:11). He gives a picture of the Christian walking around in the dead of night. Paul, in verses 12–14, describes two primary activities that take place at night. You can either be sleeping or up to no good. Disciples of Jesus should not be involved with the deeds of darkness; that's obvious. But surprisingly, Paul argues that we should not be sleeping either. We should be walking around in the dead of night as though it is the middle of the day.

What does he mean by that? It means the body of Christ is a picture of the future. It will be out of place and out of time, but that's okay. We are not to take part in the world's system and live like the world does, but neither are we to merely withdraw and be nice people who are asleep to the realities of the world around us, just waiting for God to come fix it all. We are up in the night. We are aware of what is going on, but we refuse to be part of it. We live as though we are already in the future, and we show the world what that looks like.

This principle must become one of our core guiding principles. When the world looks at our actions, our beliefs, and the way we interact with those around us, what do they see? Do they see God's future in which God's will is supreme and there is no hate, violence, abuse, or power, but only love for all? Do they see a body of people whose values are so otherworldly that they simply make no sense in the present age?

The Chapter in Review

- As Christians, we must evaluate all actions and decisions from a kingdom perspective.

- All human-run governments exist under the realm of the satan.

- All nations are under the judgment of God.

- The world right now is in need of transformation that it can only find in the kingdom of God.

- Kingdom communities should be alternative communities with a clearly alternative lifestyle.

- We should submit to, pray for, and honor the emperor.

- Because they are rooted in different ages, the present and the one to come, Israel in the Old Testament does not provide a good blueprint for how God's kingdom should function politically and societally in the modern context.

- The foundational component for kingdom life is offering ourselves as a living sacrifice.

- In Romans 12, Paul lays down clear boundaries for the manner of life of the kingdom people.

- Romans 13:1–7 is a description of how Christians can live as exiles within empire and how they should relate to the governing authorities as kingdom citizens.

- A core principle of the kingdom is that we live in the night as though it were the day, showing what the coming age and living under God's loving rule will look like.

The Big Idea

❖ The realm of the kingdom and the realm of the state are entirely different spheres of operation and allegiance.

DISCUSSION QUESTIONS

1. What is most challenging about living out Paul's description of the Christian life in Romans 12:9–21?

2. Do most Christians understand the clear distinction between the function and realm of kingdom and nations that Paul describes in Romans 12 and 13? What are the potential effects of not recognizing the difference?

3. In what ways can the modern church grow in living in the dark as though it were the day?

Chapter 11

The Beautiful Life

When I was a child, I would spend time wondering what it was like to be unable to see. I don't know where I first got the idea, but I have clear memories of walking through the mall with my eyes closed or trying to go through ten or fifteen minutes at home without opening my eyes. I learned that public places were not the greatest option for such endeavors but that at home, I could get by pretty well with a little practice.

Of course, my experiments were quite different from the real thing because I could cheat and peak anytime I wanted, and when I'd had enough, I could open my eyes and return to my sighted world. I always had a choice, but there are many who don't and for whom blindness is unending. It is not the end of the world to be blind, but I doubt there are many who would categorize it as an advantage.

Similarly, being poor does not give one lesser status as a human being, and it doesn't mean that life is not worth living if you are financially destitute, but it too, is not good news. Likewise, being imprisoned for any reason is not typically counted as good news or a desired position in life. And those who are oppressed never consider that they have received some sort of lucky break. No, being oppressed is not good news either.

But somehow, Jesus seemingly thought otherwise. Didn't he say as much in the synagogue in Galilee near the beginning of his ministry?

"The Spirit of the Lord is on me,
    because he has anointed me
    to proclaim good news to the poor.
He has sent me to proclaim freedom for the prisoners
    and recovery of sight for the blind,
to set the oppressed free,
    to proclaim the year of the Lord's favor."

Then he rolled up the scroll, gave it back to the attendant and sat down. The eyes of everyone in the synagogue were fastened on him. He began by saying to them, "Today this scripture is fulfilled in your hearing." (Luke 4:18-21)

This is so pivotal to our understanding of how Jesus thought of his coming reign and the kingdom of God that we are revisiting this passage to carefully consider what Jesus was saying here.

Three Important Symbols

If we suspect that Jesus is up to something important here, we would be right. He is making some huge claims about what he is doing in the world and what his vision of the kingdom is. But it is easy to miss if we don't follow carefully.

Many have read this passage and assumed that Jesus wants communities committed to social justice and making the world a better place. Yet this interpretation ignores the fact that, as far we know, Jesus didn't empty the jails in Israel, oppression and poverty were still rampant after he died, and he only restored the sight of a few. It doesn't seem that Jesus was laying this out as the central vocation for the church, as though the mission was to go fix the world. And Jesus himself made it clear that fixing the problems of the world was not his ultimate intention, nor would his followers accomplish that in the present age (Matthew 26:11; Mark 14:7; John 12:8).

Jesus quotes from Isaiah 61, but with some important tweaks. He has completely omitted the reference to judgment being poured out on the nations and has inserted a line from Isaiah 58 concerning the oppressed being set free. What he did, though, was to cleverly include three important Jewish symbols to reveal what type of kingdom he was announcing.

The first symbol becomes apparent as Luke tells us that this event takes place on the Sabbath. This was the day of rest. But the true purpose and point of the Sabbaths is that they were the weekly anticipation of the age to come. Sabbath was the day when people fully relied on God and stopped working, as a way of looking forward to that future age when God's people would be present with him fully.

The second symbol comes from Isaiah 58, as Jesus uses the insertion from that passage to point to the context of the entire chapter, which rebukes Israel for failing to properly embody the practice of fasting. Fasting for Jews was the practice of abstaining from eating food and renewing their complete reliance on God. But it was also a time when they were to share with the poor and care for the oppressed, practices that most clearly anticipated the coming age.

The third symbol comes from Isaiah 61, whose language is intended to invoke the Year of Jubilee. Every fiftieth year, on the Day of Atonement, the Law dictated that there would be a jubilee (Leviticus 25:8–55). Land would be returned to the original owners. The people were not to work the land and eat only what they could take directly from the fields. Those who were serving as slaves would be freed. All the provisions of jubilee pointed to the ultimate jubilee when there will be no oppression and no lack, and all creation will be restored to the state of Eden.

Jesus takes these three powerful Jewish symbols, rolls them into one and then says that this time that Jews had been waiting for centuries to come has already arrived. He is ushering in the age to come, the eternal jubilee.

What is his point? He was teaching them that the reign of God, to which all these symbols pointed, had arrived. His people would be those who would live as a picture of this age. These were not merely activities to be participated in to check off a box or make the world a little nicer place. This is how God was becoming King. As people of all nations and backgrounds submitted to his rule and began to live out this otherworldly approach, the kingdom would become a reality. It would come and grow simply through groups of people coming together to become outposts determined to do nothing more than demonstrate to the world an approximation of what it will look like to live fully under God's rule.

Lives Worthy of the Calling

This mindset of living with a different purpose and outcome than the world is on display throughout the letters of the New Testament. Here are just a few examples.

> I beg you that when I come I may not have to be as bold as I expect to be toward some people who think that we live by the standards of this world. For though we live in the world, we do not wage war as the world does. The weapons we fight with are not the weapons of the world. On the contrary, they have divine power to demolish strongholds. We demolish

arguments and every pretension that sets itself up against the knowledge of God, and we take captive every thought to make it obedient to Christ. (2 Corinthians 10:2–5)

In him the whole building is joined together and rises to become a holy temple in the Lord. And in him you too are being built together to become a dwelling in which God lives by his Spirit. (Ephesians 2:21–22)

As a prisoner for the Lord, then, I urge you to live a life worthy of the calling you have received. (Ephesians 4:1)

Be very careful, then, how you live–not as unwise but as wise, making the most of every opportunity, because the days are evil. (Ephesians 5:15–16)

For this reason, since the day we heard about you, we have not stopped praying for you. We continually ask God to fill you with the knowledge of his will through all the wisdom and understanding that the Spirit gives, so that you may live a life worthy of the Lord and please him in every way: bearing fruit in every good work, growing in the knowledge of God, being strengthened with all power according to his glorious might so that you may have great endurance and patience, and giving joyful thanks to the Father, who has qualified you to share in the inheritance of his holy people in the kingdom of light. For he has rescued us from the dominion of darkness and brought us into the kingdom of the Son he loves. (Colossians 1:9–13)

As for other matters, brothers and sisters, we instructed you how to live in order to please God, as in fact you are living. Now we ask you and urge you in the Lord Jesus to do this more and more. (1 Thessalonians 4:1)

I urge, then, first of all, that petitions, prayers, intercession and thanksgiving be made for all people–for kings and all those in authority, that we may live peaceful and quiet lives in all godliness and holiness. This is good, and pleases God our Savior, who wants all people to be saved and to come to a knowledge of the truth. (1 Timothy 2:1–4)

Our people must learn to devote themselves to doing what is good, in order to provide for urgent needs and not live unproductive lives. (Titus 3:14)

> Live such good lives among the pagans that, though they accuse you of doing wrong, they may see your good deeds and glorify God on the day he visits us.
>
> Submit yourselves for the Lord's sake to every human authority: whether to the emperor, as the supreme authority, or to governors, who are sent by him to punish those who do wrong and to commend those who do right. For it is God's will that by doing good you should silence the ignorant talk of foolish people. Live as free people, but do not use your freedom as a cover-up for evil; live as God's slaves. Show proper respect to everyone, love the family of believers, fear God, honor the emperor. (1 Peter 2:12–17)

It is not uncommon for Christianity to be reduced to a moral system. In that reductionist worldview, we believe certain important doctrines, Jesus forgives us our sin, and then our response is to leave our sin behind and embrace morally upright lives.

Why is that a problem? It is a little bit like a husband who believes that his role in marriage is to provide financially for his family but never fully invests emotionally in his homelife. That might look good from the outside, but it becomes empty within very quickly.

The gospel proclamation is that Jesus is King. We are to embrace that message and enter his kingdom, where we find a people that walk in the forgiveness and salvation that have been graciously given to the King's people. When we share in this life of faith together, we gain an "understanding of every good thing we share for the sake of Christ" as we create communities dedicated to demonstrating the life of the future age while still living in the present. That's it. That's our role. Everything we say and do should be to reflect the light of what the future will look like when we are in God's presence forever. As we discussed in Chapter 7, forgiveness and salvation are the benefit of life in the kingdom, but not the whole point in themselves.

The Beautiful Life

We can see this commitment to kingdom living and being the prophetic community clearly on display in the church in the centuries following the period when the New Testament was written. This period of the church is often called Ante-Nicene and runs from the close of the New Testament, somewhere near the end of the first century, until the beginning of the fourth century. Their response to the gospel of King Jesus, relationship to the political environment around them, and commitment to kingdom living are quite eye-opening and instructive. I will simply refer to this Ante-Nicene period as the early church. I have already referred to their faith and example several times, but it is so valuable to understand the witness of these early Christians that we will take some space here to look at their walk a little more closely.

There are two facts about the early church that are difficult for our modern minds to process. The first is that the church grew steadily during this period despite being ostracized by much of society, consistently ridiculed, and even persecuted rather heavily at times. The second is that they never wrote on the topic of evangelism. They wrote often about Christian living and the interaction between the kingdom community and the world, but not one single treatise on evangelism or mention of a global plan to share the gospel around the world, for three centuries.[24]

How could the church expand and grow throughout the world without a plan, without focusing on growth and evangelism? And this was during a time when it was no more attractive from a worldly perspective to be a Christian than in any other era. There was no obvious advantage to giving up all to follow Christ; there were no "blessings" from the Lord to accompany such a decision to live with Jesus as King.

The focus of the early church was embodying the good news that Jesus is King and living that out in every aspect of their lives. This would, they believed, show what they were about and why their life was so different, and would attract others to join. They didn't need to focus on the act of evangelism if all their energy was given to living like Christ. Christians today spend a lot of time and energy showing the world that we are relatable and not that much different from them, but the early church wanted none of that. They relished the differences and emphasized them. They believed that their entire way of life and their entire value system was and should be fundamentally contrary to the way of life around them in every conceivable manner. The truth would be shown in their living by the values of the coming age, not by being like the world or speaking great and convincing things. They pinned it all on the witness of their community life. Early church leaders like Minucius Felix and Cyprian popularized the saying that captures the heart of the formative Christian churches, "We do not speak great things, but we live them."

The early Christians presumed that their communities were only Christian to the degree that their lives looked like Jesus. Early church leader Justin Martyr demonstrated this ethic when he called for discipline for those who were "Christians in name only" but did not pursue and embody Jesus' kingship.[25] Early Christians like Justin referred to this embodied living as "good works" and noted that it was this consistent and countercultural life within the church family that intrigued others and would make them wonder what motivated people to live so selflessly and differently from the society surrounding them. The teaching in the early church was primarily aimed at instructing new disciples in how to live practically and patiently in every aspect of life in response to the truth that Jesus was their one and only King. Third-century church leader Origen envisioned the world as a theater filled with spectators watching the life of those who claimed Jesus was King to see how they lived and responded to trials like persecution or plagues. The strength of their allegiance displayed the truth of their claims about the Christ.

Third-century Christian Cyprian reminded believers often that outsiders would judge them by what they did and not so much what they said. "We know virtues by their practice rather than through boasting of them," declared Cyprian, who would go on to add that if things like loyalty and allegiance were not consistently on display "in the lived experience of humans, it isn't worth talking about."[26]

Worldly wisdom around them was put on display by writers such as the Roman philosopher Cicero, who asserted that a good man would help those around him unless provoked by mistreatment. But the early Christians held to another ethic that made little sense at first. Because Jesus was King and Caesar was not, they would do good to all people, regardless of their actions and whether they deserved it or not.

These Christians were not highly respected by the intellectuals and important people in Rome, so they were not invited often to speak publicly, and their words would have carried little weight if they did. The proof was in the pudding. Their word was in the example of their shared life, so even little things like how they chose to engage in public and political issues spoke volumes. Were they really living a different reality or not? Alan Kreider notes that "it was not primarily what the Christians said that carried weight with outsiders; it was what

they did and embodied that was both disconcerting and converting."
Rather than relying on a message or a series of logical truths, "it was
their habitus—their reflexes and ways of life that suggested that there
was another way to perceive reality—that made the Christians interesting, challenging, and worth investigating."[27]

They were right. The world did not respond with statements
of, "Look at what they write; listen to this logical message—I'm convinced." The response of the world around them, according to sec-
ond-century church leader Tertullian, was, "Look how they love one
another."[28]

The early church embraced people of every nation, tribe, language, ethnic group, and social status and lived together as one. They
shared their resources and ensured that there was no one needy
among them. They loved all people, even those who opposed or persecuted them. They believed that to complain about mistreatment was
impatient and not reflective of Jesus' kingship. They did not fear death
and so saw no terror in disease, mistreatment, sacrifice for others, or
dying. They rejected fears about the economy, rival nations, or public
politics of any kind. They advocated for anyone who was oppressed
without ever feeling any need to advocate for their own rights. They
refused to be associated with anything that would involve violence or
compulsion in any manner. They rejected any whiff of putting Christianity into a position of power that would make anyone feel compelled
to follow this way of life. They radically shared this beautiful life of
the age to come with anyone who came near, but they never tried to
change society, knowing that if they attempted that, they would fail,
but more importantly, it would take away the opportunity to be a true
alternative to what the world was offering.

"The Christians," says Kreider, "were creating an alternative
community that had nonconformist approaches to common social
problems and that imparted to its participants a powerful sense of
individual and group identity." He concludes that this "had immense
formative power."[29]

The beauty of their life and their radical uniqueness, including
their refusal to trust in the systems of the world and empire, was
what encouraged people to consider the truth that Jesus was King.
But when they failed to live out their claims, they were dismissed as a
myth. Their focus was not on recruiting and saving people. It was not

on passing laws so that society was compelled to live morally. It was on living as alternative communities that declared through their patient living that Jesus really was King. But when the Christians' claims did not match their lives, they would turn to blasphemy. When they saw Christians not loving their enemies and not even loving one another, the world would react, says third-century leader Clement: they would laugh, scorn, and call the gospel "a fable and a delusion."[30]

No, Thank You

These early Christians did not withdraw from the world. They did not turn a blind eye to suffering. Their belief that Jesus was their King, that the kingdom had arrived, and that it was their duty to live lives allegiant to those truths caused them to constantly sacrifice for the benefit of others. They cared for the sick, even if it meant that they might die. They took in abandoned children and raised them at their own expense. They loved the oppressed and outcast, although it meant being cut out of society themselves. They refused to yoke themselves with the empire and with political power, even though they were labeled as traitors and persecuted. They tore down the barriers of injustice and segregation within their ranks even while being treated unjustly and castigated by the powers around them.

Although utilizing the power of political influence may have been appealing, they consistently refused the lure of public office. "We have no pressing inducement," said Tertullian, "to take part in your public meetings. Nor is there anything more entirely foreign to us than the affairs of state."[31] He would go on to assert that a Christian could be involved in politics if they could assure that they would take no part in any form of idolatry, allegiance to the state, sitting in judgment on anyone else's life or character, taking part in condemning anyone to punishment, imprisonment, or torture, nor compelling anyone to do anything that they didn't choose. If all that was possible, which Tertullian did not believe it was, then and only then would the early Christians find it acceptable to engage in that world or take part in politics. These were things of the realm of state, and they were not to become involved in that realm. They had a different purpose and different weapons (2 Corinthians 10:3–4). It was not, wrote Origen in the third century, "for the purpose of escaping public duties that

Christians decline public offices. Rather, it is so they may reserve themselves for a more divine and necessary service in the church of God."[32]

The early church grew consistently because of the witness of their community life. Their focus was not on persuasive words but on allegiant living, which they called patience. And it was this consistently set-apart manner of living that drew the world to them and their way of life.

The Chapter in Review

- In Luke 4:18–21, Jesus appeals to important Jewish symbols to declare that the time of the coming age was now breaking into the present age through him.

- The early Christians focused their energy and pinned their witness on living lives that looked radically different from the world around them rather than on verbal evangelism. They believed in living their message rather than reducing it to mostly words.

- The early Christians believed that to get involved in worldly politics and public office would send the wrong message to the world and would not demonstrate the life of the coming age.

- The refusal of the early church to trust in the systems of the world's empires and governments was part of their testimony to the fact that Jesus was their King.

- The early church refused to take part in public office or politics as part of the witness of their community to the truth of King Jesus.

- The result was that the early church grew consistently because of the reliable witness of their community life.

The Big Idea

- ❖ Kingdom communities function to demonstrate allegiance to the King and nothing else.

DISCUSSION QUESTIONS

1. Do you see any significant differences between the way that the early church went about attracting others to join them and modern practices of the church?

2. What impact does engagement in the world's political system have on the witness of the church?

3. What would be the major challenges for the contemporary church if we adopted an approach to political systems and government that was more like the approach of the early church?

Chapter 12

The Zealot and the Tax Collector

Unquestionably, one of the most stunning developments in the world of biblical archaeology in 2019 was the discovery of ancient manuscripts that date back to the first century. After much analysis, experts in the field have agreed that these documents are an authentic written dialogue between the apostles Peter and Paul. This is perhaps the most important and enlightening historical discovery in the last 2,000 years. If you haven't been following the developing story of the partial fragments that have been unearthed, allow me to fill you in, because it is incredible. The dialogue appears to have been written in the mid-50s AD between two of the most important figures in Christianity. Here is an excerpt from the first letter written from Paul to Peter:

> Paul, a prisoner of Christ Jesus and an apostle of Christ Jesus by the command of God our Savior and of Christ Jesus our hope, and Timothy our brother, to Peter our dear friend and fellow worker in the faith. Grace, mercy and peace from the Father and Christ Jesus our Lord.
>
> As I have urged you many times in the Lord, I plead with you to consider supporting our impressive emperor Nero and his rule over the nations. I must admit that he is not perfect, but he supports many plans that align with our faith in Jesus Christ. He has been wonderful for the economy, and many brothers and sisters are prospering like they never have before. His decree to allow our Jewish brothers and sisters back into Rome, after Claudius, servant of the great dragon, banned them, has been a blessing. His reforms have allowed important leaders like Prisca and Aquilla to resume their work for the gospel. There can be little question that God has raised up a man like Nero for such a time as this. After all, if God used Cyrus the Persian for his purposes, why could he not use our emperor?[33]

Not much else survives of this first letter, but this bit offers important insight into Paul's view on politics in the first century. The reply from Peter is just as enlightening.

> Peter, an apostle of Jesus Christ. To our dear brother Paul. Grace and peace be yours in abundance. I am shocked to see you so quickly accept the propaganda of a fool like Nero. His economic reforms are shallow, and while he has pandered to the Jews in Rome, you seem to forget the constant corruption that has become synonymous with his rule and the nonstop lies that flow whenever his lips move. Those of us who were overjoyed to see the good that Claudius accomplished were grieved to hear of his leadership being brought to such a tragic end. Surely, brother, you were not swayed by the fake news and constant lies about Claudius. He was protected by God during Caligula's murderous rampage and chosen by God to be the leader of our great empire. Please tell me how you could call yourself a servant of King Jesus and support...[34]

Unfortunately, that is all that survives of this second letter. But it provides a fascinating window into Peter's worldview. Paul's response is sharp and to the point.

> Paul, a servant of God and an apostle of Jesus Christ, with Timothy, to further the faith of God's elect and their knowledge of the truth that leads to godliness.
>
> Peter, my brother, has your mind been so easily deceived by the accuser? Have your eyes been blinded to the work of the one who masquerades as an angel of light? Have you really called an honorable man like Nero a liar? Is that what Jesus would do? Claudius sat on a throne of lies and nearly crippled the economy of the great empire. Have you paid no attention to all that Nero has done for women's rights? Under his leadership, the avenues for women have increased greatly, and his building projects have driven unemployment to an all-time low. My good brother, surely you must admit that Claudius was a bigot and if you yoke yourself together with him, then you stand before God as a bigot yourself. The Lord knows that you have displayed these tendencies before in Antioch. May he have mercy on your soul. How long must I...[35]

Once again, the surviving fragments break off at this point. The part of Peter's final response that survives will not soon be forgotten.

> Simon Peter, a servant and apostle of Jesus Christ. The one who testifies to having seen and touched our glorious Lord and Savior. For those who through the righteousness of our God and Savior Jesus Christ and have received a faith as precious as ours.

I can only assume that all the beatings you have endured have left you bereft of your full faculties. How could you besmirch the memory of such a good man? Claudius rebuilt the military after it was nearly wiped out by Caligula's excesses and secured the borders of this great empire against the advances of the Barbarians and others who want to destroy the sovereignty of Rome and who are jealous of her blessings from God. May God continue to bless this nation and keep her safe as a force for good in the world. If you are going to continue to take such anti-God positions, I may have to. . .[36]

Frustratingly, that is all that remains. There is one more brief fragment from Paul, which I copied below, although the beginning of the letter remains lost to history. We simply do not know if Peter wrote anything more. Perhaps further discoveries will uncover more correspondence from these two giants in the faith.

. . . about me? How dare you? Claudius used our troops like his own personal servants. He risked their lives needlessly. Nero has used the military wisely and has had to spend much of his time fixing the foreign relations fiascos created by that idiot, Claudius. He supports the rights of citizens to bear. . .[37]

Can You Imagine?

Hopefully, you either looked at the endnotes for the letters above or figured out quickly on your own that these are not real letters. I wrote every word of them. Don't they seem absurd? Can you imagine Paul or Peter writing such things? Can you fathom a scenario in which these two apostles would become embroiled in a political debate or argument? You probably find the thought of such a thing as silly as I do. But can you imagine two Christians having a back-and-forth like that in the twenty-first century? Not only can I imagine it, I've seen countless arguments between followers of Jesus just like this, and much worse. Occasionally it has been in person, but more often it is on a social media forum of some kind. Public political arguments have become one of the biggest causes of division among Christians today as we quickly seem to forget Paul's warning to "be wise in the way you act toward outsiders; make the most of every opportunity" (Colossians 4:5).

How do we get to the place as the people of God where such controversial things like politics don't divide us? It almost seems impossible because, by its very nature, politics tends to divide. One group has a philosophy or ideology that others agree with, and a political party forms around those beliefs and values. Others have differing experiences or perspectives, which lead them to believe that they have solutions and strategies that will be more effective at driving policy or the direction of the nation or region, and they form their own party. The competing parties, whether there are two or twenty, then vie for control and power to enact their policies, which they believe will bring prosperity, however they define it. It is this competition for power, which may be peaceful or may be violent, that causes division. It is virtually unavoidable. There are some who can disagree on such issues and not allow it to impact their relationship, but our culture is definitely trending toward the inability to do that. For many, even in the body of Christ, when they find out that someone has political views that they do not share, it immediately sets off inner alarms and they question the intelligence, wisdom, and even faith of the other person.

The Impossible Becomes Possible

But consider this passage for a moment:

> Jesus called his twelve disciples to him and gave them authority to drive out impure spirits and to heal every disease and sickness.
> These are the names of the twelve apostles: first, Simon (who is called Peter) and his brother Andrew; James son of Zebedee, and his brother John; Philip and Bartholomew; Thomas and Matthew the tax collector; James son of Alphaeus, and Thaddaeus; Simon the Zealot and Judas Iscariot, who betrayed him. (Matthew 10:1–4)

Only two disciples in this list are given descriptors that would give us any hint as to their political and social affiliations. We are told that Matthew was a tax collector and Simon was a Zealot. This is quite unbelievable. Tax collectors worked with and for the Romans. They were so hated by the people that they were considered unclean spiritually. They worked for the oppressor and benefited greatly by that oppression. The Zealots were on the opposite end of the spectrum. They were dedicated to driving Rome out of Judea by any means necessary. The tax collectors were willing to partner with the pagans for their own comfort, while the Zealots were willing to sacrifice their own lives in violent revolt against those same pagans.

So how on earth did Jesus manage to get these two guys to be in the same group without huge arguments, or worse, along the way? They should have been mortal enemies, so the answer could be very instructive for our fractured and divided times.

One of the solutions I hear offered up often when brothers or sisters disagree fundamentally over passion-inducing issues like politics is to keep it to ourselves. This sounds good but is a deeply flawed remedy. What if Simon the Zealot and Matthew the tax collector had followed that advice? There would have forever been a wedge between them. They might have learned to get along and even respect one another. They might have found a way to emphasize what they had in common, namely a desire to follow Jesus. But over time, they would not have been able to remain in community together with such divergent beliefs about how to address and resolve problems in the world. Can you imagine them trying to lead a church together? How would that work?

The only way that they could have maintained such divergent beliefs is if their relationship was shallow or if their commitment to the kingdom was lukewarm. If they were completely committed to establishing God's kingdom, but one through the lens of a tax collector and the other through the lens of a Zealot, their unity would have eventually ruptured.

As Paul challenges the believers in Colossae to embrace kingdom living as their complete life, he reminds them that they have taken off their "old self with its practices and have put on the new self, which is being renewed in knowledge in the image of its Creator" (Colossians 3:9–10). It is that exchange of identity that allows him to confidently boast that in Christ, "there is no Gentile or Jew, circumcised or uncircumcised, barbarian, Scythian, slave or free, but Christ is all, and is in all." If Christians in Colossae or anywhere else had insisted on approaching the world through those categories as their identity, they would never have been able to show the kingdom to the world.

The Zealot and the tax collector were able to follow Jesus together because they dropped those ideologies and became new people. They learned to transform their minds and no longer be conformed to the patterns of the world. They accepted Jesus as their King, and that changed everything. For Matthew, he was no longer impressed by the economic opportunity afforded to those who bowed to the Roman empire. He realized that their power in the world was limited and that Jesus was the true king. Simon came to realize that Rome was not the real power in the world, but neither were they the enemy he had always believed them to be. To follow Jesus, he abandoned his faith in the power of the sword to make the world right.

They became new people to follow Jesus. They recognized that when Jesus said we must give up everything to follow him, he meant every single thing. That includes our ideologies and political beliefs. They must be left at the foot of the cross and the door of the kingdom. They are not to be clung to while cleverly hiding them just out of sight from those who think differently. Rather, they are to be transformed.

In my country, the major political division today is between liberals and conservatives. It's not hard to find both of those types of people in the same church today. And that's a problem. We think that we can be Christian conservatives or Christian liberals. Matthew notes that Simon was a Zealot and Matthew a tax collector, not to demonstrate that these two political enemies were able to set aside their differences and still follow Jesus. He includes those labels to display what they had given up to follow Jesus. He wanted to show that people of vastly different backgrounds were laying down their previous identities and making Jesus their King. They did not have two masters. They had one.

When Jesus becomes Lord, we take hold of the life of the age to come (1 Timothy 6:12; John 3:15; 10:10). That changes everything. If it doesn't, then perhaps he is not the king of every area of our lives.

This is extremely important for us to understand: The tax collector trusted in empire and the solutions of the present age. He sided politically with Rome. The Zealot opposed Rome and stood for the cause of the oppressed and those who were treated unjustly, but he simply stood on the other side of the same spectrum. He still trusted in politics, empire, violence, and power. Neither represented the kingdom of God nor were compatible with it. When they followed Jesus, they were tax collector and Zealot no more. They were disciples of the King.

Peter, Paul, and Politics

We can't envision Peter and Paul engaging in political discourse of the type I invented at the beginning of this chapter, because they were passionately devoted to the kingdom of God. Their allegiance had been given to Jesus the Christ and him alone. The early Christians did not view the world through the lens of a Christian Zealot, or a Christian who was pro-emperor, or one who was in favor of a return to the Republic of Rome. To declare Jesus as Lord meant that Caesar was not. To proclaim faith and allegiance to the Messiah's kingdom meant that you withdrew your faith and allegiance from the empires of the world. It meant you put your hope in the kingdom and not the nations and their political ambitions.

As we saw in the last chapter, the early church was quite clear on all that. Why do we seem so muddled on it all in the twenty-first century? The answer begins all the way back in the third century.

Constantine, Ambrose, and Augustine

While it lies outside the scope of this book to detail church history of the third through twenty-first centuries, it will be helpful to provide a brief sketch of the relationship between the kingdom of God and the empires.

Around AD 250, another persecution broke out against Christians in the Roman empire. This is known as the Decian persecution. When that oppression died down, conditions improved for Christians for over forty years. During that time, many grew comfortable and lost their distinctiveness. Some even accepted positions in the government of the great empire.

In AD 303, Emperor Diocletian began perhaps the most extensive and violent persecution of Christians to date. In many respects, it caught the church by surprise. The violence raged for eight years as the emperor tried to wipe the church off the face of the earth. Many recanted their faith to save their lives, but many did not, and they suffered greatly, even to the point of death. The dragon had roared one more time, but it became clear that he could not use a beast to snuff out the church. Diocletian eventually gave up and ended the oppression in AD 311. Just two years later, an unimaginable blessing occurred. Constantine and his co-ruler Licinius made Christianity a legal religion in Rome. Overnight, the threat of persecution was gone.

Over the next few years, state money flowed to restore seized land to the churches and build them places of worship. Constantine converted to Christianity (although he would not be officially baptized until he was on his deathbed), and its influence grew. It must have seemed like an incredible blessing. But was it?

Earlier, in AD 244, the emperor of Rome, Phillip the Arab, wished to attend a Christian celebration of Easter along with his wife, who had become a Christian. The leaders of the church, however, would not allow him to partake in all aspects of the gathering. Unless he truly repented, walked away from his position of power, and submitted his allegiance to Jesus, he would have to stand with the visitors and leave the church when it was time to take communion.

Unfortunately, this same level of commitment to the kingdom standard of separateness was not observed with Constantine. Once the church accepted the authority and support of the empire, it blurred the separation between state and kingdom. Before long, Constantine was inserting himself into church decisions and authority. He is often demonized today and charged with everything from deciding which books would be in the New Testament to changing the day of worship to Sunday, and many other things that are not true. But he did initiate a series of decisions that would lead the church down a path of compromise that would change the nature of the church faster than anyone might have imagined.

Within a few decades, the church was intertwining itself with the state. They went from centuries of opposing military participation for Christians or violence of any kind for any reason, to allowing the Roman army to call itself Christian and persecute heretics for holding different beliefs. The distinction between the kingdom of God and the Roman empire blurred to the point that Rome became a nation under God in the mind of the church. Many Romans joined the church, but they were no longer held to strict allegiance to Jesus and his kingdom view of the world. Right doctrine, church membership, and obedience to the authority of the bishop were now the expectation.

Constantine eventually exempted church leaders from paying taxes and called for formally paying church leaders a salary. They were also given the authority to decide many civil law cases, rather than people going before judges. Constantine did hold to the historic position of the church that people could not be coerced to be members. But by AD 380, Emperor Theodosius declared Christianity to be the official religion of Rome, outlawed all other religions, and began a program of destroying pagan temples and persecuting those who did not convert to Christianity. The church grew, but the kingdom was nowhere in sight.

The actions of the church of the fourth century were at odds with the historic teaching of Christians in the first, second, and third centuries. A theologian named Ambrose rose to prominence in the latter half of the fourth century. He came from the schools of natural law and human logic and argued that Rome was a Christian nation and to defend the Roman Empire was to defend Christianity. He introduced the philosophy that if someone was in danger, it was immoral not to use violence to defend them if necessary. This was in stark contrast to the teaching of the first three centuries.

Shortly after Ambrose, Augustine became the most influential leader in the Christian world. He taught that individuals could not control their sin and that it was up to the state to curb violence and keep order. War, he believed, was an inevitable tool that was a moral positive in the hands of a godly state. In his theology, it was now the state that would restore order in the world rather than the kingdom of peace. Augustine justified the use of violence by pointing to the violence of the Old Testament, though he did not advocate continuing other elements of the old covenant period such as animal sacrifice, a seemingly inconsistent position. He convinced the church to turn its back on the longstanding prohibition of violence in self-defense, and he eventually came to advocate for coerced conversions.

To justify the turn in philosophy toward embracing empire and advocating for violence and war, Ambrose and Augustine developed guidelines for "just war." These principles are still largely accepted and followed to this day in much of Christendom, with only minor tweaks over the centuries.

There have always been small groups that have held to the gospel of King Jesus and his kingdom of peace, operating as alternative societies. But since the revolution of Constantine, Ambrose, and Augustine, the face of Christianity to the world has been very different than it was for the three hundred years after Jesus' resurrection and ascension, and most of those small kingdom movements were harshly persecuted by the dominant strains of Christendom.

As we continue to move forward, considering the role that Christians and the church can and should play in the world of politics, there is a reason that I have spent the first twelve chapters of this book talking primarily about the kingdom of God and very little about politics. For many Christians today, our vision of the kingdom is too small.

If we do not grasp the vastness of the kingdom and what allegiance to Jesus truly demands, we are bound to develop grotesque caricatures of God's kingdom rather than the radical vision of the future that it is supposed to be. We will create Christian movements that mix Christian morals with the methods of the world and sound godly but are a far cry from what the kingdom is to be. Without a biblical vision of how the kingdom should direct our lives, values, and passions, we will get off track rather quickly when we engage the world in difficult areas like politics and justice. Without the complete transformation of thinking that the kingdom is designed to bring about, we will be conformed, in one way or another, to the patterns of the world.

First Things First

I have now spent twelve chapters laying out the case for what our vision of the kingdom community should be. The detail in this section was intentional because we must have loyalty clearly defined and determined before moving into the realm of politics. If our allegiance is tinged to the slightest degree, we will lose our way.

Earthly loyalties and identities like ethnic identity, political identification, and the desire for security will pull at us like gravity. Our kingdom identity must define everything else that we are about to discuss in this book. If Christ remains first, everything else will be appropriately secondary. But these passions are subtle and sneaky, and without us realizing it, they can take precedence over our commitment to God and his people. That is idolatry. And we must all be on constant guard.

So let us cautiously move forward with a firm resolve to "seek first his kingdom and his righteousness" (Matthew 6:33).

The Chapter in Review

- Political divisions and differences are a very real danger and threat to unity within the body of Christ.

- Simply keeping our opinions to ourselves or learning to tolerate one another's political views may work in a few cases or for a limited time but will fail more often than not.

- Simon the Zealot and Matthew the tax collector were able to follow Jesus because they dropped their devotion or allegiance to their previous affiliations and beliefs.

- Matthew undoubtedly highlights the former associations of these men to demonstrate what they gave up to follow Jesus and how people from all sides were laying down their previous loyalties to submit to his kingship.

- Early in the fourth century, Emperor Constantine ended persecution of the church and declared himself a Christian, which caused a blurring in the previously clear separation between the church and involvement in the state.

- By the close of the fourth century, the main body of the church was almost completely intertwined with the empire of Rome and had lost nearly all its kingdom distinctiveness.

- We must have a firm grasp on the allegiance that is demanded of us as kingdom people or we will be very prone to error as we engage with the world.

The Big Idea

❖ The kingdom of God calls us away from the empires, our political tribes, and our allegiance to the state and requires that we remain a true alternative to the systems of the world.

DISCUSSION QUESTIONS

1. Do you think that someone can maintain deep partisan political opinions and be fully engaged as a disciple in Jesus' kingdom? *No*

2. If we cannot imagine Peter and Paul having a political argument, even though politics were a huge passion in the first century, why are we so comfortable with that type of divide in the church today? *People don't value the kingdom above all*

3. What would be the major challenges for the contemporary church if we adopted an approach to political systems and government that was more like the approach of the early church? *We would fail to truly change the hearts of men.*

Section 2

The Realm of Empire

Chapter 13

The Idol of Nations

The constant challenge for the first prophetic community was idolatry. They were tasked with becoming the alternative to empire and being restored as God's image-bearing people, his kingdom of representatives (Exodus 19:6). But that meant worshiping God alone. This did not entail just occasional religious activity. It demanded that every aspect of their lives be devoted to trusting in God and living out his will. That is worship.

But shortly after God led Moses and the Israelites out of Egypt and gave them the charter to be the prophetic community, a disastrous moment takes place. Moses goes up the mountain to be in the presence of God and seek his direction, and when he takes longer than the people are comfortable with, they grow restless. They want something tangible to verify their allegiance and provide assurance and security. So they do something that they would have learned in Egypt. They collect gold jewelry and melt it into a golden calf. Their words that follow this action are enlightening. Those responsible for this direct rebellion against God's instructions to have no other gods before him and not make any images (Exodus 20:3–4) don't proclaim, "Here is your real god." They don't compete against Yahweh, their covenant God. They reimagine him. They present the golden idol and declare, "These are your gods, Israel, who brought you up out of Egypt" (Exodus 32:4).

For those who wanted security over true allegiance, this was enough. God had not been challenged or replaced. In the minds of the people, God had been glorified by being revealed to be with them. Now they knew he was with them because they had this idol that they could look at and revere and be proud of. How could they worship a God they couldn't see? How could they remain loyal to a God who was so different from anything they had known? In that moment, worshiping a God who didn't make sense was too much, so they made sense of the situation. It wasn't that this statue was their new god, at least not in their minds. What they did was much more subtle and deceptive. They took the God that people had encountered and mixed him with what they believed they needed to keep them safe and secure, and they then called that "God."

The Lure of Nationalism

In the opening line of his book *Jesus Untangled,* Keith Giles asks a question, "Do you know what you get when you mix religion and politics?" He doesn't give any time for the reader to ponder that, as his next words provide the answer: "You get politics."[38]

There are still places in the world where idols are statues that are revered and believed to be the representative presence of a divinity, but that has grown increasingly rare. Yet idolatry is still as rampant as it has ever been. Most of the world has grown too sophisticated for something as crass and old-world as worshiping a statue. We look down on such backward behavior. We haven't abandoned idolatry, though; we have just transformed it. Few nations of the world find security and identity in the gods or their idols. No, they find security and identity through their own idol, the political state. It is the political state that provides hope and demands the highest loyalty.

One surefire way of identifying your god or gods is to ask what can make a claim on your life. If you would surrender your life or take another life at the request of that entity, that is most likely your god. With that in mind, it is a good idea to take stock and think of what is most likely for most people to demand the sacrifice of our life if necessary. Is it not the nations in which we live? Is it not empire?

Could I Be Unpatriotic?

I was born in the United States in the latter half of the twentieth century. I am deeply grateful for where I grew up in the Midwestern portion of the US. I have lived with constant opportunities at my fingertips of a quality and quantity that few people in the history of the world have had access to. I love the people from my home and, for the most part, I enjoy and prefer the culture in which I was raised. I like other places in the world as well and enjoy the many cultures found around the globe, but I love my own place. I think that is healthy. I think that it flows from a gratitude for God and what others have done to establish the place where I live and the freedoms that I enjoy.

But there is another side to that. The history of my country is not all pleasant and pure. She is affluent, opportunity is plenty, and today the people are free. But it has not always been that way for everyone. Much of the affluence and freedom were at the expense of indigenous peoples, enslaved people, and many others. My country has a spotty record of engaging in military conflicts. Some have seemed good and opposed evil behavior, and some have seemed rather self-serving and unnecessary.

In 2017, I wrote *Crossing the Line: Culture, Race, and Kingdom.* The second chapter of that book is entitled "Two Sides of a Coin." In that chapter I present two different perspectives on the history of my country. From one perspective, it is a glorious history of freedom and blessing by God, with a few mistakes sprinkled in. But from another perspective, it is a long and painful history of injustice, oppression, and disobedience to God, all the while claiming to serve him, with a few good things mixed in here and there. I proposed the idea that we have become a divided country in many respects because groups of people accept one of those two narratives and then shape their worldview according to it, while growing increasingly intolerant of those who have experienced the other story.

Not too long after the release of that book, I was giving a workshop in a large city in the United States and someone approached me to ask about my thoughts on patriotism. They were concerned that people who believed the more negative script about the United States were ungrateful and were ignoring that we were "one nation under God."

I decided to skip right to the heart of the matter and asked this nice gentleman a pointed question: "Could I be unpatriotic and still be a Christian?" I pushed a little further and clarified a bit: "Could I believe that the United States started with rebellion, enslaved and oppressed people, and expanded its military and idealistic empire around the globe for most of its existence? And could I love the people of the United States but tell you that I do not love the government, or the political empire of the United States and I would just as soon see it crumble and communism or socialism take its place? Not that I supported those systems, but that the system of government was of little concern for me because I was devoted to spreading the kingdom regardless of the context. Could I do all that and still be embraced by you as a disciple if I followed Jesus with all my heart, soul, mind, and strength, and lived in allegiance to him and for his kingdom?"

I asked the questions as gently and kindly as I could, not wanting to come across as combative, but I think my line of questioning was a bit more than my friend envisioned when he approached me. He stammered and stalled for a minute, no doubt trying to formulate what a good response would be. He finally responded by retorting something to the effect that we are a Christian nation and are not perfect but have always tried to do God's will and that if someone were to act like an enemy to the United States then they would probably be God's enemy as well.

That is a problem, is it not? Let me be clear. Those are not my feelings. As a former history teacher, I do see both the good and bad of the country I live in. I am grateful for it. But that was not the point of my questions. Paul rebuked the church in Galatia in the opening chapter of his letter to them because they had allowed people to come in and teach them that they must hold to the Law of Moses and, in effect, become Jewish in order to be the people of the Messiah. He tells them that they have abandoned the gospel and deserted Christ (Galatians 1:6). To add in another necessity in order to be considered part of God's family is to create "a different gospel," as Paul puts it.

There are few Christians in my country who would overtly state that we must be patriotic to be a Christian, but do our actions perhaps say otherwise? Would I be treated differently by many Christians if those were my feelings?

Nationalism and Patriotism

There is nothing wrong with personal patriotism. I enjoy traveling to new places, but I always enjoy the beauty and culture of being home in the United States. It is what I know, and I appreciate it. Even within the United States, there's always a special feeling that I get when I drive back into Wisconsin, the state I grew up in. I love to bring people back to my home state and show them what is wonderful about that place. It is this perception of the beauty of home that Christian author Craig Watts, in his book, *Bowing Toward Babylon*, calls "the essence of patriotism at its best."[39]

Watts compares this kind of healthy patriotism to a child who boasts that he has the best mom in the world. That sort of hyperbole demonstrates affinity but not competition. That child loves her mom. She is not actually claiming that she is comparing her to every other mother on the planet and hers should be given preference as the absolute best in show. There is no expectation that others must come to that conclusion as well. Familiarity and a certain attachment to one's home and culture of origin is reasonable and does not conflict with allegiance to Jesus. Paul demonstrated this type of healthy familiarity and devotion (Romans 9:1–5) but his ultimate allegiance to Christ could never be questioned (Philippians 3:7–10).

Nationalism is something different. It often masquerades as patriotism, but it is competitive. Natural feelings of appreciation and patriotism melt into the belief that my country is the best one at the expense of all others or that I would favor my country and her citizens above other nations. It becomes my identity and the object of my devotion and allegiance. I would die for my country. This type of nationalism is typically defined by nationality, but it can find boundaries defined by politics, ethnic group or race, cultural identity, or other group identifications. It is the feeling that this is my group and I will act in its best interests, even to the detriment of all other groups. Nationalism of this type is completely at odds with the kingdom identity and mindset. Keith Giles, in *Jesus Untangled,* captures the problem with this mindset as he quotes Benjamin L. Corey:

> Remember: The Kingdom of God is made up of people from every nation, every race, and every language. It's hard to have unity in his Kingdom when a handful of his followers are standing in the corner, waving a flag foreign to the Kingdom and shouting, "we're number one!"[40]

Christians can fall prey to this type of nationalism, not by replacing God but by blurring the lines between faith and country. Once this blurring takes place, loyalty to country becomes indistinguishable from loyalty to God. Devotion to country then overlaps imperceptibly with allegiance to God where service to one becomes synonymous with service to the other. We then develop a theology that excuses the obvious disconnects between the ability to serve God and the nation that we love. This is precisely what Christians in the fourth- and fifth-century Roman Empire did as they sought to justify their abandonment of centuries of Christian teaching against war, violence, and even self-defense that would risk the life of another person. This nationalism becomes an almost imperceptible form of idolatry.

An illustration of this comes through the account of King Ahaz in 2 Kings 16. While in Assyria, Ahaz becomes so enamored with the pagan altar of the Assyrians that he has a duplicate built in Jerusalem and put next to the altar of God in the temple. He doesn't remove God's altar, he just sets the two up together and seeks to utilize both, never recognizing the clear idolatry of doing so. When anything is set equal with God, even if the claim is that the thing is "under God," it is idolatry. And the more powerful the idolatry, says Watts, the more unlikely that the idolater will recognize it.[41] Without realizing it, healthy patriotism can turn into a type of religious devotion accompanied by an unhealthy amount of denial and self-deception about the power that this has over our hearts and minds.

One of the great temptations of idols is in their promise to bring security. That just happens to be one of the primary benefits of nations and empires, so it is not difficult to imagine how easy it is for a nation that provides security and stability to become an idol. That was precisely one of John's concerns when he wrote the Revelation to illuminate Jesus as King and expose the true nature of the beast.

Many nations, if not most of them, will demand loyalty to the extent of giving one's life to defend them. They hold the power of life or death, asking their citizens to kill or be killed. And in instances where the lines have been blurred between religion and nationalism, people agree to give up control of their lives to the state and sincerely believe that they are doing it "for God and country."

But when Jesus calls us to follow him, he demands that we give control of our lives to him. The Apostle Paul puts it this way: "I have been crucified with Christ and I no longer live, but Christ lives in me. The life I now live in the body, I live by faith in the Son of God, who loved me and gave himself for me" (Galatians 2:20). How can I give control of my life and the ability to demand it of me to two separate entities at the same time? We are called to be Christ's ambassadors to the world (2 Corinthians 5:20). What kind of ambassador would pledge their allegiance to the land that they were sent to as a representative? The only way I could keep this type of dual loyalty is if I have blurred the lines between God and country so that I now believe that serving one is to serve the other. This is the same mistake as Ahaz made.

Is it wrong to love your country? Of course not. Is it bad to be grateful to God for the freedoms or opportunities that one has? Not at all. What is a problem is when we exalt our love for or allegiance to a nation above our commitment to God. Or we conflate the two so that we convince ourselves that service rendered to our nation is serving God. These are idolatries.

A Civil Religion

Civil religion is the description given when a nation develops within itself a sacred authority that is constantly reinforced through public rituals, symbols, sacred days, sacred places, and ceremonies. The state becomes the primary object of loyalty, affection, and trust. It is also strengthened when intertwined with a folk religion or major historical religion. This combination then becomes a new form of religion that establishes the nation itself as a sacred object worthy of veneration, which is nothing less than a form of worship. Because of the integration of the traditional religion, adherents can convince themselves that they are still practicing their religion and not worshiping the state, which is precisely what happens in a civil religion.

Civil religions have occurred frequently throughout history and to varying degrees in different places and eras. Craig Watts builds on the work of French sociologist and theologian Jacques Ellul, and suggests several questions that we can ask of ourselves to help unveil civil religions and the idols in our own time and context.[42] I will adapt those questions for our purposes here, provide my own commentary, and add a couple of questions of my own.

Where Do We Place Our Trust and Faith?

The psalmist affirms,

> In you, LORD, I have taken refuge;
>> let me never be put to shame;
>> deliver me in your righteousness. (Psalm 31:1)

Similarly, the author of Proverbs calls the reader to "trust in the Lord with all your heart and lean not on your own understanding" (Proverbs 3:5).

Do you become anxious when things are not going well in your country? Do you get worried when a political party that you don't support comes into power? Do you worry that if your nation were unable to dictate its own fate, you would be at risk?

I'm not saying that we should have no emotions when change or even calamity is on the horizon, but we have got to be honest with ourselves and examine what our faith really rests in. Is it Christ and his kingdom or is it the strength and security of our nation or political party?

Nations that operate in the realm of empires always want to believe that they can and will last forever, but only God's kingdom will not be shaken (Hebrews 12:28), so it is the only thing that is worthy of our trust and faith.

Where Do We Look for Security and Happiness?

There are two elements regarding our security and happiness that we need to consider. The first is where we find it. Do we trust our country and its military or our local magistrates and police forces for our security, or do we look to God? One challenge here for many Christians is that we have smuggled fear of death into our Christian lives, even though Christ and his resurrection free us from that (Hebrews 2:14–15). This fear then dictates many of our behaviors as we make security a much bigger concern than is appropriate for a disciple of Jesus. One of the things about the early Christians that befuddled and irritated the Romans was their disdain of their own deaths. You simply cannot intimidate and control a people who do not fear the power to take a life. That was Rome's greatest weapon, but it held no sway in the lives of the kingdom people.

The second element is not just where we go to find our security and happiness but what defines it. Many Christians go through life unsatisfied and anxious because they have allowed the culture around them to define what security and happiness look like. We must have a retirement account. We must have a house that is at least such-and-such big. We need to have a certain collection of material possessions and this much in our bank account. Without these we can neither be secure or happy. Paul warned that we should have our minds set on things of the Spirit and not things of the flesh for an important reason (Romans 8:5–8). When we let the things of the flesh create our definitions and expectations, we will spend our energy pursuing those standards. And if we are chasing after those standards in life, we can try to please God but will find ourselves unable to.

Would you become a basket case tomorrow if the military force in your country was unable to protect the border from invaders? Or would you turn in prayer, knowing that God is the true provider of what you need in the first place? And if he decided that it was proper for the defenses or economic prosperity or stability of your country to fall, would it be well with your soul because with God, you already have everything you need?

Who Has Made the Ultimate Sacrifice?

While growing up in the United States, it was constantly reinforced that I should remember and revere those who died for my freedom; they made the ultimate sacrifice by dying for me. I would never disrespect anyone who lost their lives fighting for the United States, but as a Christian I cannot agree that they made the ultimate sacrifice for my life and freedom by dying for me. My life and freedom belong to God, and he determines my steps. That means that Jesus alone made the ultimate sacrifice for me to be free, not my country or a group of people. There is no question that I benefit daily in tangible ways from people who laid down their lives in battle, but I rely on Jesus alone and revere him alone as the one who died for me. Virtually every human being in every part of the globe has benefited from the work and sacrifice of those who have gone before them and have contributed to the situations they find themselves in today. That is wonderful. It is part of the human experience. Others may have valiantly and bravely died for a cause or for the security or interests of their country. But it is important, I believe, to distinguish that only one man in all history has personally died for me in my place, and that is Jesus the Messiah.

What Guarantees Our Future?

What if the country you grew up in collapsed in the next five years? What if its economy completely evaporated or it was conquered by another country and many of the residents of your nation were carried off to continue their lives elsewhere? What if all the dreams you had for security and comfort in the future disappeared overnight as the result of a global and devastating war?

I sincerely hope none of those things happen. But what if they did? Would we still serve God? Would the kingdom still be our mission and priority? Would it devastate us if we lost the future that we now dream of and hope for? It really comes down to what is the future that we live in expectation of. Is it one in God's presence, living as a subject in his kingdom and the eventual restored cosmos?

Every other aspect of our future must be secondary to that one and is not guaranteed. That was Paul's point in saying he had learned the secret to be content whatever the circumstances, whether he was in plenty or in want. "I can," he says, "do all this through him who gives me strength" (Philippians 4:11–13). Paul was content in any situation because he rejoiced in the Lord in every circumstance (Philippians 4:4). The Lord was all he needed and all he presumed. His presence was the only requirement for Paul's joy, so regardless of what else was happening, if God was still with him (and he always would be) then Paul's future was guaranteed.

Conversely, many of us live as though our nation or way of life must be preserved at all costs. Without it, there is no hope. Former President of the United States, Abraham Lincoln, once declared that America must not fail as a nation because it is "the last best hope of earth. Citizens of God's kingdom must never allow ourselves to think that way about anything other than the kingdom itself.

Who Guards Our Liberty?

If my personal liberty were taken away tomorrow, what would that mean for me as a disciple of Jesus? Liberty is pleasant and absolutely preferable, but it is not the primary objective for Christians. The one who was a slave when called to the Lord, asserted Paul, "is the Lord's freed person" (1 Corinthians 7:22). Paul goes on to assert that the opposite is also true; the free person is the Lord's slave. The degree to which we have or need liberty is determined by God, not guaranteed by a nation. Liberty is not a requirement that we should have in order to serve God and have joy.

Can someone living under a harsh communist or tyrannical regime become a Christian? Of course they can. In fact, the church often prospers in such conditions. Can someone living in a hostile Muslim country make the decision to follow Jesus? Absolutely. Can a person living in a Western democracy follow Jesus? Yes. Slaves can find freedom in Christ. Free persons can find freedom in Christ. Prisoners can find freedom in Christ. Our true liberty is not contingent upon our life situation. That's important because it is vital that we separate preferences from necessities. God alone is the guarantor of all the liberty we need.

Whom Do We Believe on the Subject of Truth?

I will keep this point short and simple. Many people around the world hold certain beliefs and values that have been fed to them from the culture in which they grew up. Are your values and what you believe to be true determined by your country of birth or by God's word? "It is a good thing to die for your country." Does that sentiment come from God's word or from your culture?

Who or What Has the Right to Ask Us to Sacrifice Our Life?

In many places and times in the ancient world, it was believed that the gods demanded and needed human sacrifice, and they were obliged. From the dawn of time, tribes, nations, and empires have asked their citizens to die for the protection and preservation of their people. But as a Christian, can we willingly give up our lives in these types of circumstances? It might be taken or forced, but should we willingly submit to any entity other than God that demands the possibility that we sacrifice our lives if called upon?

Here is my firm conviction: When I became a disciple of Jesus Christ, I died to self. I no longer live, but Christ lives in me (Galatians 2:20). My life belongs to him. I cannot give control of my life over to another, because it is not mine to give.

Think about this. Let's say a Christian in the United States felt that it was their duty to die for their country if need be and enlisted in the military. Meanwhile, a Christian in Iran is doing the exact same thing for their country. And let's say that those two countries find themselves going to war against one another for any of the reasons that the nations rage against one another. Should these two Christians kill one another in battle? Who are they serving if they do? Is it okay to take the life of another Christian? Is it appropriate for them to potentially give their own life away to their nation? I do not want to imply that it would be okay for a Christian to kill a non-Christian. That might be even worse, but hopefully, I have made my point.

I understand there can be a fine line here. As I carry on as a disciple, acting in the best interests of others, I may find myself in a situation where I sacrifice my life to protect or preserve someone else.

That can happen at any moment. But that happens as a direct result of my service to the King. If I die protecting my wife, my child, a fellow Christian, or some person I've never met, I do so because I am acting as a follower of Jesus, and displaying the kingdom and rule of God is a higher priority than preserving my own life. But I cannot willingly give the authority of that decision over to anything other than God. [Nor should I take another life in protecting someone. Many of our early-century brothers and sisters died in horrible ways because they refused to take a life to defend a life.]

I might try to justify my actions and say that I am willing to die for my country to protect others, but I cannot control that. What if my country suddenly engages in a war that is unjust? If I have given them control over my life and feel that it is my duty to die for my country if asked, Jesus no longer has control of a life that is supposed to belong to him. And since no country can or ever will be synonymous with the kingdom of God, I need to be incredibly careful about who has control over my life.

The Chapter in Review

- In the modern context, the bulk of idolatry has shifted from statues and idols to worshiping nation-states and politics.

- To demand or expect loyalty and allegiance to a nation in order to be considered a good Christian is to add to the gospel. It is idolatry.

- Nationalism and patriotism can easily become forms of idolatry.

- Giving loyalty and allegiance to a country above my commitment to God is idolatry.

- Conflating God and country to the point where serving one is to serve the other is idolatry.

- We must trust God for our security rather than trusting a nation or military force.

- We must let God define security and happiness for us rather than our culture.

- It is easy to think that our way of life must be preserved at all costs, and to feel that way about our nation or culture rather than valuing the kingdom of God above all.

- Our true liberty, which is found in Christ, is not contingent upon our life situation.

- Christians should not give control over their own life or the decision for them to take a life to anything other than God.

The Big Idea

❖ Our allegiance must belong to the kingdom of God and not an earthly nation or civil religion.

DISCUSSION QUESTIONS

1. What are ways that nations expect and reinforce a religious-type devotion to themselves?

2. Do you see any idolatrous forms of nationalism and patriotism that have worked their way into your church? What negative effects might that have on the life, witness, and unity of the body?

3. What are some examples of us entrusting something other than God for security and happiness?

Chapter 14

American Orthodoxy

"I have always wanted to ask an American this question," she began.

I have grown quite used to getting many questions of all sorts following a weekend workshop or teaching weekend at a church where I am the visiting teacher, although the preface to this question from a young sister in the church I was visiting on the African continent caught my attention. *"This should be interesting,"* I thought to myself, before she continued.

She paused for a moment, before somewhat nervously exhaling at a volume barely above a whisper, "I don't quite know how to word this."

"It's fine," I assured her. "What do you have for me?"

She seemed to find her confidence a bit more and her volume raised as her voice steadied, "Well, what is it like to be a Christian and live in a...well, you know...such an evil empire?"

I don't get taken aback by questions very often. For any given biblical topic, there are usually a handful of questions you get wherever you go, and you get used to hearing them and answering without making it seem like that is the one hundred and twelfth time you've heard that same question. This one took me off guard. Evil empire? Wait, what?

I must interject that this was not a rabble-rouser. This was not some hyperpolitical disciple with crazy ideas and an axe to grind. She is a wonderful follower of Jesus and she loves the kingdom of God with all her heart. She is aware of political and national issues in the world but not overly focused on them. Her question was sincere, and she was being as respectful as she possibly could. She felt comfortable enough to ask me because my wife and I have built a strong relationship with her over the years, and this was something she was very curious about.

But I was not expecting it. Surely, she had misspoken. She knows I'm American. We're not the bad guys. We are a Christian nation and a force for good and God in the world. Evil empire? No way.

That was the first time I had been asked that question. It was not the last. Whether the specific phrase used was "evil empire," or "evil nation," or "war-mongering imperial country," the more I traveled outside of my home nation, the more I heard people query about what it was like to try to live a Christian life of love and peace in such a place. This was difficult for me to process for a long time. I grew up believing that the United States of America was one nation under God. My experience in evangelical America left me convinced that this was the best and most godly nation in the history of the world and that patriotism and godly devotion were virtually indistinguishable.

But questions like these offered a new perspective. Could it be that my country and its place as God's representatives in the world was not nearly the established fact that I had always presumed? This led me on a journey of discovering what the Scriptures had to say. I began to study the Bible and continued to look at many of the pro-American Christian authors that I had grown up with but studying them carefully to see if what they had taught was true. During that time, I read two books that presented the biblical case that America was not virtually synonymous with the kingdom of God and never had been and that no country could. The first was *In God We Don't Trust,* by David Bercot. The second was *The Myth of a Christian Nation,* by Gregory Boyd. I've continued to study the Scriptures and dozens of other books and have come to the realization and conviction that the country I was raised in is more of a civil religion with Christian veneer than it has ever been a faithful representative of the kingdom of God.

The Heretic Quarterback

In August 2016, Colin Kaepernick, quarterback for the NFL's San Francisco 49ers, decided to sit on the bench during the national anthem, citing his refusal "to show pride in a flag for a country that oppresses black people and people of color."[43] His actions, which he stated were largely aimed at police officers who demonstrated corruption or racism, drew a mixture of criticism and praise, but the NFL officially stated that players were encouraged but not forced to stand during the anthem. Retired Army Green Beret Nat Boyer spoke with the quarterback and convinced him that he should kneel rather than sit, as this would still register his protest but show respect for soldiers and others who had died representing America and her flag.

Kaepernick eagerly did so, pointing out that he was not anti-American and did not hate America. Quite the opposite; he argued that he loved his country and only wanted to help make it better by calling her to live up to her ideals. Then President of the United States, Barack Obama, agreed that he was bringing up legitimate issues that need to be talked about.

Kaepernick's quiet and peaceful protests garnered more attention with several other NFL players joining his form of demonstration. It was not long before athletes from other sports were kneeling, including other professionals, college athletes, and even high schoolers. At the end of the 2016-17 season, Kaepernick opted out of his contract but could find no team willing to pick him, even though much-less-talented quarterbacks were signed by other teams. Rhetoric against Kaepernick gained steam and attention, fueled further when the President of the US, Donald Trump, criticized him both in public speeches and on Twitter, framing his protest as being against the flag, the troops, and the nation, and characterizing him as un-American.

As of the end of the NFL season of 2019-20, Kaepernick remains unsigned although he has stated that he would still like to play professional football again. He has reportedly settled for a large sum of money with the NFL to avoid a collusion grievance filed against them.

A foreigner to the United States might wonder what this man did that was so terrible as to keep him out of a sport that he was well qualified to play, gather sharp criticism from conservative news outlets around the country, and be publicly chastised by the current president of the country. They might be especially confused over such treatment in a place that prides itself on being the land of the free and touts its freedom of speech and expression as the purest form of what it means to be American. What crime had he committed in peacefully protesting something that concerned him as a citizen?

More puzzling for me personally was the number of people who are professed disciples of Jesus Christ who went on social media to denounce Kaepernick and call him names. They expressed their disdain for him and rejoiced that he has been unable to find a job. Some even noted that they "hate Kaepernick" and "he got what he deserved."

He had committed no crimes and had done nothing that would seem to ruffle the feathers of or bring concern to the Christian community. Yet many Christians were furious with this young man. This is an interesting case because it exposes some important issues when it comes to our ongoing analysis of the role of Christians in the political realm.

In the last chapter we considered the blurring of lines between the kingdom of God and civil religions. In this chapter, we will look at my own country, the United States of America, as a case study to recognize what it looks like when a civil religion and the kingdom of God become intertwined in the minds of a people.

Roots of American Orthodoxy

The United States is not the first country to develop a civil religion and it won't be the last. There has been a long string of nations in the last two millennia that have come to believe that they are God's chosen vessel on the planet, the new Israel, so to speak.

America's ideological roots lie in the beliefs and intent of her Puritan founders. From their first steps on the continent, the Puritans felt that they were a special people, chosen by God for a divine purpose. Puritan leader William Bradford explicitly expressed their desire to create a place where they could establish and practice their faith without opposition. They had no interest in extending religious freedom to others. They wished to establish their own manifestation of a people in covenant with God.[44]

This was the new promised land, and they were the new Israel. From the beginning, this is how the Puritan colonies saw their quest. They believed that the church and the commonwealth they were establishing foreshadowed the kingdom of God and, while they definitely put structures of government in place, their primary concern was to set up a commonwealth to maintain themselves as a church community.[45]

Once the nation was founded and the direct Puritan influence and control waned, the ideological roots of America as the new Israel continued and could be heard preached from nearly every denominational pulpit across the burgeoning country. As the Revolutionary War drew to a close and the nation was established, it was presumed that God had given America a spot of preeminence among the nations as a physical manifestation of the new Israel and the kingdom of God. Infused with this motivation, America's role was to conquer the "promised land," and every action that the nation took was seen as an expression of divine providence.

The founding fathers were men of faith, and their tendencies toward deism are often overblown. But they were also crafty politicians in a time when the revivalist George Whitfield was more known by the average person than Benjamin Franklin was. When rubbing elbows with European Deists, they spoke their language and appealed to them. When speaking to the people, they used words that resonated with the common folk. And they appealed to several underlying elements of Puritanism, says author George McKenna, that remained alive and well in eighteenth-century America:[46]

1. America was the new Israel. They were God's chosen people set apart and sent to the wilderness to be a new light to the nations and a city on a hill.

2. American Christianity was to have an activist role. The evidence of God's grace was how intensely the mission to spread Christian culture was carried out. The purpose of God's people was to spread his will on earth and establish his kingdom in the flesh of this new nation.

3. Covenant theology was a driving force. The country would prosper if they remained faithful to their identity as the bearers of God's will in the world. If they departed from God or their purpose, they would suffer defeats from their enemies. Thus, military victories became a sign of God's continued pleasure and favor.

Armed with this identity and mission, America set out to expand both physically and ideologically throughout the world, but this expansionism was viewed, says Craig Watts, as an extension of Christian civilization. Most Americans were not bothered when soldiers were sent abroad, seeing them as a type of missionaries creating fertile ground for evangelization and humble servants of God's will.

Once a nation has formed an identity as chosen and the special envoy of God, everything it does is justified in its own eyes. They are always the good guys in the movie. They must push their way of life on others not only because it is superior, but also because it is their duty to bring their light to the Gentiles of the world. Every action is interpreted through these lenses. Watts aptly summarizes the mindset that was built into the fabric of the American mentality:

America as a chosen nation, a new Israel, was not simply the recipient of the lion's share of God's blessings and privileges. America was understood as the special instrument of God by which all the nations of the world would benefit. Hence, the military venues of the US were interpreted, not as being a quest for selfish acquisition, or economic advantage, or political dominance, but as efforts to spread universal ideas and values. For the most part, Americans have tended to be uncritically convinced of the nation's benevolence.... While the destiny of the supposedly benevolent nation was sometimes manifested in the spread of its borders, even more so it was displayed in the spread of its ideals, which were understood as being reflective of the truest and deepest values of all humankind.[47]

Christianity is not the only religion that fosters civil religions but is as prone to them as any other. When the power of political rule is mixed with the fervor of religious rhetoric and authority, the result is often a civil religion. America is not the first country to believe or declare itself in covenant with the Christian God as his newly chosen people. This despite the fact that Scripture nowhere points to the idea of a chosen people or a covenant nation, other than Israel, before the coming of Christ. There is a reason that there is no direction given to governments or rulers in the Scriptures of the new covenant, although there is much of that material for Israel under the old covenant. That is not how the kingdom is to work.

Once any country, in this case the United States, is seen as the new Israel, honoring the country is just another aspect of glorifying God. He has chosen us to be the light to the nations, and who are we to argue or shirk that duty? The mission to evangelize the world on behalf of Christ and dominating the world as Americans become nearly impossible to distinguish when this mindset is embraced. For the non-Christian nations, America and Christianity became indistinguishable. America took its place next to other empires that had become intertwined with the civil religion: the Holy Roman Empire, Russia prior to the Bolshevik Revolution, prerevolution France, the British Empire, and many others.

The articles of patriotism in a civil religion then take on a religious tone, and orthodoxy must be maintained. The American flag becomes a sacred relic and any suggestion of questioning the actions or integrity of the state are met with the swift rebuke of religious zealotry.

Israel or Babylon?

Let me be very clear. As an American, I am biased. Of that there can be no doubt. But I do believe that the United States has done many wonderful things in and for the world. It is a place of religious freedom and economic prosperity. I do believe that it has helped many other nations throughout its history. I also believe that it has often acted in direct opposition to biblical principles. It has, at times, dominated and bullied other nations into subjugation. If we were to take an honest look, the history of the United States is a mixed bag. It may be the most benevolent country in the history of the world. It may have acted with the interests of others many times, but there must be a reason that most of the world views my country very differently than we view ourselves. And we should not simply wipe away all criticism as jealousy or ignorance.

Some of you may be uncomfortable with that last paragraph. Some may even be quite angry with me. Thoughtful analysis of a nation and its impact should not be a problem. But when patriotism has become a civil religion in that nation, criticism is considered a traitorous act.

But here is an important question for us to wrestle with: Is America the new Israel? We need to determine whether we have subtly bought into the storyline that the US is the chosen nation, favored and blessed by God. Does its economic prosperity prove that it has been set apart as God's special envoy to the world?

From a biblical perspective, does the United States look more like a new Israel, the kingdom of God or a new Babylon, another in a long line of empires?

When viewed scripturally, a much better case can be made for seeing the United States as a new Babylon, an empire in which citizens of the kingdom of God reside as exiles and aliens.

I have already made the case that a Christian nation is not possible. The New Testament does not dictate any nation's policies. It is impossible for a nation to live by the principles of the kingdom as laid out in the Sermon on the Mount and other places in the New Testament.

But, writes Watts, citing author Daniel Berrigan, "Those who dwell in Babylon do not know they are there."[48] There were wonderful things about living in Babylon. It did not seem evil to her citizens. The people of Rome thought she was the best and most benevolent thing to ever happen to the world. But it was their military might and power that created their bubble of prosperity, a force that her own citizens rarely felt or saw. America is no different. Citizens of those empires were just as enamored with their own national worship as citizens of America often are. Every Babylon, notes Watts, has its redeeming features. But as religious speaker Tony Campolo once declared, "Even a very good Babylon is still Babylon."[49]

Here are some questions to consider when evaluating whether a nation is more like Babylon or the kingdom of God:

1. Does my nation give its full allegiance to Jesus as King?

2. Does my nation base its laws and policies on the Sermon on the Mount?

3. Do my nation and its leaders act like Jesus?

4. Is my nation more known for loving her enemies or defeating them?

5. Is my nation more known for militarism (the god of Mars) and materialism (the god of Mammon) than it is for sacrificing for the benefit of others?

6. Does my nation prioritize protecting its borders or loving our neighbor as ourselves?

7. Does my nation trust God to defend it or does it trust in its weapons and military might?

Answering those questions may help us discern whether our nation is a Babylon that has wrapped itself in robes of light or if it is truly a representation of the kingdom of God. Wherever we live as foreigners and aliens who follow Jesus as King, we must ask ourselves, does my nation look more like an extension of Babylon or of the kingdom of God?

Citizens of Jerusalem cried out to Pilate to free Barabbas, a man who was most likely a Zealot and an armed revolutionary. He was willing to sacrifice everything for the freedom of his people. The crowds made clear that they would rather have Barabbas free to roam than Jesus. Who would be more likely in your country to be embraced as a leader? The tough, whatever-it-takes Barabbas, or the Prince of Peace?

I do not hate my country. I love it. Please don't hit me with the old, "Why don't you just leave?" argument. I am grateful to be an American. But I must love the kingdom more than my country and not get so tangled in cords of red, white, and blue that I allow nationalism to so intertwine with the identity of the church that it no longer points people in the right direction.

Angering the Civil Religion

Once Constantine set in motion the events that led to the full acceptance of Christianity and the eventual establishment of it as the official religion of Rome, it slowly morphed into a civil religion. In my opinion, as soon as armies were sent out in the name of Christianity, it completely ceased to have any connection to the kingdom of God. The Holy Roman Empire was just the first in the long line of nations embodying a Christian civil religion.

Christian author Brian Zahnd rightly argues that the Roman world was saturated with gods. They would have had no problem with claims that Jesus was god. They even allowed Jews to maintain fidelity to their monotheistic religion, so even the claim that there was only one God was not a deal breaker. The radical and dangerous part, says Zahnd, was that they worshiped Jesus as emperor. He was their king, and it was those political implications that made all the difference. They could no longer be controlled or counted on. Zahnd writes, "It wasn't the religion of the Christians that got them into trouble per se, but the political implications of their religion."[50]

The Christians weren't persecuted for being overly religious. They were persecuted for being unpatriotic. They were criticized for not paying veneration to the gods and Caesar because of what the Romans believed would be the implications for the nation if people did not appease the gods. They were called out for refusing to take part in Roman wars and support violent actions in the society.

When did the persecution of the church end? It was not when they ceased to worship Jesus as God. It was when they ceased to recognize him as their only emperor. Once Rome became a "Christian nation," the persecution ended.

An Irreconcilable Difference

There is such a stark difference between Babylon and the kingdom of God that we should readily be able to tell the difference. Babylon loves the sword. The kingdom strives for peace (Isaiah 2:2–4). Babylon loves and uses power. The kingdom embraces powerlessness and sacrifice (Mark 10:42–45). In Babylon, the first are the most powerful. In the kingdom, the last will be first (Mark 10:31). Babylon justifies retaliation. The kingdom follows Jesus in not retaliating, suffers willingly to end cycles of violence, makes no threats, and entrusts themselves to the one who judges justly (1 Peter 2:23). Babylon kills her enemies. The kingdom loves them (Matthew 5:38, 44); Babylon uses death as a weapon to keep subjects in line and to preserve their power. The people of the kingdom triumph by the self-sacrificial "blood of the Lamb and by the word of their testimony," for "they did not love their lives so much as to shrink from death" (Revelation 12:11). From the moment that Jesus died on Calvary, God has dealt with the world through the cross.

Paul reminds us of the stark difference between the systems of the world, as good as they may be in some respects, and the kingdom of God, writing that "the weapons we fight with are not the weapons of the world" (2 Corinthians 10:4); instead we have "weapons of righteousness in the right hand and the left" (2 Corinthians 6:7), meaning that we can hold no other weapon in our hands. Pastor and author Keith Giles sums up this difference well: "So, let the state wield the sword. Let the Church carry the cross. Let the two of them never change places or merge together."[51]

I return to the case of Colin Kaepernick. Could it be that the furor against Kaepernick was religious in nature? He was a heretic against the civil religion, which is why so much ire was raised against him. He dared to challenge the orthodoxy. From that perspective, I can understand why so many Americans were deeply offended by their perception of his actions. I can also understand why so many, who view America's role in history from a differing perspective, were ready to identify with his silent protest. What is not so easy for me to understand is why so many Christians interpret situations like this based on their feelings about their country rather than letting their heart, soul, mind, and strength be ruled by their allegiance to Jesus.

The Chapter in Review

- The United States can serve as a case study of countries that embraced a civil religion into their life and collective culture.

- From its earliest days, the United States of America saw itself as a new Israel with the status of favored nation in the eyes of God. That became an integral part of its identity as a "Christian nation."

- America is one of many countries that have believed themselves to be the representative nation of God and in covenant with him.

- Criticism of a nation that has become a civil religion is typically viewed as traitorous or unpatriotic and is looked down upon sharply or worse.

- The distinction between a nation that looks more like Babylon than like a new Israel must be clear in our minds.

The Big Idea

❖ We must be careful to separate the kingdom from the civil religions of the nations in which we may reside.

DISCUSSION QUESTIONS

1. Are there elements of a civil religion that you see in your country?

2. What is so dangerous about mixing the identity of your country and the kingdom of God?

3. Does anything about the way you view your country or its place in the world need to change in light of the immensity of the kingdom of God?

Chapter 15

Two Parties

On January 15, 2017, two of the most iconic professional football teams in the history of the NFL and North American football squared off in a playoff game in Green Bay. Both were desperately seeking to return to the Super Bowl after many years of absence from the biggest game of the year. Those two teams are the Green Bay Packers and the Dallas Cowboys. The game was a tight affair all the way through, with Dallas leading most of the way. Near the end of the third quarter Dallas was leading 21–13, but then the Packers capped off a brilliant drive to bring the game to 21–20. This was good news for me because from the time I can remember, I have been a Green Bay Packers fan. My whole family was diehard Packers fans; there was never any question about that. Even though I haven't had time to watch much football in the last decade or so, I was watching that game and cheering for my team.

Things got even better in the fourth quarter when the Packers went on another touchdown drive to take the lead 26–21. But they missed a two-point conversion attempt, so Dallas had the ball with nine minutes remaining and only needed one score to win the game. This was disconcerting not only because I am a Packers fan, but also because I grew up very much disliking the Cowboys, as do all good Packers fans. So the thought of Dallas winning a huge playoff game on a big comeback drive was almost too much to bear.

In those closing minutes, Dallas drove down the field. It came down to a fourth down and 2 yards to go to get a first down from the Green Bay 32.[52] Dallas quarterback Tony Romo threw a pass down the left sideline to a sprinting wide receiver, Dez Bryant, who leaped into the air over the defender, pulled down the pass, and then went lunging headfirst into the endzone. It was a touchdown, and now we were trailing 27–26.

But then something wonderful happened. The announcers noted that the Packers had thrown a challenge flag to demand a review of the play. Replays then showed that as he lunged toward the goal line, Bryant's hand that was holding the ball hit the ground and the ball momentarily squirted up in the air before he regained control while rolling over. The replay officials shocked everyone by announcing that the play was ruled incomplete. There was no catch. There was no touchdown. The home crowd burst into jubilant celebration, and the Packers went on to win the game 26–21.

I know many Dallas Cowboys fans who will go to their grave claiming that they were robbed and that it should have been ruled a catch and a touchdown. No Green Bay fans I know agree. According to the rules at the time, we will tell you, it wasn't a catch. The fact that they changed the rule the next year as a result of that play is irrelevant. By rule, it was not a catch, and we won the game as we should have. Besides, even if they had ruled it a touchdown, we had nearly five minutes left on the game clock and would have easily gone downfield, gotten a field goal and three points and won the game anyway.

There's a term for this phenomenon in sports. It's called being a homer. Whenever a play or call from the officials goes your team's way, it was the right call. And whenever it doesn't, it was clearly a wrong call and one of the greatest atrocities in the history of human civilization. Being a homer is one of the fun parts of being a sports fan. You can suspend all objectivity and give wholesale support to your team no matter what. If a player from your team does something questionable, you like his spunk. If a player from the other team does the same thing, he is dirty and needs to be banned from the game. If a touchdown play is ruled to not be a catch, it was the right call when it goes my team's way. But if the roles were reversed, you can believe I would have been screaming my head off that it was clearly a touchdown and the game was stolen from us.

Making the Same Mistake

Not all countries are built on a two-party system as their underlying political structure. My country is, so I will consider that type of system in this chapter, although I believe the general principles will apply to most situations, since there are most often two or three main choices that we are encouraged to make when it comes to political groups and who has power, although some live in countries where the choices are limited or illusory.

Those who identify as Christian in the United States are just as divided politically, it seems, as America itself. Many Christians identify as liberal or Democrat, while many others identify as conservative or Republican. There are others who may identify as libertarian or some other smaller group, but most Americans fall into one of those two political parties or ideologies.

As a child growing up in a typically conservative evangelical church in Wisconsin, life seemed pretty simple. Good Christians were Republicans. Non-Christians and liberal Christians were Democrats. That's a simplification, of course, but that's mostly what I grew up hearing and believing from every direction that I knew.

As I grew older in years and in my discipleship to Christ, I questioned where that assumption came from, especially since it didn't seem to be such a no-brainer anymore.

If you'll allow me to speak in broad generalizations at this point, it would seem that what we would now call evangelical Christians had largely retreated from the public square and the marketplace of ideas in the 1930s and resigned Christianity to something of a personal and private faith that need not interact with the world at large. This led to what most evangelicals saw as a sharp decline in public morals that by the 1960s had reached alarming lows.

Things changed in the late 1960s and into the 1970s. The Republican Party spoke out about the problems that they saw in America that needed to be fixed. America's real problem, they argued, was a moral one. The nation that was "under God" had drifted sharply from its moral moorings and needed restoration. Many who were associated with the conservative wing of the Republican Party began to call out America's problems, and many evangelicals got excited because what they were saying sounded an awful lot like naming sin. And they were championing the two things that evangelicals loved most: God and country. They spoke out against things like abortion, immorality, divorce, crime, and the decline of the family. The Bible has much to say about these issues, and they understandably felt that it was about time that some politicians cared.

Finally! Someone in power was speaking the language of the devout and they were calling sin as sin. In droves, those who identified as Christian made their way into the Republican camp with visions of restoring the one nation under to God to its glorious past. That became so normal, as I mentioned above, that in my world, if you were Christian, at least a white Christian, it was assumed you were

Republican. The term "Democrat" almost became synonymous with "pagan."

What never made it onto the radar for most was the fact that the party held to many other positions that were not biblical. They blurred the lines between the kingdom of God and their country. They took a position toward war and military that should make Christians quite uncomfortable. They strove for power and exalted economic greed in a way that Jesus never encouraged. But none of that mattered. They were correctly identifying the problem, in the eyes of these Christ followers, so this was their political home. And in the blink of an eye they became active and powerful as a voting bloc.

What also escaped their attention was that the solutions to these problems that were being offered were decidedly not kingdom focused or biblically derived. They may have identified some of the very real problems in society, but their answers were not Christ-centric and quite often were not rooted in love for neighbor.

But it was too late. Many evangelical Christians had been drawn in by the siren's song of identifying the problems and had yoked themselves together with a political movement.

If we fast-forward to the decade of 2010–2019, we see a similar phenomenon happening. This time, though, it is the liberal faction of the Democratic Party that has started to call out the problems in society, and to a growing number of Christians, these sound like the real sins that plague us. They denounce racial and gender injustice, intolerance for others, mistreatment of immigrants and the economically disadvantaged, and a host of similar issues. The ears of many have perked up. The Bible has much to say about these issues, and it's about time some politicians care.

Finally! Someone in power is speaking the language of devoted Christ followers who love their fellow man and are calling sin as sin. History is repeating itself, as droves of Christians are now making their way into the Democrat camps and identifying with the issues that these camps advocate for the loudest. It's not that there weren't self-identifying Christians who were Democrats, but it has become more and more acceptable in the eyes of other Christians. It has become normal.

And while they have now emotionally and politically yoked themselves together with this philosophy and party, they have failed to notice or care that there are many other things that this party stands for that are opposed to the word of God. This party embraces the abortion of unborn children, and they increasingly oppose God's intent for his humanity in the realms of marriage, gender identity, sexuality, and much more. They seek political power over others to bully or force them into accepting their positions.

These Christians too have been drawn in by the siren's call as they heard a party denounce as problems the sins that they hate the most and want to see done away with. But just like the generation before, they have failed to discern that most of the proposed solutions are not rooted in biblical thinking or coming from a kingdom perspective.

The two sides have made the same mistake, and neither one has recognized it. To make matters worse, it has created a sharp division in the body of Christ and even in many local congregations. This growing divide has created a massive amount of tension in many local churches.

"How can they call themselves a Christian and support the Democratic Party?"

"How can they call themselves a Christian and support the Republican Party?"

And in unison: "If you think that way politically, you can just go ahead and unfriend me on Facebook."

Do you see the problems? It's not just the tension and division. When Christians yoke together with one side of the political spectrum or the other, we lose the ground of being prophetic to the culture. We become just another player in the partisan games. And it's easy to dismiss us, because there is no obvious distinction between the kingdom of God and whatever political side we have tethered ourselves to.

In my country, we have missed that in many respects the conservative movement is a parody of the morality, security, and allegiance found in the kingdom of God, while the liberal movement is a parody of the justice, compassion, and inclusion found in the kingdom of God. But they are just parodies. Neither offer the real thing. If you live outside the United States, the configurations of the specific parties and agendas will be different, but they likely parody aspects of the kingdom while falling far short in their own way.

Let me be clear here. I do not favor either of the two major political parties in my country. Both have sincere, well-meaning pec who work for what they believe will be the best for the country. Both have greedy, manipulative politicians who will lie and seize power wherever they can. Both have positions that will, at times, overlap with a kingdom agenda, and both have positions that are diametrically opposed to the kingdom. If at any point in this book, you feel that I am going too hard on one or being unfair while letting the other one skate by, that is not my intent. I am not trying to demonize either party but to show that from a kingdom perspective, neither one seems to be a solution. Whatever country you are in, I think you will find that to be the case with your options. If at any point, though, I appear to favor one side of the political spectrum over the other, that is a result of my deficiencies as a writer and not a hidden agenda.

Our Role in the Two-Party System

We are still working our way toward what the Christian role in secular affairs and politics might be, but the question for now is what should be our role in two-party or similar systems? How do we know which side to support and identify with? Which partisan political affiliation should we yoke ourselves together with as either individuals or more collectively?

My simple suggestion would be neither side. There are significant difficulties both internally and externally when the church takes on a worldly political identity. That does not mean that we do not engage with the issues of the world. This is about how we engage and the identity we maintain when we choose to do so. There are at least eight reasons that Christians should avoid political party affiliation of any kind.

The first problem is that it can cut our evangelism field in half. When we share that meme, make that politically partisan post, or put a sign supporting a candidate in our yard, we have that right in most countries. I certainly have the right to do so in mine. But just because things are permissible does not mean that they are beneficial (1 Corinthians 10:23–24). We might feel better, but how much closer have we brought anyone to the kingdom of God? Is our preferred candidate focused on calling people to discipleship of Jesus and forming them to the image of Christ? And I'm not just talking about paying lip service to God. Does their economic agenda embody the kingdom in people's lives? Does passing that law they support help transform someone's heart? And once our public declaration has been made, it is quite possible that we have angered a neighbor or online friend from a different political persuasion and have lost all credibility in their eyes. Was our post or yard sign worth cutting off an opportunity to share the kingdom with them?

The second problem is like the first. When we become identified with a worldly political party or ideology, it can give the impression to those whom we want to reach with the truth of the gospel and an invitation to join the kingdom of God that they must also convert to our politics as they convert to following Christ. Of course, we cannot please everyone, and being a church body that takes a stand as a prophetic community will turn people off and anger others, but that should come only when we are living out the kingdom and not because of unnecessary political affiliations or opinions.

The third problem is that it risks us being yoked together with unbiblical agendas or solutions, as I described above. Paul asks a series of probing but related questions in 2 Corinthians 6:14–16 after declaring that believers should not be yoked together with unbelievers: "What do righteousness and wickedness have in common? Or what fellowship can light have with darkness? What harmony is there between Christ and Belial? Or what does a believer have in common with an unbeliever? What agreement is there between the temple of God and idols?"

Early church leaders of the first three centuries consistently and unequivocally called the church away from engagement in public office and Roman politics. Leaders like Tertullian in the late second century argued that Christians were free to partake in party-based politics if while doing so they could avoid supporting other religions, public support of any pagan festival, taking part in any activity or judgment that would cost someone their life for any reason, condemning anyone to physical punishment, prison, or torture, or supporting any position that would stand opposed to the purposes of God and his kingdom.

The fourth problem is that engaging in typical partisan politics causes us to rely on the weapons of worldly power and coercion that do not bring people closer to a relationship with the King or entry into his kingdom. We must not confuse moral behavior or laws that prohibit personal immoral behavior with drawing people into the transformation of the kingdom of God, which should be our primary and only goal.

The fifth problem with engaging in a party-based system is that we lose distinction from the world. I had grown up going to the same church my whole life, but when I was seventeen, I served as a volunteer for the Republican Party in my county. Very few of the organizers or politicians I met through that position ever seemed to be particularly spiritual or religious, yet their worldview, politics, and engagement with the world were largely indistinguishable from the church folks I had always known. When we engage in politics, we can easily look like or even become just one more voting bloc vying for power and influence.

The sixth problem is that we run the risk of inflating opinions that are not biblically rooted. Christian theologian Tim Keller argues that "most political positions are not matters of biblical command but of practical wisdom."[53] Speaking out prophetically against sin or oppression or on behalf of the poor are necessary for the church. But Keller rightly asserts that there are many ways to help the poor, for example, and the Bible does not give the exact recipes for every time, place, and culture. To become impassioned or divide over matters of practical wisdom is not acceptable for Christians.

This leads into the seventh problem with two-party politics becoming intertwined in the church: taking sides politically will cause division within the body of Christ; and we must not allow divisions to threaten our unity (1 Corinthians 1:10) over matters that are not our primary affairs (2 Timothy 2:4).

Divided Loyalty

Finally, the eighth problem with embroiling ourselves in the political fray is that when intermingling our identity within a two-party system, our passions will be raised and our focus will be lost for what matters when it comes to the kingdom of God, which is to live out the life of the coming age, provide an alternative to the world, and call them to take part in this reality. In other words, we take the very real risk of ceasing to be the prophetic community.

This is no small consequence. It might be the most damaging of all. We lose a large degree of our saltiness and no longer shine as light in the darkness. We look like just another special-interest, politically motivated group.

Party loyalty and identification in the church can become devastating to our function as the prophetic community. We can hardly speak out against any injustice without fear of being leveled from friendly fire within our own community claiming that we are being political, but really meaning that we have stepped on their partisan toes. The kingdom will be political, but it should not be partisan.

But, as a biblical teacher in God's community, if I were to stand up and speak out against something that the political right believes in because I feel it to be opposed to the purposes of God's kingdom, I will get torn down and attacked by fellow disciples of Jesus because I have "become political." Yet if were to turn around and denounce some aspect of liberalism, I will get destroyed by left-leaning disciples because I have gone against their political orthodoxy. The result of this partisanship in the church is the loss of the ability to be the prophetic community without causing great controversy, being attacked from within as leaders, and losing members who get angry because the idol of their party politics has been assaulted.

In the past year, I have wanted to write an article detailing how deeply sinful I feel that our current president is and the damage that devotion to him among disciples has caused. But I know that if I do that, it will cause enormous controversy in the church. I also very much wanted to write an article making much the same point about leaders in the Democratic Party, but the response would be almost the same. I don't think the problem is that my kingdom-focused critiques are wrong. The problem is that too many who call themselves Christians also worship at the altar of their political gods and would be as ready to strike at me if I challenged them as were the people of Ephesus when Paul took aim at their goddess Artemis (Acts 19:23–41).

Without even realizing it, Christians can easily get sucked up into the homer effect that has seeped into modern politics these days. Under this mindset, everything the other side does is wrong, hypocritical, immoral, or illegal. But when our political side does the exact same kind of thing, it is justified, and we excuse the behavior. This has led to enormous hypocrisy in contemporary politics, spurred on by media outlets that have fallen prey to the same my-side-versus-your-side mentality. When my convictions from studying the Scriptures led to me taking a huge step back from secular politics and down the road of a different approach, the hypocrisy that results from this homer position became glaringly obvious. If you are emotionally invested in partisan politics and deeply convinced that the other political side is obviously more morally corrupt than are the politicians on your side, you are very likely a victim of the homer effect.

The Lesser of Two Evils?

Many followers of the King will justify participation in the two-party system by utilizing two arguments that are similar. One is the lesser-of-two-evils philosophy. Proponents of that way of thinking will argue that Christians have a responsibility to be good citizens and take part in their civic duty of voting. Fulfilling that responsibility may, and often does, demand that if we cannot find a candidate that will do good, we hold our nose and choose a candidate that will do the least harm.

Walking arm-in-arm with that philosophy is the one that is built on the famous quote, "The only thing necessary for the triumph of evil is for good people to do nothing." This presumes that if Christians simply sit back and embrace a righteous pietism that keeps us from voting or engaging in the political spectrum, it will allow the forces of secularism and evil to run amuck.

So is it necessary, although less than ideal, that we will sometimes, if not all the time, find ourselves voting for the lesser of two evils?

I personally do not find knowingly voting for a lesser evil a good position for a Christian to take. We often couch it in language that sounds palatable and grace-filled, saying things like, "Sure, he has flaws, but no one is perfect, and God can use anyone."

Note that the lesser of evils is still evil. Scripture encourages us to overcome evil with good (Romans 12:21), not to overcome evil with a slightly more palatable version of evil. The lesser-of-two-evils argument will sound more convincing, I believe, if we lose sight of the fact that our goal is to call people to the alternative world of God's kingdom, not strictly to make the world a better place.

We have been taught in modern Christian circles that we should always do the most good, or if it is our only option, the least harm. This teaching has armed us with the idea that a bad decision is better than no decision or that to choose the lesser evil is more important than making no choice at all.

I find at least four important flaws with that line of thinking that we should consider.

First, what matters more, the country or the kingdom of God? The interests of those two are not always mutually exclusive, but they often are. If it comes down to it, does the temporal good of the country matter more than the damage done to the reputation of Christ and his kingdom? I have talked with many Christians over the years who justify their support of a party or candidate because they like some of their positions, often ones that benefited them personally or that enforced a certain moral perspective that they hold as a Christian, but they did not consider the damage done to the reputation of Christ by supporting someone who did not represent Jesus in character or methods.

Let me be blunt here. In the eyes of many in our contemporary culture, the fact that so many Christians have supported Donald Trump has completely removed any possibility of those people ever considering Christianity as a viable option. But before his detractors get too happy, the same could be said of those who supported Barack Obama. The problem is not that the world needs to change its perspective. The problem is that we have done unnecessary damage to our own cause by engaging in politics in a destructive manner.

I think this point is inestimably important. We are not trying to curry favor with the world, but we also are called to be careful what messages we send to those outside the faith (Colossians 4:5; 1 Thessalonians 4:12; 1 Timothy 3:7). If a candidate or party does not strive to fully represent the truth of the King and his kingdom in every way, then supporting them can and probably will damage our witness, even if we think they are spot on in a few areas. And don't be fooled by politicians who utilize religious jargon and their position on one or two issues to claim to be allies or Christians themselves, but whose life and many of their other positions don't look anything like Jesus.

Second, yoking with unbelievers is still yoking with unbelievers. It does not matter what fine-sounding arguments we might put forward. When we support a candidate, we are helping to institute every position they hold and will fight for. Admittedly, I used to be a single-issue voter. I would vote for whatever candidate held to my same beliefs about the issues I felt were deal breakers. The problem with that is that, in effect, I wound up also voting for many things that work against the values of the kingdom of God. For myself, I can no longer do that in good conscience.

But don't we yoke ourselves together with a company when we buy their product or a movie company when we watch their movie? I don't think so. We could have a conversation about what we support in those types of situations, but I do believe that joining or supporting a political party is in an entirely different category. When we support a politician, we are advocating to give them rule and authority in the world (to whatever degree that may be, based on the office they seek). That is a big thing and does give us a certain amount of responsibility for what that politician does in quite a different way than supporting a company or watching a movie does.

Third, there is an important distinction between coming to a compromise solution and compromising principles. Not all compromises are equal. A diverse family of people like the church will find that compromise is its life blood. We must be all things to all people and find the middle ground on many matters of life together. That is good. But that does not justify compromising principles. To vote for the lesser evil smacks of compromising principle rather than reaching a compromise with someone else that does not do damage to my faith or principles.

I find it interesting that we will quickly point out the compromise of principle when a young Christian seeks to justify dating a person who claims to be a Christian at some level but whose life does not consistently bear witness to that. We will tell them how foolish and dangerous it is to put their desire for a relationship over their principles of whom to be potentially yoked with. But do we make a compromise of principle when it comes to supporting a candidate or party? I think so, but you'll have to decide for yourself.

Finally, the argument falls flat that we do nothing and let anti-God forces have their way if we fail to vote for a candidate who does not fully represent the kingdom of God. This presupposes that the kingdom alternative to politics means that we are doing nothing or being ineffective. In effect, it is to argue that God will only or can only work through the two-party system or through politics. Can God not move through the kingdom methods of alternative living, self-sacrifice, prayer, and being the prophetic community? Being the kingdom does not mean doing nothing. It means fighting with weapons other than those the world uses. It is to the question of kingdom engagement that we will turn in the next chapter.

We Can Change the World

The kingdom of God will always be political from a certain angle. We are called to loyalty to Jesus as Lord. For the first Christians, that declaration by itself was a strong political statement. It meant that Caesar was not Lord and that Jesus was the King of kings. He held the highest authority. For the first three hundred years of Christianity, they consistently avoided yoking themselves together with politics. And even though they were roundly criticized for that position, they knew that it was their job to offer the world a true alternative. They knew that they were to stand up against injustice but not use the weapons, power, or politics of the world to fight that injustice. They grasped the reality that the kingdom of God was the solution, and they called people to come join them as they lived as an alternate society, guided by the values and standards of the kingdom. They knew that the kingdom of God, not politics, changed lives and communities.

The early Christians resisted the temptation of latching themselves onto a political philosophy for solutions. They stood up and spoke prophetically against any solutions or identification of problems that were not rooted in the new and otherworldly reality of the kingdom.

And they radically changed the world.

The Chapter in Review

- "Homerism" is fun in sports. It is divisive and destructive in politics.

- Party-based political systems give the illusion of choice to Christians, but none of those options can ever fully represent God's kingdom.

- When Christians yoke themselves with one side of the political aisle or the other, we cease to be the prophetic community.

- Becoming politically aligned or yoked with a worldly political party or group can severely damage our kingdom witness to the world and erodes our distinction from the world.

- Political groups rely on the weapons of the world, something that we are not to use as disciples.

- Being associated with political movements damages our ability to shine as a light in the darkness.

The Big Idea

❖ There is no place in a party-based political system for citizens of God's kingdom if they are going to maintain their voice as the distinctive prophetic community.

DISCUSSION QUESTIONS

1. How might political affiliations harm your witness for the kingdom? How might political affiliations help your witness for the kingdom?

2. What damage does the homer effect have in your country's political atmosphere? Does it negatively impact the church?

3. Do you believe that God could make significant changes in the world through his kingdom means without the help of political solutions?

Chapter 16

Politics in Its Place

It was a warm night in early September in Oklahoma. The year was 1994. We were celebrating the beginning of what was my senior year in college. There was a big event that we had all participated in on campus that welcomed the incoming class of first-year students and helped them get oriented to life on the somewhat smaller campus of the private university that I attended. After the event, a group of about twenty-five or thirty of my friends hung out in a central area of the campus until well after midnight. We should have gone to bed at that point. That would have been the sensible thing to do at that time of night. That's what most of the other students did or had already done. But someone brought up the idea of driving about fifteen minutes away to the cliffs and, for some reason, that seemed like a good idea.

So we piled in several cars and drove to a cliff that was situated about thirty to thirty-five feet above a lake, with the intent of jumping off the cliff and into the water. By the time we all arrived it was after 2 a.m. As we approached the edge of the cliff, I realized that it was a dark night and when you peered over the cliff, you could not even see the water. But before I knew it, one of us had jumped off and a few moments later, we heard the splash and then heard him give a "whoop" that let us know he was fine. I didn't want to jump that night, but being that there were a good number of girls with us, I didn't want to look like a coward, so I eventually took the leap. On the way down, I failed to keep my legs straight, bringing my knees up to my chest a bit, which caused me to hit the water so hard with the backs of my legs that I had huge bruises on the back of both thighs by the next day.

Cliff jumping that night was fun, but it was dangerous. During the day, it would have been a pretty normal activity, but it should not have been an activity that we engaged in during the middle of the night.

We have talked about Romans 13:11–14 already in Chapter 10, but I want to return to it briefly to begin this chapter as we talk about the role and realm of politics. After describing the very different realms of the Christian community (Romans 12; 13:8–10) and the governing realm of the state (Romans 13:1–7), Paul calls the body of disciples to wake up even though it is the middle of the night and embrace the activities of the day rather than those that would be more appropriate for night.

Significantly, Paul isn't just calling them to recognize that, even though it is night, they should wake up and wait for the day to come with great anticipation. He calls for them to behave as though they were in the daytime. When people are either sleeping or engaging in late-night carousing that takes place under the cover of night, the faithful are to get up and live as though it is the middle of the day and plough their fields or go to the well and draw water, or whatever else people do in the middle of the day. In a modern context, go cliff jumping. Go to the beach and sunbathe. Go play soccer in that field. Paul is calling us to be people who know that the day is coming and, even though it is night, live out the reality of the coming age as though God's presence were already wholly filling his creation.

Politics

According to the good folks at the Oxford Dictionary, the standard definition of politics is simply, "the activities associated with the governance of a country or other area, especially the debate or conflict among individuals or parties having or hoping to achieve power."[54]

So far, so good. Societies need to be governed and well ordered, and the best way that humans have discovered to do that is through rules and laws that facilitate that order. Some societies are run politically better than others, but all societies have politics of some sort. It is necessary for a person or group of people to hold and wield a certain amount of power to pass and enforce those laws; and the existence of power almost always creates conflict of some sort. Power must be passed along through means of competition or maintained through strength, so conflict of one kind or another is virtually inevitable.

On the surface, none of that seems problematic. However, although Jesus could certainly have embraced political power in Judea and beyond, he didn't. He could have become king, but consistently and persistently refused. Paul could have stayed engaged in the political and powerful religious world from which he came in Jerusalem, but as soon as he was confronted with the truth of the gospel, he gave all that up. The New Testament confirms that governing power is a legitimate realm that should be respected and honored by Christians and that they should not seek to overthrow it, rebel against it, or undermine it. They should do their best, in fact, to live in peace with that realm.

Yet we must make note of the fact that there is not one single New Testament directive for God's people to become actively involved in that realm either. Paul directs Timothy to maintain his focus on the work of the gospel and not get distracted with the things of the world—and we can assume that this would include political issues—writing that "no one serving as a soldier gets entangled in civilian affairs, but rather tries to please his commanding officer" (2 Timothy 2:4). Paul certainly wasn't encouraging involvement in the military. He was speaking of their engagement in the affairs of empires. I will admit that our context is quite different from Paul's, so there is not always a one-to-one correlation. But it should at least give us pause that engagement in the New Testament seems to be clearly in the direction of not seeking political power.

As we have seen, the early church of the late first, second, and third centuries clearly steered away from the realm of politics, patently refusing to become involved in the military or take public office. Responding to a third-century critic of the church named Celsus, a church leader in Northern Africa, Origen, captures well the early church's attitude toward the civilian affairs of state. First, he counters Celsus' attack that Christians are not patriotic and will not help in the defense of the country, by stating that they do indeed help in the defense of their homeland by praying diligently for their leaders and country. In response to the critique that they will not participate in the political life and well-being of Rome, Origen responds powerfully:

> Celsus also urges us to "take office in the government of the country if that is required for the maintenance of the laws and the support of the religion." But we recognize in each state the existence of another national organization, founded by the Word of God, and we exhort those who are mighty in word and of blameless life to rule over Churches. Those who are ambitions of ruling, we reject; but we constrain those who, through excess of modesty, are not easily induced to take a public charge in the Church of God. And those who rule over us well are under the constraining influence of the great King, whom we believe to be the Son of God, God the Word. And if those who govern in the Church, and are called rulers of the divine nation—that is, the Church—rule well, they rule in accordance with the divine commands, and never suffer themselves to be led astray by worldly policy.[55]

He goes on to explain that Christians don't decline participation in this realm for any other reason than one.

> And it is not for the purpose of escaping public duties that Christians decline public offices, but that they may reserve themselves for a diviner and more necessary service in the Church of God—for the salvation of men.[56]

Origen then sheds light on the purpose of the Christian community, arguing that they restrict themselves to the realm of the Messiah's kingdom so that those within the community may "lead better lives," and that they may cause those outside their ranks to see their radically different way of living and seek to join them.

Why Did They Avoid Politics?

We can be easily tempted to dismiss the relationship of the early church to the political realm on two fronts. We can make note of the prevalence of pagan worship that was wrapped up in the politics and public life of Rome and presume that this is the primary reason that Christians for nearly three centuries refused to take part. The other presumption we can make is to point out that our early-century brothers and sisters lived under a harsh empire, while many of us today live in representative governments of one kind or another. They had no say in their governance, but we do, so we have an obligation to participate.

I will respond to those assumptions in inverse order. Roman political life, even during the time of the emperors, was robust. Although influence and participation were limited to official citizens of the empire, it was expected that they play an active role in governing the society. Refusal to do so was seen as treasonous and looked down upon. It is for that very reason that the early church needed to occasionally defend their position and affirm that they were not unpatriotic, and more importantly, they were not planning a rebellion. They were deeply engaged in the public sphere as far as helping those in need and defending the oppressed, but they quite intentionally seemed to have refused, as a general policy, engaging in politics at any level to do so. They believed that kingdom methods were more effective than Rome's. So, if there was a fear of an enemy attack, they didn't sign up for the military; they engaged in intentional and focused prayer for the safety of the nation and believed that the relative peace of that time was a result of their prayers and nothing else. The bottom line is that they could have participated in the public life of politics but chose not to because of their convictions about what the kingdom of God was.

Can we presume, though, that their example does not apply to us because the Roman Empire was awash in pagan worship and because we don't have that problem in the modern context? It is true that paying honor to the Roman gods was expected as a routine part of social participation. Refusal to do so was an affront to the state because it might risk angering the gods, who would then rescind their protection of Rome, which put everyone at risk.

While our gods and idols may not be as overt as they were in the Roman Empire of the first three centuries, they are just as real and compete for predominance in our lives every bit as much. We give our idols different names, but they have no less pull on our lives. The gods of power, materialism, war, comfort, and sex rule in our society just as they did then.

If I once again turn to my country, the United States, as an example, there can be little question that politics has taken on a religious fervor. Of course, we have the gods of materialism, power, war, and the rest, but politics itself has taken a role that is religious in its nature. Contemporary Americans decreasingly look to politics simply for governance, viewing differences in opinion as minor. Our political passions take on a spiritual fervor; we look to politics for meaning, identity, comfort, deliverance, and safety. Rather than leaders taking on a divine status, it is politics itself that now provides our hope and demands our allegiance. We often judge the moral character of others based on their political affiliations and ideologies.

According to psychologist Jonathan Haidt, humans seek societal righteousness through six foundations, which he labels as "moral taste buds": Care/Harm, Fairness/Cheating, Liberty/Oppression, Loyalty/Betrayal, Authority/Subversion, and Sanctity/Degradation. Liberal philosophies emphasize the first three almost exclusively. Conservative approaches stretch across all six but put a much higher priority on the last three. Two competing versions of what constitutes moral rightness then develop, and those on the other side of the fence are not just people with a different way of seeing things, they are immoral or amoral heretics. They are the problem with the world and what stands in the way of our society reaching utopia.[57]

The only thing worse than the moral heretics are those who refuse to engage in the system at all. They become the atheists of this political religious state and are thought of with a disdain similar to how the Romans viewed the Christians who refused to honor the gods and participate in public life. Those who thoughtfully withdraw from the political system and seek another way threaten its supremacy.

The religious intensity is only cranked up higher as we mix this political orthodoxy with tribalism. Nothing brings us together more effectively than a common enemy. We seek out news stations that denounce the heretics on the other side, and the feeds in our social media reinforce our beliefs through an echo chamber or bubble effect where we slowly block out dissenting voices as "dangerous" to our psyche and well-being and will no longer subject ourselves to such heretical attacks on the orthodoxy. Before long, asking someone about their politics takes on the same stakes as asking someone their religion in the middle ages. If you are not with my tribe, you are against us and should be dealt with. How long is it before verbal assaults on dissenters give way to something much darker?

And when we subtly give our allegiance to our political ideology, it becomes the source of our hope and deliverance. Failure to institute our policies means darkness and destruction for the land, and that cannot be tolerated.

When followers of Jesus allow this idol into their lives, the effects can be devastating to the body of Christ. Suddenly, we find ourselves dividing tribally within the church based on these gods of politics. First, we argue with one another. Then we ignore those "others" and hope the problem (or they) will go away. The next step is to interpret everything against the grid of our political beliefs. We judge others based on their politics. If a preacher speaks out against injustice, we applaud if the words match up with our political orthodoxy but become vitriolic if they cut against the dearly held doctrines of our god of politics.

We will have, at this point, completely lost sight of the vastness of the kingdom, of Jesus as our only deliverer and hope, and of our allegiance to him alone as King.

Finally, we separate and leave our church or demand that others do so if their politics, or perceived politics, become hostile to our deities. Eventually, even the kingdom itself comes to be viewed through the lens of this political orthodoxy and religious fervor, and those who are sincerely trying to live in allegiance to it will be shouted down as nothing more than political heretics just like the rest. Allowed to continue, the god of politics will rip the church to shreds.

Other Things That Divide

[A major problem that political engagement in the traditional sense poses for the body of Christ is that it preys upon the differences with which we come into Christ and slowly turns those differences into division.]

With the six foundations above from the work of Haidt in mind, we can easily come into the kingdom with different affinity for any combination of those six, although it often lies along the traditional liberal or conservative tendencies mentioned above. One person will most value liberty over oppression, while another will see sanctity of life over degradation as the greatest moral good. Both may root their values in biblical thinking to some degree, which will lead them to have differing passions. Both of those inclinations can find a home within the values and ethos of the kingdom of God, but if they are funneled into the political machine, their partisans will cease to work together and see value in the other emphasis; rather, they will fall on different sides of the political spectrum and become enemies. The worst part is, both will cover their politics with a veneer of Christianity and convince themselves that their positions are biblically based and God-honoring.]

But it is not just these values of righteousness or the spiritualizing of political passion that cause division among believers engaged in politics. There are other important differences between believers that can be overcome in Christ but when mixed with politics tend to separate us beyond repair.

National Identity

Scripture is clear that within the kingdom, one of the things that should no longer bring us identity or status, or cause division, is our national or tribal identification. "Here there is not Gentile or Jew, circumcised or uncircumcised, barbarian, Scythian, slave or free, but Christ is all, and is in all" (Colossians 3:11). When we become citizens of God's kingdom (Philippians 3:21), that should become the source of our ethics and values and the object of our affection and loyalty. We live as members of the holy nation (1 Peter 2:9) who are foreigners and exiles (1 Peter 2:11) in the places where we live. We no longer represent those nations but are ambassadors for the kingdom of the Messiah (2 Corinthians 5:20). We are no longer citizens of one nation, showing fidelity to that one above all others. We are part of a family that consists of members of all people groups, all tribes, all cultures, and all nationalities.

It makes sense that Christians who grew up in or live in different nations would have different experiences and differing political views of the landscape of the world. For example, a disciple of Jesus from the United States might think that representative democracy and traditional capitalism are the best forms of government and economy, while a Christian from Western Europe might wholeheartedly believe in socialistic models. Those types of differences might lead to interesting discussions if they are kept in their place, but if we allow politics to play too large a role in our lives and hearts, these can quickly become divisive.

But the greater threat by far is nationalism. When my country becomes an idol that in all honesty holds a bigger claim on my loyalty and allegiance than does the kingdom of God, that is a huge problem. That is one of the major struggles that I have with Christians voluntarily joining the military in their nation. Once that is done, they give up control over their allegiance. Most wars are fought in the best interests of their own country. That is simply at odds with the worldview of a kingdom citizen. Violence is not a weapon allowed in the kingdom (Isaiah 2:1–4; Matthew 5:38–48; Romans 12:9–21, etc.), and that soldier might now find themselves being ordered to take the lives of Christians who live in another country and serve another national interest. It seems to me that in most of these cases, it is the beast that wins in these scenarios and not the slain lamb.

When there is no clear-cut pecking order between the fidelity and allegiance reserved for the kingdom and a subsequent proper role of loyalty to our homeland, the kingdom loses, or perhaps more accurately, we lose the kingdom. If nationalism and national loyalty are not curbed and put in a healthy role, subservient to the kingdom in our lives, our patriotism will take an inappropriate role in our hearts and cause separation and division among the global family of God. Should disciples in Russia and those from Ukraine be at odds because of the positions that their nations have taken against one another? [If we let these identities and passions into the kingdom, they will surely devour us]

Historical Experiences

Different groups of people have had very divergent experiences historically. That may seem obvious, but it is easy to overlook how that past can determine varied political views and perspectives.

As I mentioned in Chapter 14, there have been many occasions when Christians from countries other than my own have asked me what it is like growing up in such an evil nation. From their perspective and experiences, America is an empire that either militarily or economically forces its will on the rest of the world. They are familiar with incidents in the past sixty or seventy years when the United States has been responsible for a coup d'état in their country or had leaders assassinated. We might view our own nation as the good guys, while other countries might have a completely different understanding.

These variant experiences can be a factor within a nation as well. For example, historical events in the United States have been totally different for most white Americans and most black Americans, which can lead to opposing political views. Black Americans have suffered through hundreds of years of enslavement, segregation, and policies that kept them in an inferior status economically and in access to education, fair employment, equal housing, and much more. This system has made it possible that a small number of unusually talented or lucky people have escaped and broken through, but the odds have been stacked for so long that it has been an impossible task for the entire community to break out simply through determination.

On the other side, white people in America have the same sorts of struggles that anyone might have that can make life difficult, but the color of their skin has never been one of those things. So it is easy to believe that anyone can make it if they just work hard enough. Because they have never had to approach life with these many other obstacles, they simply don't know what it's like. The need to hear and believe one another's perspective is paramount.

If our trust in politics is exaggerated, we will believe that the presence of laws will guide the system to equality, or an absence of laws will allow the system to work to bring equal opportunity to all. I am not saying that laws cannot and do not have a major impact in these issues. They can and do. Politics can address certain aspects of injustice, but it will never speak to the hearts of people or cause transformation, and that is what is truly needed. Only the kingdom can do that.

If we trust in political solutions, we can quickly become mortal enemies of one another, divided by our partisan politics that have been cultivated by divergent historical experiences. Our histories are important—we should not just pretend that they don't exist when we become Christians. But they must be informed by the kingdom solutions.

Paul was a proudly Jewish man in the first century with no love for the Roman Empire. He could easily have continued to view the world through the eyes of a marginalized and oppressed people. He could have seen Gentiles as the enemy. But instead he saw them as his brothers and sisters in Christ. Then he became the apostle to the Gentiles and spent the rest of his life being often persecuted by Jewish leaders for his advocacy for Gentiles. Based on that experience he could have easily become hostile toward Jews. Yet he spent a large portion of his ministry to the Gentiles encouraging them to take up collections to support Christians in Jerusalem who had undergone difficult economic oppression. Paul never became a prisoner of the differing histories and partisanship of his day. Rather, he continued to call people to understand those differences and address them through the life-bringing kingdom of God.

Cultural Differences

Considering our cultural perspectives is never an exact science nor easy. There are always exceptions. Cultural groups, however, do tend to have certain characteristics or commonalities. Those tendencies of a group are classified as archetypes. A stereotype, though, is when someone else assumes that all members of a group adhere to all archetypes of that group. That means that our various cultural backgrounds will indicate how many of the people in a group might act, but there are many factors that can change that expected typical behavior as well.

There are many ways in which culture might impact our political views, but allow me to give one salient example. For people who were raised in an individual-focused culture, two of the chief virtues are personal responsibility and making your own way. Perhaps the cardinal sins are attempting to hold the individual responsible for something that others did and not taking care of one's own load.

Those who were reared in collectivist cultures, however, have different tendencies and values. Those cultures emphasize group identity, and taking care of others in the group is expected. Also highly prized is taking responsibility for the actions of your group, past or present. The entire group is responsible, in many ways, for actions of anyone within the group. The chief sin for people in these types of cultures is to shirk group responsibility or not care for others who find themselves in need for whatever reason.

Once we are aware of these cultural values, it doesn't take a lot of mental work to see with what great impact these assumptions and ethics would inform someone's political views. Those with individualist backgrounds will have very different political sensibilities than will those from a collectivist background, and it will be extremely difficult for each to understand the other, let alone respect or be willing to work with them.

In the world of partisan politics, this simply results in those groups tending to support opposite political platforms, and then the two will fight it out for power and influence in the political system to gain the upper hand and implement their policies. But in a diverse church, these variances, left unchecked, will rip unity apart at the seams. Cultural differences like these may lead us to emphasizing disparate values that can have an impact on everything from how we approach the benevolence ministry in our church to our political instincts. If we don't become aware of these differences and embrace submission to Jesus as King as our duty in his kingdom, we will threaten the unity of his church.[58]

The Chapter in Review

- All societies must be governed and ruled through laws and politics of some type.

- There is no place in a party-based political system for citizens of God's kingdom if they are going to maintain their voice as the distinctive prophetic community.

- The stance of the early church was to avoid the political realm, not just because of the nature of that realm, but also so that they could solely focus on kingdom responses and solutions to the issues in the world.

- The role of politics in much of the world today has become a religion in itself.

- The religious fervor of modern politics threatens the identity and work of the church.

- Nationalism, differing historical experiences, and cultural backgrounds are all major threats to the unity of the kingdom and its mission in the world.

The Big Idea

❖ Much of politics has become religious in nature, and many worship their political ideology or government without realizing it, but kingdom citizens must resist this temptation.

DISCUSSION QUESTIONS

1. What examples can you give of a religious devotion that many people have today regarding politics and political systems?

2. If Jesus could speak to your church today in the flesh, would he more likely urge you to join one of the political parties in your country, or would he call people out of their political devotion to follow him and advance the kingdom alone?

3. What do you think about the assertion that Christians who have accepted politics into their life at a religious level can get to a point where they see even those who are trying to remain loyal to the kingdom alone as political antagonists and denounce them? Do you agree or disagree with that assessment? What impact could that type of attitude have on the church?

Chapter 17

Living in the Right Realm

I recently watched a clip of an American football player completely out of his realm. He was a celebrated running back in the National Football League during his career and part of a Super Bowl champion team who found great success in running through defenses and being very difficult to tackle and bring down. But in this clip, he was playing a different game with professionals from that sport. This time he was playing what my fellow Americans would call soccer, but many serious fans around the world would argue is the real football.

As the clip wore on it was obvious that his athletic skill and years of training in American football were doing him little good in the realm of soccer. The two sports are so significantly different that he simply could not operate well against these highly trained soccer players. It was just a brief exhibition, though, so it was all in good fun. But things changed in an instant when he switched the game entirely. Without warning, he bent over and picked up the soccer ball with his hands, something that is strictly forbidden in soccer but is an integral part of American football. Then he ran through the defenders the way he would in his own sport, stiff-arming them and pushing them out of the way. They laughed as he bullied his way through them but were helpless to impede his march toward the goal. Once he arrived at the goal, the goalie tried to stop him but stood no chance as he effortlessly spiked the ball past the goalkeeper and into the net.

It was a humorous display but a brilliant example of how the two realms of those two sports are at such odds with one another that they simply cannot be merged. When you attempt to play by the rules of one while surrounded by the other, it is so out of sync that it is immediately obvious and laughable.

The Two Ages

I have already talked about the two ages at several points throughout this book, but allow me to briefly summarize for the purposes of this chapter. Both the ancient Jewish people and the early Christians

Do I believe in the Messiah this way?

understood the world to be broken into two ages. The Jews believed that the present age was the age of sin, death, division, and suffering. But one day, God would send his Messiah and resolve the problem of evil by paving the way for the world to be repaired and restored by God. This would usher in the age to come, a time when there would be no sin, death, evil, or pain. There would be nothing but God perfectly ruling with his human image bearers over his creation.

When Jesus came, he spoke often of this age to come, or what is often translated in English Bible versions as "eternal life." The massive twist that Jesus brought to this concept was that he was ushering in this realm now, in the present age. Through him, his followers could access the life of the eternal age while still living in the present. The age to come in its fullness was still in the offing, but it had arrived in Christ, and now these two ages could be found overlapping in the communities of his disciples. His people would live by the values and certainty of the coming age while surrounded by the present age.

This is precisely what Jesus meant when he said that the way the kingdom would come in the lives of his people was as they did God's will on earth as though they were directly in his presence, which is what he meant when he said "in heaven" (Matthew 6:10). That verse is tucked into the middle of the Sermon on the Mount (Matthew 5–7), which is perhaps the most comprehensive description that Jesus provides on what it will look like to do God's will on earth as if we were in heaven. This is what it will look like for the age to come to overlap the present age.

During Jesus' life, the age to come was contained within him. As his friend John put it, "in him was life" (John 1:4). But when he walked out of the grave, that life became "the light of all mankind" and was now available to all people.

For the first time in the history of the world, there were now two distinct realms available. For the people of God, that changes everything.

This is important to note because it means that even the examples that we can look at in the Old Testament have to be interpreted through this lens of the two ages. Men like Joseph and Daniel who served God and worked through the political empires in which they lived did not have the alternative reality of the age to come available to them as we do. While we can take certain principles from their lives, we cannot just turn to these situations as though their context is the same as ours. This is at least some of what Jesus meant when he said that "whoever is least in the kingdom of heaven is greater than [John the Baptist—who represents all the prophets and those who did not have access to the kingdom]" (Matthew 11:11).

Embracing the Kingdom's Realm

Understanding this difference between the present age and the age to come is so important to what I believe is the role of the kingdom when it comes to engaging with the world of politics and the world in general that I keep returning to it. In my opinion it is the lynchpin of how we operate in the world. Jesus has rescued us from the present evil age (Galatians 1:3-4), and we are to take hold of the life of the age to come, to which we were called (1 Timothy 6:12).

When we read the Sermon on the Mount it looks crazy. Bless those who curse us? Love enemies? Those who are said to be blessed and experiencing true prosperity, according to Jesus, seem to be the opposite of what we see around us. It doesn't make sense. It's not meant to, at least not in the present age. That's because it is what it looks like to live the future right now.

We are to be outposts that show the world what it looks like to live under God's rule. We are truly foreigners and exiles (1 Peter 2:11), and not just in some vague spiritualized sense. We have our realm and live by its values, and the moment we cease to do that, we are no different from any other group of people operating within the present age.

Many Christians struggle with the teaching of Jesus in the Sermon on the Mount and similar concepts in the New Testament because they are trying to hold on to the values of the present age and are not foreigners and exiles. They want religion that will make the present more tolerable and then usher them into heaven after they leave this age. But they don't want to die to themselves and the comforts of this age now. This makes them unable to fully process things like loving our enemies, not using violence to resist evil, and overcoming evil with good. They feel the need to reinterpret what Jesus said or water it down. "The Sermon on the Mount was just an ideal that we can strive for but can never attain." Or, "Jesus only meant for this to apply to instances of religious persecution." Or even, "Jesus meant for us to embrace these teachings in our personal lives, but in our public lives we can embrace the values that are necessary for states to function."

What we miss is that the nations and empires are operating in the present realm, but we should not be. That does not mean that the nations are automatically evil in every case, but they are not and never can be the kingdom. They cannot be "Christian" nations, because the nations are God's governors of the present age. But the kingdom is his appeal to the world to enter the age to come. The methods available to the kingdom are radically different from the world's because they emanate from a different reality. The kingdom is for the world, but not of the world. We'll examine this difference in methods and focus in the next chapter.

Perhaps it will help to look at the two ages in a visual format.

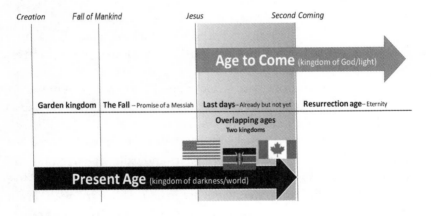

What About My Country?

We may love our country. We can and often should be grateful for where we live. I am thankful that I have the freedoms and opportunities that I do in the country where I was born. Some nations provide more opportunity and freedom to their citizens than others. Some provide more safety and security. Admittedly, that can get complicated because, at times, many of those benefits came at the expense of others. But the important part is that regardless of how appreciative we may be for our homeland, the nations are part of the present age. They are not the kingdom.

A constant temptation for kingdom exiles is to be pulled back into the present age. Sometimes it is the fear of death that can do it. Sometimes it is the allure of comfort and pleasure. Sometimes it is patriotism and love of country that rivals our allegiance to God's kingdom. We lose perspective that the role of the nations is to operate in the present age and the role of the kingdom of God is to operate in the realm of the age to come. And this is devastating because when the kingdom is no longer functioning by the values of that realm, it quickly ceases to become the kingdom.●

I want to return to Romans 12 and 13 again to make this point crystal clear.

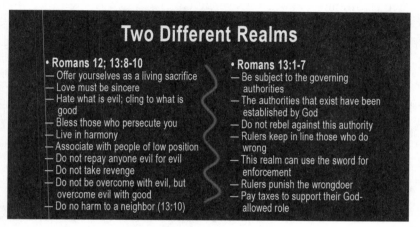

Two Different Realms

• Romans 12; 13:8-10
— Offer yourselves as a living sacrifice
— Love must be sincere
— Hate what is evil; cling to what is good
— Bless those who persecute you
— Live in harmony
— Associate with people of low position
— Do not repay anyone evil for evil
— Do not take revenge
— Do not be overcome with evil, but overcome evil with good
— Do no harm to a neighbor (13:10)

• Romans 13:1-7
— Be subject to the governing authorities
— The authorities that exist have been established by God
— Do not rebel against this authority
— Rulers keep in line those who do wrong
— This realm can use the sword for enforcement
— Rulers punish the wrongdoer
— Pay taxes to support their God-allowed role

On the left of the diagram above we see Paul's description of the realm in which we are to operate as the prophetic community. He details it in Romans 12:1–21, then moves on to the realm of the nations in Romans 13:1–7, only to return for a final sketch and summary of the kingdom realm in Romans 13:8–10.

Take note of the otherworldly life that this directs us to. This is Sermon-on-the-Mount living. We are to offer our whole selves to this realm. This is what it looks like to worship God. Our love must be sincere as we cling to the good. We do our best to live in harmony with all people as we bless our persecutors. We associate with those in low positions, reject revenge and do not repay evil for evil no matter the circumstances. We take care not to turn to the weapons of the world or utilize evil to overcome evil. We overcome evil with good, using nothing but what is available to us in the kingdom realm. And no matter what, we do no harm to our neighbor for any reason.

This is what it looks like to be salt and light. The one thing that salt and light have in common is that you are certain when they are present because they change what is around them so much. This is different from anything the world can offer because it does not come from the present age. It cannot. In fact, it is foolish in the present age. Living like that might get us killed! Yes, it very well might. It did for Jesus. It has for countless Christians since the cross. But we do not fight with the weapons of the world (2 Corinthians 10:3–4); rather, we triumph like the saints described in a deadly battle with the great dragon who triumphed "by the blood of the Lamb and by the word of their testimony; they did not love their lives so much as to shrink from death" (Revelation 12:11).

Paul describes this realm and life in Romans 12 with no exceptions, no dilution, no indication that this only applies in certain situations. This is the life to which we were called.

He then switches dramatically to another realm, calling Christians to be subject to the realm of the governing authorities. The fact that he calls for the kingdom realm to be subject to the realm of nations demonstrates that we are looking at two different entities. We are not to be immersed in this world or participate in it, but submissive to it, meaning we don't fight against it and do not take the position that it must be eliminated.

There are opposite temptations here. One is to become so radical about the kingdom realm that we feel we must get rid of the nations and leave only the kingdom. The problem with that mentality is that it belies the nature of the kingdom, which is to be an alternative to the nations. The second temptation is to be wooed by the realm of empire and mimic its tactics, smuggle its methods into the kingdom, or become enmeshed in that realm, thinking that we can live with one foot in each realm with no problem. But exiles live in the nations to be light to them and call them into the light, not to become part of them.

Paul then describes the purpose of the realm of the governing authorities quite clearly. They are allowed and established by God for the purpose of limiting evil in the present age. That is their ideal purpose. Some nations stray from that and become corrupt themselves. Others live up to that calling more fully. But they exist to keep evildoers at bay. That is the purpose and function of the laws and the power that they wield. As part of the present realm they can utilize the sword, that is violence and coercion, to enforce their power. As Christians, we should not demonize or delegitimatize that realm. We are even called to support it with our taxes when those are demanded, but that is the only aspect of participation that is hinted at here. Beyond paying taxes and living at peace with our nation, the Christian has no obligation. We might have freedoms beyond that where we live and would need to carefully consider the impact of engaging in those freedoms, but we are not required to participate in any of those by Scripture. We must also ensure that any actions we take borne by our freedoms are aligned with the purpose and function of God's kingdom.

The authorities and nations have their realm, their purpose, and their tools to complete their job. But none of those are ours. We have our own realm, purpose, and tools to be the alternative prophetic community that we are called to be.

The Bottom Line

The function of the state is to restrain evil in the present age. We are to allow and respect that. But we should be very wary of attempting to force or influence the state to implement values and morals of the kingdom. There will be some values and morals that are common between the kingdom and the nations, and we should encourage that. Restraining murder, for example, is a positive for any culture. But the way of life that is unique to those who have chosen the kingdom of God should not and cannot be forced. The kingdom is very different from mere morality.

We might be tempted to pass laws that enforce the kingdom morality or way of life, but even if we succeed, people under those laws are no closer to the kingdom of God. Morality does not usher us into God's kingdom. I am not arguing that moral laws do not have a benefit and bring good. They do, and to that extent should be encouraged. But we must be careful with that. Laws function in the realm of the present age and can be useful tools at times, but we must never lose sight of the purpose that we wish to usher individuals into the age to come, not make them more moral and good people but without the kingdom.

So we can honor and submit to the role that the nations play, but because these realms are so divergent, it will be impossible for us to fully participate in and embrace the realm of nations. Politics can restrain evil and bring order to the present age, but they can never bring about the kingdom, nor should anyone try to make them.

Because the kingdom realm is focused on demonstrating the age to come, everything we do should be a display of Christ's reign. We must stay resolute that we can only establish and maintain the kingdom as an alternative society through kingdom means. The moment that we venture into present-age solutions or tools to establish the morals or values of the kingdom is the moment that it is no longer a choice and the instant it ceases to be the kingdom of God. That road is littered with forced conversion, crusades, inquisitions, an intermingling of church and state, embittered people forced to live by values that they don't share, and a kingdom lost.

The Chapter in Review

- Since the kingdom of God came through Jesus, those who follow him now have access to way-of-life options from the age to come that were simply not available to those who came before.

- This life of the age to come, described succinctly in the Sermon on the Mount, does not sync with or make sense in the present age.

- Nations and empires operate in the realm of the present age; the kingdom of God operates in the realm of the age to come.

- The only scriptural requirements for kingdom people in their response to the nations is to live in peace and pay taxes. Anything we might do beyond that is based on the freedoms we have in our own country and is a choice to wisely exercise those freedoms insomuch as they align with our kingdom purposes.

- We must remain steadfastly focused on our purpose and role as people of a different realm and not trust in or rely on solutions that are rooted in the present age.

The Big Idea

- ❖ When considering the role of political engagement for the kingdom, we must understand clearly that we are to operate within the values and solutions of the age to come and allow the governing authorities of the nations and empires to carry out their function within the realm of the present age.

DISCUSSION QUESTIONS

1. What are the possible negative results if kingdom people lose sight of our purpose and begin to trust in and fight almost exclusively for solutions to problems utilizing the methods of the present age?

2. What are the biggest challenges in your heart about trusting only in God's methods to change the world through his kingdom?

3. How might living in this two-realm model change the negative perceptions that many in the world today have about Christianity in general?

Chapter 18

Planting Our Feet

In 1976, Baptist minister Jerry Falwell Sr. initiated a series of I Love America rallies across the United States that continued for several years. I can recall attending one in my hometown when I was no more than six or seven years old. They were aimed at breaking down the traditional separation of church and state that most American churches had respected for two centuries. Falwell eventually turned the momentum from those rallies into a national organization, launching the Moral Majority in 1979. This was arguably the rise of the Christian right in the United States. The national group aimed at coalescing Christians into a political force to enact their political agenda throughout the state and national governments. By the early 1980s, they had so captured the imagination of at least the majority of white evangelicals in America that they had become a political force of a size and type never seen before.

Soon, if a Republican politician wanted to stand a chance for election to a national office, it was a necessary journey to seek the endorsement and backing of the Moral Majority. They were pro-America, in favor of legislated morality, unwaveringly pro-life, and unquestionably conservative. They wielded their political power and inaugurated a series of culture wars across the country as they sought to flex their political muscles to get their agenda put into law. Like the Pharisees of Jesus' day, they would help the nation become pure again by stamping out sin. Their primary tool? Political power.

Ed Dobson, vice president of the Moral Majority in the early years, now admits that the movement had a distinct lack of a coherent and biblical political philosophy. The approach that they utilized, according to Dobson, was "ready, fire, aim," buoyed by a belief that America had a favored-nation status with God, all the while "neglecting what the Bible teaches about the poor, unfairly attacking enemies, and using manipulative fund-raising techniques."[59]

The Moral Majority rushed into the political fray and seized political power as a Christian movement without having a clear theology on the role of the kingdom of God in the world or on Christians utilizing political power. Self-admittedly, they rushed in without a well-thought-out position. Not having a clear philosophy of the kingdom and our role in politics can be rather detrimental and is not a mistake that we can afford to make in the times in which we live. Before we consider further what our positions might be, let's look at a few other Christian political philosophies down through history.

Geneva

In 1536, John Calvin was invited to join the Reformation that was swelling in Geneva, Switzerland. By 1541 he was offered an invitation to lead the church of the city. Calvin quickly shook past early opposition and instituted new forms of church government. In short order, he forced out his opponents and had an iron grip on the government of Geneva itself. Calvin set about creating a secular government that was informed and instructed by the church alone. He believed that the purpose of secular government was "to foster and protect the external worship of God, defend pure doctrine and the good condition of the church, ...mould our conduct to civil justice, reconcile us one to another, and uphold and defend the common peace and tranquility."[60] The church and state became virtually indistinguishable under Calvin, who argued that the responsibility of the state was to nurture human flourishing and cultivate upright conduct and behavior.

Geneva was to be a Christian utopia, but it didn't work out that way. In theory there was a separation of church and state in Geneva. In day-to-day reality, it was a virtual theocracy and a stifling authoritarian state in many respects. Calvin's Geneva did not take kindly to opposing thought. Critics were executed, like Michael Servetus, who was burned at the stake for heresy when he would not repent and embrace Calvin's views on Christian living and beliefs. In supporting such action, Calvin was united with the thinking of other Christian groups of his day, whether Lutherans, Anglicans, or Catholics. In the seventeenth century, heretics were to be executed.

The Amish

Not more than a couple of hours from where I grew up is a community of Amish believers. The Amish are a Christian group whose roots can be traced back to Swiss German Anabaptists. They believe that technology that is not spiritually helpful to the group should be rejected, so they have become known for simple living, plain dress, the use of horse and carriage, and a tendency to reject most modern conveniences and advances. There are over one-quarter million Amish spread across the United States and Canada, with the highest concentration in the state of Pennsylvania.

The Amish are strict pietists, meaning they have largely withdrawn from active engagement in the affairs of the world. They live rather insulated lives and remain separated from the culture around them. Citizens who live in areas where the Amish reside will see them from time to time and may interact briefly with them through one of their businesses, such as crafting and selling fine furniture, but on all practical levels, the Amish try not to be impacted by the culture, and they have virtually no impact on it.

The Amish have grown increasingly distant from modern society. They educate children in their own schools, pay taxes that they must pay, and have been given exemption from participating in Social Security. They do not engage in politics as a general rule, do not participate in the military, and have minimal influence on modern society outside their own community.

Wilberforce

A young man named William Wilberforce was radically changed from listening to the preaching of a former slave trader named John Newton, widely known for penning the beloved hymn "Amazing Grace." The England of Wilberforce's youth was built on the slave trade and ever-expanding colonialism. Wilberforce, a promising young politician, was mesmerized by Newton's presentation of the gospel and was convicted to turn from his sin and declare Jesus as Lord, wanting to leave politics to spend his life in service to his King. Newton dissuaded him from that, convincing him to use his influence for the benefit of others, calling him to an Esther-like role of considering that God may have placed him into public life for such a time as this.

Wilberforce became fixated on ending slavery and slave trading in the British Empire and was determined to use his political life toward that end. In describing the lasting impact that Wilberforce's career had on British society and history, Steve Monsma highlights five principles that guided Wilberforce throughout his life.[61] First, his deep personal commitment to Jesus' kingdom transformed every aspect of his life. Second, he did not act emotionally or without thought. He was part of a group that would come to be known as the Clapham group. This group prayed, planned, and thought through their actions carefully, seeking to do nothing more than show the kingdom of God to the world in which they lived. Third, they understood that they would face fierce opposition and persecution but would continue to work for the benefit of others despite the hardship. Fourth, they worked for the good of the oppressed first and then the greater good of society. They avoided becoming a special interest group that sought only to protect the narrow interests of their fellow Christians or a particular social class. Fifth, they took up causes very slowly and only after careful examination of the facts and a tremendous amount of prayer and Bible study. They often took years before taking a position and deciding to take up a cause publicly.

Wilberforce and his compatriots always stood up for the oppressed but sought justice for all, including the oppressors. Even when seeking to bring an end to slavery, although they despised it, they worked toward compensating slave owners so that they would not be left penniless or treated with spite or vengeance.

Political Philosophy

Each Christian movement or group has a political philosophy, whether they realize it or not. Some groups have had systematic theologies and approaches to secular politics. Other groups have not clearly examined their approach or have attempted to avoid political thought altogether; but not having a philosophy is a philosophy of its own.

The Christian right and groups like the Moral Majority took the road of political power as a means to an end but did not have a political vision driving or setting the boundaries for them. As a result, they have found themselves shackled together with one political party at a great cost to the kingdom of God. Poll after poll demonstrates that most Americans now regard Christianity more as a political bloc than a spiritual movement, often citing judgmentalism and forced morality, and hypocritical morality at that, as the primary characteristics of modern Christianity. That is a tragedy. Even critics of the Christians of the first three centuries did not charge them with judgmentalism.

Their chief criticisms were that they were reckless in their lack of fear of death, they foolishly lived like they were family with people of all social classes and nationalities, and they undiscerningly loved all people. The rush to impose Christian will through political power has left our modern society with a bad taste in its mouth and zero understanding of what the kingdom of God truly is.

Calvin's Geneva purported to be a Christian utopia, and in many ways it was wonderful, but it eventually developed a dark, oppressive side and could not be maintained because they attempted to establish the kingdom through means not appropriate for the kingdom. Today, Sweden is one of the most atheistic cultures in the world, though at one time the official state church there followed Calvin's teaching.

A more modern example of this approach would be Zambia of the early 1990s. In 1991, the southern African country selected Frederick Chiluba to be its next president. Chiluba declared that Zambia would be "a Christian nation"; he "filled his cabinet with evangelical Christians, and issued a decree that said, 'I...submit the government and the entire nation of Zambia to the Lordship of Jesus Christ. I further declare that Zambia is a Christian nation that will seek to be governed by the righteous principle of the word of God.'"[62]

Historically, when a country purports itself to be a Christian nation and vows to govern itself according to biblical standards, it never shows the world the kingdom of God. Chiluba's administration was no different. Ronald Sider notes that "Chiluba violated human rights, tortured opponents in custody, bought votes, and allowed widespread corruption so he could run a third term. He even used tear gas on groups who opposed him." Although he was exonerated of any charges in Zambian courts despite overwhelming evidence, he was eventually found guilty by a UK court of stealing $46 million. So much for the lordship of Jesus Christ.

The Amish instinct to withdraw from society owes more to tradition than to carefully thought out philosophy, although that is not to imply that they have not carefully thought through their positions. They seemingly have been so swayed by the desire to not be corrupted by society and so informed by a past of persecution that their withdrawing has left them practically incapable of being salt or light. They are ineffective at bringing anyone beyond their own children into their version of kingdom living and give little thought to the life of the world.

Wilberforce represents another approach. It was an attempt to apply the values of the kingdom to the public sphere. He fought his whole life to defend the oppressed, believing that in rare cases, the political sphere would need to be entered to make change. Few have been able to follow his model without becoming part of the system themselves and losing any kingdom distinctiveness they may have had.

There is yet another strain of thinking, one for which I did not provide a specific example here. That is the philosophy of the dominionists. They tend to believe that the entire Scriptures, including the Israel model and the Old Testament, provide the blueprint for what human government should look like and that it is the duty of Christians to take over their countries, province by province if need be, and apply the rule of the kingdom of God to all aspects of their land. This, they believe, will be for the benefit of all society, even if people do not want such a ruling force.

⌐My own spiritual community falls into the category of not having a systematic approach to politics and modern society. We are a group that is very committed to living with Jesus as Lord and takes seriously the call to spread the gospel to people of all nations, but a systematic approach to politics is nonexistent, and the topic is usually ignored altogether in fear that bringing it up may cause disunity.⌐

That leaves us in a vulnerable and untenable position for the long haul. We are a diverse fellowship that has churches around the world, and each congregation is committed to reflecting the diversity of its area. That means that these diverse local churches all have a wide variety of backgrounds, cultures, and experiences on display in the lives and histories of the members. It also means that two distinct strands of political approach have become part of our communities. Some eschew politics altogether and maintain that we need only worry about the gospel. Politics doesn't matter, according to this group. The other approach is to maintain political involvement but to do so uncritically, bringing in whatever political beliefs and approaches we had when becoming a Christian, sometimes with slight changes based on certain convictions formed after our conversion. As you can imagine, this can leave a church deeply divided. That is not to imply that we all can or should think the same, but I do believe that it is naïve and dangerous to ignore political philosophy and largely take on a "don't ask, don't tell" ethos. ⌐

This vulnerability was exposed quite clearly in the churches in my tradition in the United States during the 2016 presidential elections. Many disciples who had kept quiet their political beliefs for years were suddenly quite visible in their support for Donald J. Trump. Some of his rhetoric appealed to them, and they were emboldened by other members who had been quite vocal in their support and approval of President Obama. Thinking that it was okay to let their affiliations be known now, the Trump supporters in the fellowship spoke up but were shocked to find that this support deeply hurt the feelings of others, especially brothers and sisters of color. Suddenly, a deep rift was exposed in the fellowship. Was the problem that one group was supporting the wrong party or person? Or was it that both sides had embraced political beliefs based on their backgrounds and experience that remained unchanged and untouched by a consistent approach to the kingdom and politics throughout our fellowship?

Should We Just Leave Politics Alone?

The world of politics and political engagement is complicated. There are no clear-cut answers that hold true in every situation. That makes it even more challenging for the Christian community because most of us prefer a few easy steps or principles that we can apply simply in every situation without having to give things much thought. That sort of lazy approach is not available here.

Due to the complications and headache-inducing complexities of these situations, many who have pledged their life to King Jesus are tempted to throw up their hands and leave politics "out there" for the world, thinking they can safely ignore it within the secure confines of the church.

But it is a mistake to attempt to completely ignore the world of politics or just withdraw into a pious shell, claiming that the only legitimate function of the church is evangelism that is focused on personal salvation and showing people how to be forgiven of their sin. I can see at least six reasons why doing so would be a huge mistake for kingdom citizens.

Withdrawing looks like the church does not care about the problems of the world. God plans to renew his beautiful creation one day (Matthew 19:28; Revelation 21:1–5), not just ball it up and throw it away for a disembodied spiritual realm called "heaven." Letting the world burn while we engage in an evacuation-style evangelism that can't be bothered with the issues that people face every day is offensive and hurtful to a world that currently knows only the present age.[1]

Completely withdrawing from all things political is tantamount to wishing the world to keep warm and well fed while doing nothing about their immediate needs (James 2:16). We should take care not to become so enamored with issues of justice and other political engagements that we lose sight of the kingdom and being the prophetic community, but we are called to be a light to the world, and that starts with offering samples of the age to come right here in the real problems of the present age. We can never offer complete solutions, but we certainly have samples to attract people to the future reality of God's kingdom that has broken into the present realm. The problem here is that it is far too common to call anything controversial and in the public square a political topic these days. If our instinct is to withdraw, then all we need is to hear the word "political" and we check ourselves out. We need to find a way to be engaged in the world without being drawn into the political power struggles of the world. Thus, we don't withdraw, but we also refuse to use the weapons of the world.

Complete withdrawal leaves the world without the true salt and light. Bland food with no saltiness can be hard to eat, and a room with no light is dangerous. The kingdom offers salt and light by being visible in the real world and showing them a different way. We are the blueprint to God's future, and without it the world is left to build with no vision for what things should look like.

For many, withdrawing from the world of political engagement means that we simply will not engage in thinking about politics, but that does really mean that we will not be affected by it. Nor does it mean that there are not issues in which we should engage. We need to have a well-thought-out approach, because not having one opens us up to mistakes and being constantly duped and swindled by groups seeking to use the church for their own purposes. It leaves us to become pawns of the con men who have learned to speak our language, rather than being representatives of the king. When a church community refrains from having a vision of political engagement, it becomes prone to the divisions and varying worldly political views that its members bring with them into the church. We must remember that becoming active in issues that are political or have been labeled political is not the same thing as being political or becoming involved in partisan politics.[1]

Withdrawing causes the kingdom of God to lose the voice of the prophetic community. Taking up that role in the world takes tremendous thought and effort as we consider how the principles of God's word for his people will apply in each generation and situation.

And finally, withdrawing will rob the world of a chance to see the sacrificial love of Christ in action and deny them an opportunity to see what it looks like when he is King. This means that they will not have a true choice between living an empire-approved life or the kingdom alternative.

I don't believe that any of the above examples from Geneva, the Amish, or the dominionists provides a clear vision of how we might engage in the twenty-first century. Wilberforce's example is a much closer approach, although he engaged in the political system more than I would advocate in normal circumstances. He was faced with unique times and seemed to largely keep his purpose focused on the sacrificial means and methods of the kingdom to achieve the specific goal of bringing the slave trade to an end.

One of the greatest influences on Christian theology and political theory of the twentieth century was Reinhold Niebuhr. His contention was that the church had an obligation to bring its social agenda to bear on secular society to transform it for the better. The assumption being that the best way, and maybe the only way, to achieve justice was through politics. So, into the fray the church must go. On the other end of that argument was twentieth-century missionary and philosopher Leslie Newbigin, who argued that once Christians buy into the concept that every human has the right to develop their potential to the greatest extent, it is a short jump to believing that the only reasonable means of securing and protecting those rights is through the nations. Whatever means we then must utilize to establish and preserve those rights, we willingly swallow.

The kingdom must neither withdraw from society nor accept that its purpose is to transform it. To accept Niebuhr's premise that our role is to transform society is to invite the wolf into the hen house. In their seminal book, *Resident Aliens*, Hauerwas and Willimon assert that "the church does not exist to ask what needs doing to keep the world running smoothly and then to motivate our people to go do it."[63] They argue that "the political task of Christians is to be the church rather than to transform the world."[64] When our obsession becomes to transform the world, we will hardly notice "that in fact the world [has] tamed the church."[65]

Hauerwas and Willimon demonstrate how Niebuhr brought a Constantinian approach by setting the discussion as though our only two options are "a world-affirming 'church' or a world-denying 'sect.'"[66] These are still the only two options in the mind of many. We either enter the fray completely to transform the world by being part of the system or we withdraw completely. These two options are so entrenched in people's minds that I can almost guarantee that I will be accused, by some who read this book or hear me speak on the topic, of advocating for withdrawal from society simply because I call for an alternative. We are to be what Hauerwas and Willimon call the community of the cross or what I have referred to as the prophetic community. It is a group that understands that the most effective and resilient thing the church can to is to be an alternative community. It is to that alternative mode of engagement that we will now turn.

In the next two chapters, I will propose nine principles that will guide us toward a philosophy of engagement with the world. But first, a few additional thoughts.

Three Anchors

As we consider principles for political engagement for citizens of God's kingdom, there are three guiding truths that should anchor our thought process.

The first is that the values of empire and the values of the kingdom of God are at complete odds with one another. Trying to pretend that they can overlap or that a nation can be a Christian nation is simply to erase the true kingdom from the equation.

The second is that the more a nation purports to be Christian, the more likely it brings disrepute to the name of Christ. Nations can try to fulfill their role in a just and kind way. Some nations will be far more moral than others. The kingdom can encourage that and call for it. But nations cannot be Christian. They have a role to play that is rooted in the present age. As an alternative of the age to come, the kingdom will always stand as a stark contrast to even nations that seek to be benevolent and kind. However, even the best-meaning nations are a mixed bag and typically have a dark side.

I have seen this in my own country. For centuries now, the United States has claimed to be a Christian nation, virtually synonymous with the kingdom of God. Around the world, other nations have taken that message at face value. They look at the immorality, the massive pornography industry, the greed that the US has shown around the world, the way the majority has treated indigenous people and minorities, and the military machine, and many have associated those things with Christianity. It is difficult to deny that this association has played some part in the resurgence of Islam and other non-Christian religions around the world. We must make a clear distinction in our mind between our country of residence and/or birth and the kingdom of God. They are not the same and will not ever have the same agenda.

The third is that the degree to which anything is Christian is the degree to which it acts like Jesus. Jesus' friend, John, revealed that, "Whoever claims to live in him must live as Jesus did" (1 John 2:6). That is simple and straightforward and must be our standard of evaluation for anything or anyone that claims to be Christian. Does it echo Jesus' teaching? Do they love like Jesus? Do they sacrifice for the benefit of others the way Jesus did? Simply using religious language or appealing to the Bible on occasion doesn't make us part of the kingdom any more than putting a Lamborghini logo on a Toyota Prius makes it a Lamborghini. When we embrace a nation or even a church that behaves in ways that are foreign to or even in flat opposition to the principles of the kingdom of God, we transform that entity into a potentially destructive force that serves as a double danger because not only are people robbed of the chance to see the true kingdom, they are shown darkness and told that it is light. That will make them hesitant to being open to the true light when it arrives. Again, what I am aiming for here is a clear understanding of the difference between the nations and the kingdom. Even when a nation does good, it is not the kingdom of God.

Just to be clear, that does not mean that I am saying that any institution that is not the kingdom of God is evil or must be avoided like the plague by Christians. A group that fights for justice for wrongly accused prisoners on death row, an agency that provides food for those in need, or a country that acts benevolently toward another are all good things. We should encourage, applaud, and even potentially partner with their work. But we must take extreme caution not to confuse them with the kingdom of God, not to become enamored with solutions that are rooted in the weapons of the present age, and not to yoke ourselves too intimately with any institution or group, especially any that exercise power over others.

What should the kingdom of God look like in each situation? That is difficult to say precisely, although I will propose the nine principles in the next chapters, but surely a great start would be to look for actions that embody the fruit of the Spirit, which is "love, joy, peace, forbearance, kindness, goodness, faithfulness, gentleness and self-control" (Galatians 5:22–23).

What Is the Empire Cooking?

In considering the first chapter of the book of Daniel, author Brian Zahnd notes Daniel's refusal to eat from the king's table. His primary reason for that was to remind himself and his fellow exiles of their identity and that their true provision came from God. Daniel and compatriots were sending a message to themselves more than they were worried about communicating anything to the empire.

How does this apply to our modern situation? Zahnd notes that Christians don't have dietary laws that help establish their identity and teach them about God's ways, but we do have a battle to maintain our identity while immersed in empire. He argues that the main meals being served up from the kitchen of the empires are a steady diet of consumerism and militarism, which he refers to as Mammon and Mars.[67]

Empires worship at the altars of the economy and national security. Those become sacred concepts in the world of empire. In the empire, "It's the economy, stupid," and "We need to maintain our way of life," will always trump "Love your neighbor as yourself."

Zahnd writes, "Prioritizing the economy above principle changes Christians into de facto pagans. The other sacred obsession in the American superpower is security. We guarantee our prosperity by a demonic devotion to the capacity to unleash hyper-violence upon our enemies."[68] He notes that despite the scriptural call for Israel to trust in God rather than military might (Psalm 20:7) and the commands for the kings of Israel not to multiply their warhorses, they simply ignored it "just like every so-called Christian empire has ignored Christ's command to 'put your sword away.'"[69]

What that means is that for many of us, at least my fellow Americans, there will be a constant tug toward economic prosperity and national security. These will feel like nonnegotiable must-haves. But we must resist those urges and seek to truly see each situation through the lens of the kingdom of God and not allow these shades to cover our lenses and distort our view.

Moving Forward

The Christian community needs to have a consistent stance on politics and political engagement. Without such, we will be prone to being blown back and forth by the prevailing winds of our culture and easily duped, becoming completely ineffective in the world in which we live.

Are we going to aim for Calvin's theocratic utopia? I believe this model to be deeply flawed by not allowing for dissent and choice. What about the Amish withdrawal strategy? That is a clear failure to be salt and light for the world, so it falls short of being a prophetic community.

Some may think we should strive for something closer to Wilberforce's engagement with the world but for the good of the world. There is much to be admired in his efforts and we may, in some rare instances, find that his approach is necessary to help others, but engaging fully in the world of politics and laws does not seem to be a consistent and clear fulltime approach for a kingdom community.

And the dominionist approach? This method completely ignores the difference in the coming of the kingdom of God and the age to come through Jesus and tends toward coercive methods, which we must reject.

We also must recognize that much of our instinct toward politics, at least those of us in the United States, comes from an entitlement that our culture should be dictated by Christian values. Simply because the founders of this country wished for that to some degree and presumed Christian values does not mean that they used kingdom methods or even established anything close to a true outpost of God's kingdom. Simply appealing to a time when the country was dominated by a morality rooted in Christian culture is not necessarily the most kingdom-coming approach. It might make us feel more comfortable, but that doesn't mean it is right.

With our feet planted in the orienting truths and other reminders that we have considered in this chapter, it is time to move on to consider the simple principles that will help guide our actions in a complicated world.

The Chapter in Review ✦

- Christian movements that do not have a theology and philosophy of political engagement are susceptible to the political ideologies of the present age.

- We must find an approach to politics that provides principles that will help us to live out the reality of the kingdom but still realistically be in the world without becoming of the world.

- Completely withdrawing from politics and the world is not a viable option for kingdom communities.

- Withdrawing from society robs the world of the prophetic voice and a chance to see the alternative community as a light.

- We must remember that the values of the empire and the values of the kingdom are at complete odds.

- The more a nation claims to be a Christian nation, the more it brings disrepute to the name of Christ and his kingdom.

- The degree to which anything is Christian is the degree to which it acts like Jesus.

The Big Idea

- ❖ Kingdom movements must have consistent principles of political engagement that do not mimic the values of the nations.

DISCUSSION QUESTIONS

1. What is the current political philosophy of your church? Is there an informal but dominant political leaning that most congregants in your church hold?

2. If you consider the three models that were discussed briefly in this chapter, Calvin in Geneva, the Amish, and Wilberforce, which is the most appealing to you personally and why?

3. What is the common impression of Christianity that most nonchurchgoers have in your country? Why should what they think matter to the church?

Section 3

Engaging with the World

Chapter 19

Principles of Engagement, Part 1

There is a big difference between principles and rules. That thought may have never occurred to you before, but it is quite important as a Christian to know the differences. Rules are rooted externally to the individual. They are easy and convenient because we don't have to think much in response to rules. We can simply appeal to the rule and do exactly as it says. Rules typically compel our behavior through the threat of punishment or another kind of threat. If you break the rule, then "this" will be your consequence. Rules remove the element of discernment, but they also are inflexible. A rule stands firm even if the context or situation changes. Rules do not adapt to fluctuating conditions. They don't allow for maturity and growth, because they simply tell us what to do and don't demand much from us.

Principles are quite different. Principles guide us but not through force or threat. They are rooted internally and motivate or direct us toward good behavior that applies the heart of the principles to ever-changing situations. Principles are much more difficult to live by, however, because they demand that we apply wisdom, thought, and discernment as to how and when to apply them. They cause us to mature and grow as we utilize them, because they demand a great deal from us every time we seek to employ them.

We might rather like the idea of a few simple rules that tell us what to do when it comes to engaging in the world of politics and justice as Christians. We don't want to have to think about such complex and difficult things. The world is a messy and often ugly place full of sin, oppression, lack, hate, violence, and so much more. Determining how to be the prophetic community in such a morass is rarely clear. It can cause spiritual vertigo. How nice it would be to simply have a short list like the Ten Commandments that would tell us exactly how to respond in any and every situation.

But that is not how the new covenant works. God doesn't give us rules, he gives spiritual principles to guide us and help mature us as we discern how and when to apply those principles. For example, rather than giving us five rules of human interaction, God simply tells us to love our neighbor as ourselves and then expects us to wrestle with what that will look like and what it will demand of us in every situation in which we might find ourselves. Or he tells us to love our enemies and then lets us go to work with that one in our back pocket.

No, we will not find rules of political engagement in or even implied in the Bible. What we have are biblical principles that we must think through and apply. Because they are principles, that means that the principles themselves have been gleaned and crafted for this situation, which means that they may be imperfect or incomplete. I do not offer these as the definitive word for all time. We may find down the road that they need to be added to or adjusted to fit the real world. I welcome that ongoing conversation.

Before we begin, I will mention one important foundational principle that will help keep the others properly rooted. In Matthew 22:15–22 we find an incident when the Pharisees tried to capture Jesus in one of the hottest political debates of his day. Should the Jewish people pay the oppressive Roman taxes? This is a lose-lose question they have posed Jesus. If he says yes, he infuriates the Jewish crowds. If he says no, he marks himself as an agitator and opens himself up to a rightful charge to be punished by Rome. There is no good response.

But Jesus flips the Pharisees' game. He appeals to Genesis 1, which teaches that humans were made in God's image to represent him fully with every part of their lives and who they are. That is what is important to God. He also appeals to a coin with Caesar's image imprinted on it. That is what is important to Caesar. If Caesar wants his little coin with his image on it, that's part of his realm, so give it to him. But God wants our devotion. He wants us to be restored to his presence and realm. And we should be focused on giving that to him.

As we consider when to engage and what it might look like to do so, we will do well to remember that it is easy to value things like coins that belong to Caesar's realm, but we must avoid the temptation and remain fixated on giving to God what is God's.

Principle of Engagement #1 – Focus Allegiance

Any act of involvement or engagement must begin with properly aligned allegiance. I believe that is why Daniel 1 begins with the account of the young exiles rejecting the food from King Nebuchadnezzar's table. They were aligning their allegiance to God in this setting, which would challenge that at every turn. Every experience they had in Babylon would tempt them to turn their trust to Babylon and find identity, security, and provision in this new and mighty king. But they set their allegiance to God first, which would enable them to order the rest of their steps.

God is pleased to save those who give allegiance to his crucified king (1 Corinthians 1:21). There is a reason that when describing the conversion of those who would follow Jesus and embrace the kingdom by calling on his name and being baptized into his life (Romans 10:13; Acts 22:16), Paul asserted that Christians declared publicly that "Jesus is Lord."

True allegiance is the starting point for everything else. And the nature of allegiance means that there is only one subject of our ultimate loyalty. You cannot have competing allegiances, or you will have none at all. When we pledge our allegiance to Jesus as our King, there can be nothing else that would vie for our heart. In good conscience, I cannot pledge allegiance overtly or tacitly to anything other than the kingdom of God. I cannot pledge or give my allegiance to another country, ruler, party, or philosophy. The only thing that is truly "under God" is his kingdom, so that makes it quite clear for me.

If our allegiance is not properly oriented, it will get off track quickly. If I set out to walk ten miles due North but am off even a fraction of a degree, by the time I reach the ten-mile mark, I will have veered a great deal from true North without ever realizing it. If our allegiance is compromised even slightly, it will have massive implications as we move forward into a highly politicized world full of complex challenges and problems.

It might make sense to ask definitively here and clarify, what role does a Christian have in a party-based political system? Virtually none, in my opinion. To throw our allegiance to or align ourselves with one political party or philosophy is to compromise the values of the kingdom. Political parties are rooted in the values and solutions of the world. Their agendas may temporarily overlap with a portion of the values or agenda of the kingdom of God, but much more will not. It is dangerous waters to attach ourselves to any one party or candidate, because we will find ourselves yoked with so much that does not align with the role of the prophetic community that we will quickly lose the saltiness of the kingdom.

Instead, we need to operate as the kingdom. That means that, together, we should align our loyalty to Jesus and then work through thoughtfully and prayerfully what allegiance to King and kingdom will look like in each situation.

Can we vote in national elections and the like and still be allegiant to the kingdom as our number one agenda? Possibly. Although I believe that to do so would take an incredible amount of discernment, if that is a course we wish to navigate. Can we become loyal to one political party and throw our lot in with them no matter what and keep our loyalty and mission focused on the King and his kingdom? I don't see how.

Let me not beat around the bush and get right to the heart of the matter: Should Christians vote? We are certainly not required to. Personally, I doubt that the early Christians would have, although we will never know for sure. Most of us today have that freedom, and I understand that many have sacrificed their lives so we could have it. As deserving of honor as that is, it cannot by itself dictate our behavior. Many Jews before the time of Christ (especially during the time of Antiochus IV) died in order to preserve the right of the Jewish people to maintain their food purity laws, but Jesus wiped those away when they were no longer necessary in the kingdom.

At the same time, I don't think a strong case can be made that it is inherently wrong for Christians to vote. Certainly, there may be great value, particularly in local school board or city elections. When engaging on a larger, national stage, however, we must show great caution and put the kingdom first. If we can discern a specific reason that keeps in line with the values and principles of the kingdom of God without yoking us to unrighteousness, and maintain our trust in God rather than laws and politicians, then perhaps there could be times and places to vote. One thing is for certain, though. There is not a hard-and-fast rule that can be applied in all situations.

I think we need to consider the other principles below before developing a final thought about voting, so I will return to this idea at the end of Chapter 20.

The key decisions with this principle are:

❖ Does our allegiance to Jesus lead us to refrain from engaging in the world in these issues or does it dictate that we should engage?

❖ If we are engaging in a specific area, can we do so and maintain our allegiance to Jesus and the values of kingdom living?

Principle of Engagement #2 – Understand the Purpose of the Kingdom

Everything about the kingdom of God is a choice. If God wanted to force us to honor and praise him or to live by a certain set of morals, he could have done that. It seems like that would be light work for the Creator of the universe if that were the road he wanted to go down. But he does not.

From the story in Genesis 3 on, humans have been given a choice to live with God as their king. Adam and Eve chose to exalt their own will over God's, and most of society has continued on that path ever since. Yet God patiently and lovingly offers us the freedom to decide.

Freedom and choice are important aspects of the purpose of the kingdom of God as we seek to expand its borders and reach throughout the world. This will be more challenging than we might suppose because it is so easy to establish laws and rules that we sincerely believe are in the best interest of others but that take away their freedom to choose. There are some things that are universally unjust or harm others and cannot be a legitimate choice. We will look at those concepts in the next principle. States and nations may outlaw things and take away choices, whether it is just or not, and back it up with the power of the sword, but the kingdom must avoid those tactics.

Whenever we ponder whether the prophetic community should get embroiled in an issue or take a stand, or consider how we should engage, one of our guiding principles must be to mirror God's consistent ethos in the world to allow people to choose whom or what they will serve. One of the characteristics of God's love is that it is noncontrolling and never forces anyone to obey.

That is not to argue that laws or even most laws are illegitimate or wrong. Remember, we are not arguing political science here or what is best for the nations. We are talking solely about the role and involvement of the people of God's kingdom, which must be an alternative to the world.

That also does not mean that the church cannot have the highest of standards and expectations for life within the kingdom. People choose the life of the kingdom and can leave if they want. What we cannot do is to confuse society with the kingdom and then begin a mission of mandating and legislating the morals and values of the kingdom into the world. Nor do we want to let society dictate what our morals and values will be.

Politics and laws work through entirely different means than the kingdom of love and self-sacrifice. Sociologist Robert Woodberry has done thorough and peer-reviewed work in which he has demonstrated something very interesting and perhaps unexpected.[70] According to Woodberry, his extensive research and data crunching reveal a stark difference between the type of missionaries that went to locations around the world and the nature of those societies today. He distinguishes between missionaries who came from Protestant, non–politically affiliated movements and those who came from state-run churches and the Vatican-run Roman Catholic missionaries. The Protestant, non–politically connected missionaries were much more critical of colonialism and fought with the people against such oppression. This aversion to political structures and abuses had a lasting impact. According to Woodberry's work:

> Areas where Protestant missionaries had a significant presence in the past are on average more economically developed today, with comparatively better health, lower infant mortality, lower corruption, greater literacy, higher educational attainment (especially for women), and more robust membership in nongovernmental associations.[71]

According to Woodberry's findings, missionaries who were funded by the state or the Vatican had "no comparable effect in the areas where they worked."[72] While this is complex, it does seem to lend credence to the idea that freedom and kingdom solutions offer more long-term hope than political solutions.

In short, we are not trying to be the world, and we are not trying to turn the world into the kingdom. We are offering the world a choice to see a different way of living and offering samples of that life wherever we can so that they will choose it. The kingdom cannot be forced. Jesus directed his disciples to leave a town and shake the dust off their feet if their message was rejected (Luke 10:8–12) and urged them to not throw their pearls to pigs (Matthew 7:6). If people do not choose the kingdom, they must be allowed to make that choice without it then being forced upon them through legislation or any other means.

The key decisions with this principle are:

❖ Would our course of action preserve individual freedom where appropriate as well as maintaining the ability for people to make choices about their own life?

❖ Would our course of action continue to present the kingdom as an alternative to be chosen, with no sense of coercion?

Principle of Engagement #3 – Stand for Justice

Before we jump into this third principle, I will freely admit that this may be the most difficult one to navigate and come to agreement on. That probably means that this is where we should invest the most time as the people of God in communicating, humbly listening to one another, and truly learning about the perspectives of others. It is quite shocking to me how quick we are in the modern context to think we understand what is going on in the world without ever immersing ourselves in the background and perspective of those who think differently. This is especially vital for those of us who come from a privileged background. We receive a great deal of privilege or lack of privilege from what country we were born into, what ethnic group we come from, and even quite often the color of our skin. It is important to not be defensive about any privileges that we may have been afforded in our life. Don't feel guilty about it. You didn't ask for those things. But you have been given them, and that means that as a Christian you can use them for the advantage of those who have been less fortunate.

An important principle for us to consider as we decide when and where to engage as both individuals and as a community has to do with justice. Does this issue involve a matter of justice or injustice? There are at least three elements of this that must be considered.

First, does the issue at hand bring harm or injustice to another? There are, of course, two levels of justice. The world has one vision of just and unjust, and God's word has another. I don't think that means that we automatically categorize things as neatly as that and only care about issues of justice that are absolutely outlined in God's word.

[Certainly, things that are unjust by God's standards should be matters that we care about deeply and meet our standard of involvement. But there may be times when the world or part of a population views something else as deeply unjust, and to simply ignore that issue may seem unnecessarily callous or unloving and damage the witness of the kingdom.]

For example, the Bible does not say much about voting or list it as a universal right. Yet, for a hundred years after the Civil War in the United States, voting rights were denied to the black population of the US as well as many other persons of color. That is not a biblical instance of injustice, at least not directly; however, it is an obvious case of oppression. We will discuss this further in principle #5, but standing up for the oppressed is a central feature of the kingdom of God, so that should have been something that was on the radar of every group of people that called themselves citizens of God's kingdom. Sadly, most opposition to that situation came only from black churches while the rest of American churches remained silent for nearly a hundred years.

Second, does the action in question bring enough harm to the actor or others in the situation that their choice should be taken away? Many Christians might feel that it is not a good thing for an individual to have a weapon, but is the danger inherent enough that the right to choose a weapon of self-defense should be left up to the state and not the individual? It would not seem to meet that criterion. We may have personal feelings about the rights of individuals to possess firearms, but if a country were to restrict access to them, this does not seem to rise to the level of an injustice against humanity.

Or, many Christians would argue that a homosexual lifestyle is harmful and destructive not just to society but also to the practitioners of such a lifestyle. Yet that hardly seems to rise to the level of harm or creating oppressed victims to the point where the Christian community should feel that they would be justified in partnering with a state to take away the individual's right to choose. A case could be made that if Christians lived in a nation where such choices were outlawed, they might find themselves advocating for those freedom-denying laws to be removed, even though they do not support that behavior within the kingdom of God itself. We cannot foist the morality of the kingdom on those outside the kingdom, but we are still driven by the freedom that God affords humans as a basic human right.

Third, is the issue in question a case of universal injustice and harm? Murder, rape, slavery, and false imprisonment, just to name a few, are universally unjust even if a society has made such actions legal. Nazi Germany legalized the murder of many groups of people, most infamously, Jewish people, but it is clearly unjust. Rape is de facto legal and acceptable in some societies but is unjust. Slavery has been legal in various places and times but is a clear injustice and something that should not be tolerated by Christians, although we will need to consider certain nuances in responding to this atrocity and things like it in principle #8 below. During the Jim Crow South, black people were often arrested for the nonspecific crime of "vagrancy." In practical terms, that meant they could be arrested anywhere, at any time, for almost any reason. Like the others listed above, this is an obvious injustice that should immediately alert kingdom people that involvement and engagement in some form is on the horizon.

⌈The biggest challenge for diverse communities when it comes to applying a principle that involves discerning what is unjust is that we will have such different backgrounds and sensitivities to issues.⌋Alleged systematic mistreatment of one segment of the population by police will be an obvious matter of injustice to kingdom citizens from that segment. Meanwhile, people from another segment of society might tend to dismiss these claims and support the authorities and see it as a crime issue or something exaggerated by the media. How do we move forward through such divides? I will return to this in principle #6 below and attempt to answer that.

The key decisions with this principle are:

❖ Does the situation so oppress a person or group of people who cannot fully stand up for themselves that God's people need to step in and help them?

❖ Does the situation involve a clear injustice so that ignoring it would be to partner with the injustice?

❖ What course of action can we take to mitigate or stop the oppression without violating kingdom principles or using worldly weapons?

Principle of Engagement #4 – Mercy Triumphs over Judgment

Mercy strives for peace and wholeness. Judgment strives for justice first and foremost. Jesus was clear that our interactions with the world should be marked by mercy (Matthew 5:7) rather than characterized by judgment (Matthew 7:1–5).

Peace is a tricky phenomenon. Jesus was the Prince of Peace who was ushering in a kingdom of peace. He never committed a harmfully violent act in his life. He allowed himself to be killed rather than to kill. He prohibited his disciples from using violence to defend his life. As far as it could depend on him, he lived at peace with all people. Yet he also said, "Do not suppose that I have come to bring peace to the earth. I did not come to bring peace but a sword" (Matthew 10:34). Jesus wasn't suddenly cutting against everything else he taught and advocating for war and violence. Rather, he makes clear in the subsequent verses that he is referring to the controversial nature of his message. It would divide and cause controversy between those who accepted it and those who rejected it. But it was always seasoned with grace and mercy rather than being judgmental.

This principle reminds us that the kingdom people should always be the voice of peace. We should use peaceful methods and seek peace for others, knowing that the result won't always be a life of peace for ourselves. But it also means that when we engage with the world, even on difficult subjects, that the world feels the love and mercy of a peacemaker rather than the judgment of a people that prefer peace for themselves. Peacemakers are willing to get uncomfortable for others. People who want to experience peace for themselves are often unwilling to do so.

I applaud my brothers and sisters in Christ who have become experts in conflict resolution and now go into government facilities and secular corporations instructing them how to work through conflict. Christians should be leading the way in these matters.

Sadly, though, Christians in modern society often are not the voice of peace. As a collective, Christians have often been known for their judgment of others and have been the loudest supporters of war and violence to keep security and tranquility without discerning that those are weapons of the world and not of the kingdom of peace. It sends a strange and contradictory message when we then turn around and sing "Peace on earth, good will to men" at Christmastime.

Christians are more known in modern society for being judgmental than merciful, and that's a problem.

I know of no one, ever, who has become a genuine citizen of the kingdom of God through legislation, political might, violent action, or judgmentalism. And if something is not demonstrating and building up the kingdom, then it is adding to the empires. Let us not forget that.

The disciples in Revelation, we are told, triumphed over the dragon with nothing more than the sacrificial blood of the lamb and the word of their testimony. They did not endanger other lives but were willing to risk their own as "they did not love their lives so much as to shrink from death" (Revelation 12:11).

Kingdom peace may look different from the world's vision of peace, which often comes through force, might, and at the end of an exceptionally large stick. We will have to work out what that might look like in each situation as we allow Jesus' words to echo in our ears: "Peace I leave with you; my peace I give you. I do not give to you as the world gives. Do not let your hearts be troubled and do not be afraid" (John 14:27).

The prophetic community will speak mercy and peace, live peacefully, and advocate for peace for others, knowing that it may disrupt our own peace at times or even cost our own lives. We should keep in mind that the biblical concept of peace is not just an absence of conflict; it is wholeness, completeness, harmony, and balance.

The key decisions with this principle are:

❖ Take a long look at the form of engagement or proposed engagement. Does it display the mercy of God to others?

❖ Does the engagement demonstrate the fact that judgment is reserved for God and is not our domain?

Principle of Engagement #5 – Display Solidarity and Empathy

In Daniel 4, King Nebuchadnezzar has a dream about a large tree, and it puzzles him. Daniel finally explains it to him, and the meaning must have taken him by surprise. Daniel explained that the king was that large tree and that God had given him power and authority for the benefit of others, but instead, he used it for himself, to make himself great. He would answer for that folly.

The principle holds true for kingdom citizens. Humans were designed by God to put the interests of others first. That is unquestionably how Jesus lived (Philippians 2:1–8).

Don't forget that when Jesus gave his first recorded public speech, he highlighted Isaiah 61, saying,

> "The Spirit of the Lord is on me,
> > because he has anointed me
> > to proclaim good news to the poor.
> He has sent me to proclaim freedom for the prisoners
> > and recovery of sight for the blind,
> to set the oppressed free,
> > to proclaim the year of the Lord's favor." (Luke 4:18–19)

If I could challenge you to take the next few weeks or months and read through the entire Bible, both the Old and New Testaments, you would quickly find that God takes the side of the oppressed and marginalized. He never demonizes the rich, but throughout the Scriptures, those who are deemed the least desirable and worthy by society are the ones God wants us to care for the most.

James, the brother of Jesus, spends a considerable amount of space in the second chapter of his book challenging the allegiant to not show favoritism toward the wealthy and powerful in society. There are many ways that we can do this, so we must be ever vigilant.

James brings it altogether in 2:13 when he simply states, "Mercy triumphs over judgment." The last principle called us to ensure that we aim for mercy rather than judgment. When judgment triumphs over mercy, we become critical of the poor and wonder what bad decisions they made to get into this situation. When judgment triumphs over mercy, we speculate as to what the oppressed have done to deserve their condition. When judgment triumphs over mercy, we care more about punishment, imprisonment, and our own safety than we do loving those in need. *Oof. I can be this way.*

In Matthew 25, Jesus could not have been clearer. When we act on behalf of the marginalized, we do it to and for him. And when we don't, it his him that we neglect.

Taking the perspective of the outcast and oppressed is a massive shift in worldview for many Christians; at least it is for many in my faith community, which tends to be middle class and up. We must strive for reconciliation with God, reconciliation with others, and reconciliation for others. But to do that, we must see the world through God's eyes and through his love for the poor, the prisoner, the outcast, and the unloved.

We must not shrink the gospel into a reconciliation that only focuses on that between God and humans. These individualistic versions of the good news are "reconciliation with memory," which Christian authors Katongole and Rice describe as "an approach that ignores the wounds of the world and proclaims peace where there is no peace (Jer. 8:11)."[73] This approach is too quick to abandon the past wounds that have not been reconciled and healed in search of a future that cannot be until we are realistic about the past. The result, say Katangole and Rice, is a superficial discipleship that separates personal salvation from social transformation and a vision of what the kingdom can accomplish in the world. We must remember, though, that true reconciliation of any kind without God as the foundation will remain vague and elusive.

When considering political engagement, both in what issues to take up and then how to approach those areas, we must train ourselves so that our godly instinct is to care for and stand up for the oppressed rather than fight for the rights of the comfortable and "deserving" portions of society.

We must not let ourselves slip into the anesthesia of occasional collections and a few volunteer work days to help the poor, but then the rest of the year pushing for policies and laws that continue to hold down the poor and marginalized, or simply ignoring their plight. We must stop judging the health of the economy by how well the big corporations and the rich are doing and advocate for those on the lower rungs that often don't matter to the mainstream. Those are the very people that God wants us to care about the most.

This principle of standing in solidarity with the marginalized in empathy should lead us to at least three things as the life of the kingdom is realized among our own and then spread to those in the world that are not yet citizens of God's realm. The first is economic love for neighbor that starts with caring for our own people but then overflows to the least in the world. Second is a love within the church community for the oppressed, the marginalized, and the most vulnerable that extends to those in that same position in the world. Third is a commitment to advocate for those in need and a refusal to show favoritism of any kind to the well off and comfortable.

The key decisions with this principle are:

❖ Do our actions demonstrate a heart of compassion and love for the marginalized and oppressed?

❖ Are we acting on behalf of those who are left behind by society or who have gotten themselves into bad situations, showing them mercy and solidarity?

❖ Do we advocate for the poor, the struggling, and those who are cast away by society, and do we show them special honor and dignity?

The Chapter in Review

- As Christians who are called to engage with the world, we must remain focused on giving to God what is God's.

- **Principle #1:** We must have a properly focused allegiance.
  - o Does our allegiance to Jesus lead us to refrain from engaging in the world in these issues or does it dictate that we should engage?
  - o If we are engaging in a specific area, can we do so and maintain our allegiance to Jesus and the values of kingdom living?

- **Principle #2:** We must understand that the kingdom of God is always a choice and can never be compelled.
  - o Would our course of action preserve individual freedom where appropriate as well as maintaining the ability for people to make choices about their own life?
  - o Would our course of action continue to present the kingdom as an alternative to be chosen, with no sense of coercion?

- **Principle #3:** We must stand for justice and be anti-injustice.
  - o Does the situation so oppress a person or group of people who cannot fully stand up for themselves that God's people need to step in and help them?
  - o Does the situation involve a clear injustice so that ignoring it would be to partner with the injustice?
  - o What course of action can we take to mitigate or stop the

oppression without violating kingdom principles or using worldly weapons?

- **Principle #4:** Mercy must triumph over judgment.
  - o Take a long look at the form of engagement or proposed engagement. Does it display the mercy of God to others?
  - o Does the engagement demonstrate the fact that judgment is reserved for God and is not our domain?

- **Principle #5:** Solidarity and empathy must be displayed, especially for the oppressed and marginalized.
  - o Do our actions demonstrate a heart of compassion and love for the marginalized and oppressed?
  - o Are we acting on behalf of those who are left behind by society or who have gotten themselves into bad situations, showing them mercy and solidarity?
  - o Do we advocate for the poor, the struggling, and those who are cast away by society, showing them special honor and dignity?

The Big Idea

- ❖ As we discern when to engage with the world, we must be guided by well-thought-out, kingdom-focused principles.

DISCUSSION QUESTIONS

1. What are the areas in the lives of contemporary Christians that most vie for their allegiance?

2. How engaged has your church been with issues of injustice and oppression in the world? What has that engagement or lack thereof communicated to the world about the kingdom?

3. Which do you tend to emphasize more in your actions: mercy or judgment? Which does your church tend to emphasize more?

Chapter 20

Principles of Engagement, Part 2

I was part of a group a few years back that was tasked with studying and reporting on a rather complex and difficult topic. We spent many months researching and wrestling with what the biblical approach and teaching on the topic were. But it wasn't just an exercise of pulling out biblical truth and leaving it at that. We then had to recommend how to apply the scriptural principles in the modern world. That was no easy task. Our world is as challenging and muddy as it has ever been; but that was our role, so we pressed on.

Throughout the time we worked on that and considered how we might apply our findings, we had a saying that was repeated often and that guided us through our process: "The right thing done the wrong way is the wrong thing." As the old saying goes, that will preach. The statement is a bit of a hyperbole, of course. It doesn't mean that we should throw the baby out with the bathwater. But it is a guide to being careful how we go about things.

When it comes to principles of political engagement for the people of the kingdom, we would do well to keep the appropriate principle of this truth in mind. Finding the right and good is half the battle. But if the right thing is applied in the wrong way, it can quickly become counterproductive.

Principle of Engagement #6 – Be Angered by the Right Things

Pastor and blogger Darrell Lackey recently penned a rather provocative article about the things that upset Christians. He begins his article with a controversial quote from author and speaker Tony Campolo:

> I have three things I'd like to say today. First, while you were sleeping last night, 30,000 kids died of starvation or diseases related to malnutrition. Second, most of you don't give a shit. What's worse is that you're more upset with the fact that I just said "shit" than you are that 30,000 kids died last night.[74]

Campolo's quote has become famous for both its shock value and the stark truth behind it. In Lackey's article he goes on to pose several propositions to those who call themselves Christians, to demonstrate that we can easily lose perspective and get angry about things that should pale in comparison to more dire issues. When we do this, we often become more known for our anger or judgmentalism over the comparatively insignificant items and look quite petty and ridiculous to the world. I will adapt several of Lackey's challenges to the shallow, simplistic, and legalistic reduction of kingdom values for our purposes here to demonstrate this sad but all-too-frequent behavior.

If you become upset about gay marriage being made legal or a transgender person using a public restroom but are apathetic about the hate, violence, and discrimination leveled against these same people, then you may have lost the kingdom perspective.

If you get enraged when store clerks greet you with "Happy Holidays" instead of "Merry Christmas" but don't give a second thought to the wasteful use of resources, rampant materialism, and out-of-control consumerism while many live in abject poverty in your own area and around the world, then you have lost the kingdom perspective.

If you get irritated by someone at the grocery store using food stamps or vouchers but care little about a system that has caused many to be in need or dismiss those in need because "they should have worked harder," then perhaps you have lost the kingdom perspective.

If you become upset when you see people smoking cigarettes or vaping or drinking alcohol but have never even thought about how much food our society wastes daily while countless numbers of children and adults go to bed hungry every night, then you may have lost the kingdom perspective.

If you get angry about all the swearing in Hollywood movies, but the excessive and voyeuristic displays of violence don't bother you a bit, you may well have drifted from the kingdom perspective.

If you become more irritated by homeless people being allowed to beg on the streets than you are with the fact that there are so many homeless people in your area, then you may have lost the kingdom perspective.

If you become angry about young people who commit crimes and want to see them locked up with the key thrown away but have little or no concern over the devastating and heartbreaking conditions in which they were forced to grow up, because hey, "other people have overcome tough circumstances," then may I propose that you have lost the kingdom perspective.

I could go on, but hopefully you get the point by now. I'm not saying the things listed first above are fine and we should just accept or jump into those behaviors ourselves, but it is about perspective. When judgment triumphs over mercy, we tend to lose perspective on what is truly important, get angry about the wrong things, and fail to act in the areas that might display the true light of the kingdom. We can easily become moralists who spend more time being irritated by others than we do having empathy for those stuck in sin and being willing to lay down our lives for them. For this very reason, right in the midst of the Sermon on the Mount, Jesus teaches that if we are going to mourn over sin (Matthew 5:4), then it must start with our own life and shortcomings, lest we become judgmental (Matthew 7:1–6).

We must be careful about being led by our emotions. On the other hand, anger is an emotion given to us by God for the primary purpose of inciting us to take action against sin and injustice. For this reason, Scripture does not discourage anger, only sinning in response to it (Ephesians 4:26). Anger has its place among kingdom people, but we must recognize that proper anger is in response to true injustice and aimed at dealing with the source of that injustice. Anger can be an important motivation, but it must be controlled and directed properly.

The key decisions with this principle are:

- ❖ Are we angry about the things that anger God?

- ❖ Are we focusing our energy and potential engagement in societal issues on genuine injustices?

Principle of Engagement #7 – Use Kingdom Weapons

God's wisdom and ways are not the same as the world's (Isaiah 55:8–9). We often make the mistake of thinking that God is just like us, but he is not (Psalm 50:21). When God pointed to the coming of his kingdom, he gave hope by promising a time that would be radically different from the present age. It would be an age when the nations would come together as one and would transform their weapons of the world into instruments of peace (Isaiah 2:2–4).

The kingdom is characterized by freedom of choice, peace, power under rather than over others, and equity. That means that any solutions that we offer to the world to address what ails us, whether it be within the kingdom confines or for the world itself, must embody those values.

We must offer solutions that maintain the integrity of the individual to choose. The kingdom cannot be coerced, and morality cannot be legislated. The world of politics is all about power and control. Behavior is regulated through laws and enforcement. Not so with the kingdom. It will be tempting to fight to legislate the morality and values of the kingdom, but as soon as someone is forced into behaviors due to legislation or societal pressure, the kingdom is like a mist that vanishes. Urging laws that protect the oppressed is good, but utilizing laws to legislate morality, take away personal choice, or enforce preferences is not good.

The kingdom must be an advocate of peace. We can respect and submit to the worldly realm of governing authorities that use the sword to mitigate evil and keep peace, but those are not our weapons, and if we forget that, poof, the kingdom is gone. And if we can only imagine methods of violence to overcome the violence of the world, then perhaps we have lost any semblance of the prophetic imagination and creativity of the kingdom of peace.

The nations lord their authority over others, but not so with disciples of Jesus (Matthew 20:25). The kingdom is populated with servants, not masters. Again, it will be tempting to simply seek and gain political power so that we can implement the benevolent rule of God in society. Surely it would be to their advantage if they lived by God's values. And arguably it would. But that is not how God operates. We cannot establish the kingdom by means and methods that are off limits to us. We must overcome evil with good (Romans 12:21).

Most nations operate through the strength of a small minority. They are the ones with power and influence to direct everyone else. This concentration of power and authority can be intoxicating. Yet, as kingdom people, we must be on guard against such things. The kingdom strives for and models a community of equity that has no surplus or lack (Acts 2:44–45; 4:32–37; 2 Corinthians 8:13–15; James 2:14–16). We cannot and should not resort to methods that prove advantageous only for a few or for just a portion of the society.

Perhaps most importantly, our role in the world will be to advocate for others and point the world to the wholeness offered in the kingdom. Our primary goal is not to fix the world. There will be times of great injustice when we may feel we have to make attempts to intervene for the life of the world, but those should be rare, and we should be wary of doing so and very careful to use kingdom weapons when we do.

The key decisions with this principle are:

❖ If we were to engage in a specific issue, would our action model the kingdom values of freedom, choice, love, and mercy?

❖ Is there a way to accomplish what we seek without utilizing weapons, violence, power over others, coercive laws, or the like?

Principle of Engagement #8 – Strive to Be Sacrificial

In some respects, this principle might be the key to all the others. This is the way of the Lamb. It is following the path of the one who lived the principle of the cross his entire life and laid his life down for others. Every action we take as the people of God is to be informed by the call to be self-sacrificial in everything we do. The Son of Man came to give his life as a ransom for others (Matthew 20:28). To follow Jesus, we must first pick up our cross daily (Luke 9:23). Jesus Christ laid down his life for us and we, in turn, are called to lay down our lives for others (1 John 3:16).

We know all that, of course. But it is stunning how quick we are to forget or to relegate it to the status of a platitude.

We will overcome the dragon only through the blood of the Lamb and the word of our testimony about King Jesus. It can be difficult to remember that because we live in a world that constantly tells us differently. Power changes things. Might changes things. Great arguments and ideas change things. Vision changes things. Being the biggest and the best bring change. But not lowly self-sacrifice. What good is that going to do?

Everywhere we turn, we see different versions of the same basic message: Be true to yourself. Look out for number one. Have it your way. If you don't take care of yourself, no one else will. Jesus, however, calls us to just the opposite. Rather than be true to ourselves, he calls us to deny self.

This is the part that is so often missing when Christians seek to engage with the problems of the world. Don't get me wrong, there are many followers of Jesus who live with this sacrificial heart and mind every day. But far too often, when we jump into the political arena, this ethic of self-sacrifice is conspicuously missing. This is so true in the minds of so many, even professing Christians, that we often label self-sacrificial kingdom methods of bringing about change as "doing nothing," right before calling for actions that do not match the values of the King.

In the ancient Roman world, if someone didn't want an infant that they had just given birth to, they could simply leave it outside to die. The practice was called exposure. Many of the infants died, and some were scooped up by slave traders and assigned a grim life of enslavement. The Christians could have sharply criticized the Romans who engaged in this practice. They could have protested and mocked them for their cruelty and inhumanity. They could have railed against the disturbing callousness toward life and affirmed unflinchingly that they were pro-life. Perhaps they could have even tried to push for Caesar to outlaw this practice. They could have played the long game of gaining political control so that they could enact change through the Senate. But they did none of that.

They worked out what love and self-sacrifice might look like in the face of such a terrible situation and simply took these children. They saved them from death and slave traders and raised them in the Christian community. It's not easy to raise children. It's expensive and demanding, but they did it. Time and again, they did it. There is no way of knowing how many infants the kingdom citizens took in over the first few centuries of Christianity, but some Christian historians have surmised that it was in significant enough numbers that it was a contributing factor to the steady and impressive growth of the early church in those first three centuries.

In the first century BC, a gladiator and slave named Spartacus led a slave uprising against the Roman Republic in what is known as the Third Servile War. The rebellion nearly succeeded as the oppressed in Rome fought back against their powerful oppressors.

I mention this solely as a point of contrast. At times in the first three centuries, the citizens of the kingdom of God faced economic oppression and social ostracism. At other times they faced harsh and brutal persecution. True stories of Christians being dipped in tar and lit on fire as human torches or ripped apart by wild beasts in the Roman Coliseum have become well known to history. The Christians could have risen up and fought back as Spartacus did, seeking their own safety or to bring down the rule of their oppressors. They never did. They asserted that they were sheep, and no one would give the name sheep to those who fell in battle, sword in hand, defending their own lives. They proclaimed that they would willingly yield themselves to the sword rather than betray their calling to self-sacrifice and being the kingdom of peace. They argued that there was no difference between provoker and provoked if the latter used the same violent methods as the former. They were far more interested in changing the violence and oppression of the world by their resolve and commitment to overcoming evil with good than they were in preserving their own lives. They were a living, breathing example of self-sacrifice.

This stands in stark contrast to modern Christianity, in which much of the typical engagement with the world is about fighting for and preserving our own rights. We moan and howl if the tiniest slight comes our way. We rabidly defend our rights and fight for them far more than we advocate for others. Self-sacrifice seems to be in short supply as we turn to the shortcuts of power and influence. We flex our muscles rather than our faith and engage in culture wars with the intent of winning them wholesale. Because if we don't, whatever might become of Christianity? What could God possibly do to expand his kingdom if we don't stand up for ourselves and ensure that we have every ounce of our rights and freedoms? It seems that many of us would rather pick up a gun to defend ourselves than a cross to sacrifice for the benefit of others.

It seems that Christians may have forgotten that we are to fight for the life of the world rather than our own comfort and security.

The key decision with this principle is:

❖ Would this action or engagement be self-sacrificial, or does it rely on power over others?

Principle of Engagement #9 – Determine Where Action Should Occur

We have talked often in this book about the kingdom being a blueprint or demonstration of the life that will exist in the coming age. We are to be a foretaste and a sample that compels people toward a life under the reign of King Jesus. For Jesus and for Paul and the other apostles, the good news was the kingdom of God and the alternative way of living that was now available in the kingdom. The good news was not that the kingdom was some new religious order that would slowly move through the world and fix the nations, one by one.

Economic justice, for example, was to take place primarily in the kingdom of God. Widows and the neediest were taken care of by the body. Churches that had provisions to spare shared with those that did not. No one was to go without. Disciples viewed their wealth and possessions as common to all and shared with anyone in need. That was the standard ethos of the church for the first three hundred years. The poor outside the Christian community were then given what they had left over, but that was just a sample of the generosity and love of the alternative community. Jesus told them that they would always have the poor around (Matthew 26:11). Wiping out poverty in the world was not the function of the kingdom. The kingdom offered the solution through their countercultural way of life. Giving to the world was a sample.

Likewise, slavery was an ever-present specter in the first-century world. It was as integral to their society as electricity is to ours. There were some areas in which citizens could put pressure and make changes in the Roman world, but this was not one of them. It was a fact of life, so Paul did not waste time trying to fix the world. But Paul makes it clear in his letter to Philemon that when the principles of loving one another and putting the interests of one another first were put into action, slavery could not exist within the kingdom itself. It took some time for them to work it all out, but it was the inevitable conclusion. Slavery was incompatible with kingdom life. Yet, because many slaves had become allegiant to Jesus but could not control their freedom, Paul gave them instructions about how to think about their freedom (1 Corinthians 7:21–24) and how to live with the kingdom on display even though they were enslaved (Ephesians 6:5–8). And he instructed Christian slave owners how to treat their slaves (v. 9), because simply telling them to free them, if there was no brotherly love behind it, could induce them to cruelly cut their slaves loose and remove them from all they had ever known with no way to support themselves or their families.

After deciding to follow Jesus, a number of Ephesians who had practiced sorcery brought their scrolls and burned them publicly (Acts 19:19). What they did not do was demand that the people of Ephesus do the same because it was a sin.

The point is that most of the world-altering kingdom life is to be demonstrated and lived out within the kingdom. If people want the life of the kingdom, then they can choose to make Jesus their King and become part of his people.

Attempts to officially address and engage issues in the world beyond the boundaries of the people of God should be judiciously thought through and limited. The situations in which we do deem public engagement necessary should be such egregious violations of God's plans for the world or against human rights that we have no other choice. Just to be clear, when I speak of engagement, I am not talking about basic acts of benevolence or working for those in need, which should not be controversial.

But there are times when the church does need to work for change in the world. Why? It is simple, really. If we say that we believe in a biblical standard of sexual morality that is given to us as choice by God and is consistent with the way he designed us, then to allow others to either choose that way of life or not is consistent. To mandate it is not consistent with God's character. But if we say that we believe no one should be violently forced into sexual acts, but that is only our concern within our own kingdom communities, and we ignore those in the world who are abused and oppressed, that is not consistent. It looks like hypocrisy rather than consistency. In those cases, to demonstrate the life of the kingdom, we must stand up for the oppressed that are not part of our community where they cannot stand up for themselves.

Most white churches before the Civil War that did not overtly support slavery remained silent about it, often claiming that it was a political matter and not something that the church should become involved in. It was "political" and a matter of choice, so they would refrain. While the solution to first-century slavery was to be found in the alternative community, transatlantic slavery was so unjust, so evil, and so destructive that for the church to sit by and do virtually nothing was monstrous and callous. It did not display the kingdom, but quite the opposite. The enslaved could not advocate for themselves.

In England, men like Wilberforce who were dedicated both to the kingdom and the methods of the kingdom engaged politically sole- ly for the purpose of standing up for the oppressed. Using kingdom methods, they succeeded. I firmly believe that the unwillingness of those who claimed to be Christian in nineteenth-century America to get involved on behalf of one of the most wicked examples of oppres- sion in recorded human history contributed to the violent and deadly war that would eventually abolish the institution. Kingdom methods were not employed, so it eventually came down to the weapons of the world because the world finally realized just how evil the slave trade was. That is not to imply that there were no Christians who advocated for the enslaved, but not even close to enough utilized kingdom en- gagement the way that Wilberforce did.

Some will argue that it was just, then, for Christians to pick up guns and kill as they protected the lives of these slaves. That is pain- fully flawed logic. We cannot stubbornly refrain from acting and sacri- ficing on behalf of others for so long, refusing to be the kingdom, and wait until the only option left seems to be the violent options of the world, and then use that as justification for Christians to be disobe- dient to the King and his kingdom values. England didn't have a war over slavery, because Wilberforce brought a kingdom solution to the table before it got to that point. And it should go without saying that if all those who claimed to be Christian lived out the kingdom, there would have been no slavery.

Very few situations in life are ideal and without messiness. I un- derstand that it is easy to create a mental vacuum and call for ideal peaceful kingdom solutions in any situation. The real world will often be more complex and challenging. I cannot say that there will never be exceptions that must be made. But that should not change, I don't believe, the standard for which we aim.

But what about something like segregation? Many places in the world are segregated along tribal, socioeconomic, or racial lines. These various forms of segregation can lead to injustice and inequity. Yet this does not seem to rise to the level of a form of evil that creates victims that cannot speak or fight for themselves. It might become that in some instances, but usually it does not rise to that level. The church should speak out against segregation, but perhaps the most effective course it can take in this issue is serving as a light and exam- ple to the world. Segregated churches do not reflect the gospel call to gather the nations, and they fail the gospel in that respect. When the church is not only diverse but committed to radically modeling the gathering of the nations found in Christ, the body of Christ will stand out in the world.

Imagine if large groups of American white Christians moved into predominantly Latino or black neighborhoods so that the small groups in their church were geographically integrated and diverse. What if large numbers of South African white Christians moved into black townships, living lives that were intertwined with their black brothers and sisters, just to be a city on a hill for the world? If actions like these became normal among Christians, the impact would be far greater than any legislation has proven to be.

When considering engagement, there are two sets of options from which to choose that Christians will need to consider regarding our response. The first set of options covers how we speak about the topic and the second deal with how we act in response to the issue.

The first option of rhetoric is to remain officially silent on an issue rather than speak out. Some issues are better left to the individual conscience of kingdom citizens and do not need a public voice. The second option is to speak prophetically against the culture, emphasizing the alternative choice of the kingdom and how it is different from what the world offers; or in some cases, it may overlap significantly with the approach of one political group. That doesn't mean that this group now becomes our new political home. It simply means that there may be overlapping philosophy in one area.

When it comes to our actions, we also have two options. The first is to address issues strictly within kingdom life by modeling a different way than the world typically does. We may choose to model racial or economic justice within the community without attempting to change the world's system in any significant way. In so doing, the kingdom becomes a true alternative. This response can be paired with either speech option above. The second action option should be rare. It is to seek change in society. This must be done considering all nine principles and be used in tandem with the option from above to speak prophetically.

The key decisions with this principle are:

❖ Will our primary response be to model and embody a radically different alternative to what the world can offer?

❖ Or will our primary response on some issues need to be to engage with the world and stand up for the oppressed or disadvantaged?

❖ If we do need to engage with the world, how will we employ the previous principles to direct our actions?

Should Christians Vote?

I have tried to discuss issues related to voting throughout these two chapters, but now I will attempt to bring it all together as concisely as I can. I don't believe there is ever a one-size-fits-all answer to whether we should vote or not.

On one hand, voting can easily turn into yoking ourselves with a party or ideology that does not express the kingdom of God consistently. Choosing the lesser of evils is still choosing evil. Whether we like it or not, to consistently vote is to enter the world's system of power and partisanship.

On the other hand, some will argue that not voting may result in tyrants coming to power or situations worsening in our countries. If all Christians stopped voting, what would be the result? Voting is a right and a responsibility and one that could potentially be utilized to bring about good in the world. Sometimes, using the power of the vote could be a force for good or to keep dangerous ideas at bay. As my friend James Becknell reminded me, sometimes voting can be a faithful act.

I do believe that our primary role in the world is to shine the light of the kingdom. It can shine in good times and bad, and quite frankly, has historically shined brightest during some of the darkest periods. Should we continually fight for a dim glow rather than darkness or should we concern ourselves primarily with creating a kingdom that is a true alternative to the darkness of the world? I tend toward focusing on the kingdom and the desire to build it into the true prophetic community. I find that most of the time, my energy is better spent trying to build up and draw people into God's kingdom rather than engaging in political solutions. Some will call that naïve.

I would then adapt the principles from above, utilizing those that apply, to help guide an approach to voting. My proposal is that before a citizen of the kingdom votes they answer these questions:

1. Does my vote reflect complete allegiance to Jesus' kingdom and what it stands for?

2. Am I voting to preserve or expand freedom, or would it be to exercise power over others?

3. Does my vote reflect God's vision of justice rather than mere worldly justice?

4. Does my vote reflect mercy for all, or is it driven by judgment of some?

5. Does my vote seek to consistently protect the marginalized, oppressed, and innocent?

6. Does my vote help my witness or harm it?

7. Does my vote avoid promoting or supporting worldly weapons?

8. Is my decision of who or what to vote for driven by a willingness to sacrifice for the benefit of others, particularly those in the most fragile positions?

9. Does my vote glorify God and advance his kingdom in some way?

The Chapters that Follow

With these nine proposed principles we can now look in the closing chapters of this book at specific, hot-button issues in the modern world and how these principles might help us think through and develop consistent approaches to some of the more challenging problems in society today.

The Chapter in Review

- As Christians who are called to engage with the world, we must remain focused on giving to God what is God's.

- **Principle #6:** We must get angry over the right things.

- **Principle #7:** We must use kingdom weapons and not trust in the weapons and methods of the world.

- **Principle #8:** We must employ self-sacrifice to bring about true change.

- **Principle #9:** We must determine the context and setting of our engagement and action.

The Big Idea

❖ As we discern when to engage with the world, we must be guided by well-thought-out, kingdom-focused principles.

DISCUSSION QUESTIONS

1. Have you ever found yourself getting angry over the wrong things? What causes us to lose perspective at times?

2. Have you ever found yourself tempted to call for Christians to use weapons of the world because, deep down, you just were not sure that kingdom methods would do anything? What is the cause of that lack of faith and how do we address it?

3. Do you truly believe that self-sacrifice is the means of true change in the world? What is most difficult about that for you?

Chapter 21

Engaging in Personal Social Issues

If you are heading out to a church service in the city of Boston, Massachusetts, you had better leave your bag of peanuts behind. It seems that there is a law on the books in Boston that prohibits churchgoers from munching peanuts during a church service. Those with peanut allergies would probably be in favor of that law being enforced.

In Texas, you will want to leave your costumes and disguises at home, because it is against the law to wear a disguise to church. Similarly, it is strictly against the law in Alabama to wear a fake mustache that causes laughter during church. No word on whether it is legal to wear a mustache that does not cause people to laugh.

And my friends in Omaha, Nebraska shouldn't get too condescending toward their brothers and sisters in Texas and Alabama, because it is illegal to sneeze or burp during a church service there. I hope you're not coming down with a cold. New York City has laws against bodily functions as well. In the city, it is technically against the law to intentionally pass gas in church to cause a disturbance. I would love to know the story behind the incidents causing this law to be put into effect.

In Mississippi, any private citizen can arrest anyone who disturbs a church service. Wouldn't it be great to walk into a police station with a group of chatty college students in custody? Speaking of things that the law allows you to do in church, the state of Maine one ups that and requires church attendees to bring a shotgun to church in case Native Americans attack during a service. Good thing they hadn't yet beat their shotguns into plowshares.

Many of the above laws might not make sense, but this one surely does: in Ohio, if you plan to kill a housefly within 160 feet of a church building, you had better have a license, or it is an illegal kill. Because... of course. I don't think the wisdom of this law needs any explanation.

And finally, be very wary if you climb into the pulpit in Nicholas County, Virginia. It is against the law in that whole county for a clergyman to tell jokes or humorous stories from the pulpit during the church service. I would request that no one who ministers in that county read this section during a sermon, just in case I could be charged as an accessory.[75]

While all these laws may have made sense to the people who passed them at the time, they seem absurd now. Not all laws are absurd, of course, but trying to legislate right and moral behavior in church through the laws of the state is a highly problematic undertaking. Paul seemed to understand this even in the first century when he taught that the fruit of the Spirit cannot be established through laws because they simply cannot transform the heart, which is the whole point of the Spirit's work in the kingdom of God. Transformation is a choice and happens internally through the work of the Spirit. Trying to accomplish that through external laws is an exercise in futility and one that will block the coming of the kingdom rather than establish it. We would do well to remember this as we consider how and when the body of Christ might engage in hot-button social issues of the day.

LGBTQ

There are over fifty countries in the world where homosexuality is an outlawed activity. If you look at a world map, most of those countries are in Africa and the Middle East, with a few sprinkled in Southeast Asia. In several countries, the penalty for engaging in homosexuality is death. That might sound shocking at first, and it is, but we must also be honest about the fact that the book of Leviticus calls for that precise penalty for those who committed acts of homosexuality.

Throughout the Bible, in both the Old and New Testaments, homosexuality is condemned. It is never spoken of positively or encouraged as legitimate behavior for God's people. Yet it was clearly something that existed through the entire course of biblical times, although it was strictly discouraged in Israel and so was quite rare in that specific context. In the New Testament, Jesus confirms that marriage was ordained by God as a covenant union between one man and one woman (Matthew 19:8). Paul mentions homosexuality on three separate occasions. In Romans 1:18–32, he argues that the acceptance of homosexual behavior in a society is a sign that they have rebelled against God's design for humanity and have been turned over to their own desires. In 1 Corinthians 6:9–10, Paul confirms that those who choose homosexuality are among those who have rejected the life to which God calls humans in the kingdom of God. In 1 Timothy 1:8–10 he asserts that homosexuality is one of the behaviors that demonstrate that someone is in active rejection of the life that God wants for them.

Some recent attempts have been made to demonstrate that Paul's concern was not homosexuality in general but abusive practices that were associated with pagan cults. Paul knew nothing, they argue, of consensual and loving homosexuality, and so he would have no problem with mutual homosexual relationships or gay marriage today. It is outside the scope of this work to delve into those arguments, but I will simply state that they are extremely unconvincing and fail to make the case. The truth is that there were consensual and committed forms of homosexuality outside of the pagan temples in Paul's day. It was an accepted practice in many parts of Roman society. [Paul's rejection of homosexuality as legitimate behavior for the self-denying kingdom citizen worked against the prevailing culture and toward a tighter view of sexuality. There simply is no legitimate way that someone can read the Bible at face value and determine that it condones or encourages this choice.]

As a child growing up in a typical American evangelical church, there was no mistaking the fact that homosexuality was a sin. The way it was presented, it was as though it was one of the worst sins imaginable. Homosexual people were often mocked from the pulpit, and the religious culture of the 1970s and 1980s warned churchgoers constantly that these were depraved people who should be avoided. Gay marriage was illegal, and it was not unusual to hear calls to ban homosexual behavior if it wasn't already illegal.

The world has changed drastically in the intervening decades. In most of the world, outside of Africa and the Middle East, not only is homosexuality legal, so is gay marriage. In fact, homosexuality is often celebrated now, and a society's acceptance of homosexuality, gay marriage, and gender fluidity in all forms is now considered a plumb line for how advanced the culture of a nation is. Societies that still discourage or outlaw these types of behaviors are considered "backward," dangerous, and "still living in the dark ages."

Many church denominations and faith traditions around the world have now changed their stance on homosexuality and have not only accepted it as tolerable behavior, they have allowed practicing homosexuals full rights of membership within their churches, and many now accept practicing homosexuals as members of their clergy. And the ranks of churches that have moved to this position seems to be growing each year.

What should be the position of the kingdom of God when it comes to homosexual behavior? What about gay marriage? What about the rights of LGBTQ people for everything from equal protection under the law to more specific issues such as bathrooms that are not gender specific or leaving gender open to choice and self-identification?

These matters related to homosexuality are certainly not the only controversial social issues that Christians will face, but I will utilize them as an example for how we might think through these and similar controversies both now and in the future.

Responses to the Issues

As we examine possible kingdom responses to important political issues in this chapter and the next five, I will group the first three principles of engagement into a section that I will call "Kingdom Mindset." Here we will examine what it means to maintain our allegiance to Jesus and hold tightly to the conviction that the kingdom cannot come under compulsion but must be a choice, while balancing those two principles with the call for kingdom people to stand up for justice even in the present age.

Principles four through six I will label "Kingdom Compassion." In these sections, we will examine what it means to preserve mercy over judgment in everything we do, all the while seeking solidarity with the marginalized and taking care to be angered by the right things.

The final three principles I will call "Kingdom Action." Here we will consider what kingdom weapons might look like in specific situations. We will also examine how we can implement the Christian ethic of self-sacrifice and whether action should primarily be something that we model as an alternative within our own Christian communities or if the situation demands that we seek change and offer assistance to the world outside our own alternative community.

Kingdom Mindset

When deciding how kingdom communities might respond to social issues such as these homosexuality-related topics, we must first consider our loyalty to Jesus and his plan for humanity. Jesus is not interested in what is popular. He certainly wasn't when he was physically on earth and he doesn't seem to have developed much of a taste for that since then. Jesus calls us away from being true to ourselves and toward self-denial. In embracing Christ-focused self-denial we will find the true selves that God intended for us to be. This will usually cause us to be in a countercultural posture. When it comes to these types of issues, homosexuality is not a sin worse than any other sexual expression that goes beyond the confines of God's ideal plan for sex to be reserved for one man and one woman in a covenant marriage with one another. We are all called to deny ourselves in order to follow Jesus. It is that which should be emphasized.

The kingdom is about making the decision to recognize Jesus as King. Our response to these types of social issues is to give the world a picture of fulfillment in Christ through self-denial and offer them a choice. That means that love for Christ will be emphasized rather than being all about demonizing their specific sin. If people don't love Jesus first and want him as their king, then simply bashing them for their behavior will have little effect in the long term. Any responses that we take must be focused on choice, which would seem to steer us away from coercion through legislation.

An important distinction must be made with topics like the ones we are considering in this chapter. Homosexuality and related issues are, we believe, outside of God's plan for humanity. But they are not an injustice against other humans inherently. In other words, without the word of God, homosexuality is not inherently unjust and oppressive toward a group of people who cannot defend themselves. Some might argue that these actions might be harmful to the individual who chooses them, but they are not oppressive to others. As Christians, then, we believe that active homosexuality cannot be accepted into kingdom communities, but we also find little reason to crush it outside the kingdom. That does not mean we condone it, but simply that we respect that people outside the kingdom have the God-given freedom to choose.

There needs to be an important clarification here. When I say that active homosexuality cannot be accepted, I refer to it being endorsed as a good and right behavior for members who have fully chosen to make Jesus King. But this behavior does not remove the dignity of a person. It does not strip them of their humanity. It does not make them any less worthy of respect and love. Any person should be welcomed and feel welcomed into our midst the same as anyone else. Quite frankly, that will take some recalibration on behalf of some of us. Loving people as they are and welcoming them into the life of our fellowship without judgment and allowing them to experience the

Escaping the Beast: Politics, Allegiance, and Kingdom

life of the kingdom before they have fully learned what it might mean for them to deny themselves to follow Jesus is something that many Christians have applied inconsistently. Some people experience this type of welcome. Other people's lifestyles make us uncomfortable, so we give them the talk about the need to repent of their sin up front before they've ever had a chance to know Jesus at all.

Kingdom Compassion

The twentieth century was characterized by judgment toward issues of homosexuality and gender fluidity. The world heard the message loud and clear, and it sounded to them like Christians were trying to force their morals on others. The reason that it sounded that way is because that's exactly what was happening. It was all judgment with little mercy. The homosexual and transgender lifestyle offended most Christians far more than did the shameful, often hateful, and oppressive treatment that these people received.

The treatment that homosexuals and transgender people received is something that the church should have spoken against and did not. We should be ashamed of that. Christians were more angered by the sexual choices of adult non-Christians than they were by the consistent dehumanizing treatment of a segment of the population. We failed to stand up against the oppression, mistreatment, and ridicule they received. We have an opportunity to do that now. We should work for dignity and freedom of choice while at the same time not compromising within the kingdom what Jesus has called people to if they would like to follow him. This has become more complex with the wholesale acceptance of homosexuality by some religious organizations, but it is not impossible.

Kingdom Action

Because the prophetic community is to be the alternative society and does not seek to coerce morals, laws regarding homosexuality do not seem to align with kingdom values. Nations have the right to make laws, and then we must consider whether those laws are humane and provide freedom and protection. A nation may very well decide to restrict marriage as an institution to a man and a woman, while allowing those who choose homosexuality another option outside of marriage. That is not, however, the way that the world is going right now. Marriage has been opened in much of the world to both heterosexual and homosexual unions. That should not be the business of the church. If the nations want to embrace homosexual marriage, it is their choice and does not harm others or inflict injustice upon them. Being a Christian does not mean that we get to police the behaviors of the rest of humanity.

It is very possible for kingdom people to be in situations where they work against a law that lines up with their values within the kingdom. For example, if there is a kingdom community in a country that has outlawed homosexuality and imprisons violators, that is an unjust law. It legislates private behavior of individuals and personal morality. It leads to oppression. Those Christians might seek to have those laws mitigated as unjust. At the same time, the message within the church would be that active homosexuality is not part of God's plan if you wish to make Jesus King. They could affirm those who have unwanted same-sex attraction while holding to the standard that one will not engage in homosexual behavior if they choose to live within the kingdom community.

Some might object that to not oppose gay marriage laws leaves the church in the vulnerable position of possibly being forced to accept, endorse, or perform these types of weddings. Whether that is true or not only becomes an issue if we feel that we must have official state approval and benefits in order to exist. That is an unnecessary assumption, so this should not be a concern that dictates our behavior.

Imagine if Christians decided that it was not their role in society to deny people the right to marry someone of the same sex. If they want to do that in the world, what is that to us in the kingdom? Instead, as a collective, we have sought to bolster laws that prohibited gay marriage and we have embittered millions of people toward the kingdom way. We demonstrated judgment, not love. What was missing significantly from the Christian response in the twentieth century to homosexual and transgender issues was the measure of compassion. We failed to stand up for the dignity and freedom of others.

What has also been missing in large measure is self-sacrifice on our part. When the HIV/AIDS virus began to rampage through homosexual communities in particular, Christians should have been on the front lines of serving and loving victims and seeking a cure. Instead, the Christian community was not at the forefront as a collective. The homosexual and transgender community felt Christian judgment far more than compassion or respect. In the early days of HIV/AIDS, many people avoided those who might have these illnesses because they feared contracting it themselves. Many others even shamefully denounced the outbreak as God's judgment for sinful behavior. It is interesting that God seems to judge in the present age the sins that we don't like, but he always leaves alone the ones that we tend to be fonder of, like greed or gossip.

This would not have been the response of the early church. They often stayed in areas where diseases had broken out when most others scattered, because they wanted to show Christ's love even if it meant they would die. Had this type of self-sacrificial love been shown to the homosexual and transgender communities in the 1980s and 1990s, imagine how different things might be today.

What if the primary Christian response to the homosexual revolution of the last half decade had been to affirm the humanity of all people and to rush into the gay communities that were being ravaged by HIV/AIDS and lovingly care for victims of this deadly disease? What if we had not singled out and demonized homosexuality as the worst of all sins? What if we had acted both corporately and individually to protect all people from mistreatment and stood up for those who were being mistreated? What if we had remained silent politically on the issue of gay marriage, refusing to conflate personal morality with the worth of a person and not imposing our choices onto others? If you want to follow King Jesus, then there is a different way to live. That is true for all of us who must learn to deny ourselves to be the true selves that God created us to be. Paul never called for Rome to ban homosexuality. He simply stated that there was no place for that active behavior within the kingdom life. Those who followed Jesus worked to leave those behaviors behind along with all the other behaviors that don't match up with the kingdom ethos.

The current debate in many states surrounds issues like universal bathrooms. I see no reason for the Christian community to engage publicly in that issue. Our role is to be an alternative society, not to act paternalistically to the empires. We might feel that it is a mistake and the wrong thing to do, but that doesn't mean that we need to change the world to fit our morals. If we are concerned about who might be using a public bathroom, first, let's make sure that we are treating everyone involved with humanizing love. And second, consider the self-sacrificial move of quietly finding another bathroom for our child or whatever the case may be.

I will offer an illustration of what I am arguing here. The halftime show for Super Bowl 54 recently became the hot topic of discussion. It featured well-known singers Shakira and Jennifer Lopez. We watched the game with our small group in our church family. We didn't pay much attention to their halftime performance. Most people left the room during the show and were busy doing other things. Evidently, one of the two ladies utilized a stripper's pole to dance on during the halftime show, although I didn't see that personally. I saw several Christians the next morning posting very snarky comments about their dancing and the amount of clothing they decided to wear. That's a typical modern Christian response. The world should adjust to our morals. They should wear more clothes. They should ban stripper's poles from events like this. If these ladies had decided to make Jesus King and then went and did that, it might be our place to talk to them. But what really happens in situations such as these is that we want to be able to partake in entertainment just like the rest of the world, but we want them to accommodate to our sensitivities so that we can watch in comfort. Do you not see how hypocritically and judgmentally that comes across to others?

But shouldn't our first response be to adapt our behavior to stand out rather than dictate morals to the world? It might feel good to lecture the world about their morality, but it accomplishes little to nothing except confirming for the world that Christians are judgmental, and often hypocritical as well. How has the kingdom been displayed? If we don't like exhibitions like that, then perhaps the Christian community should stop watching the Super Bowl and respectfully make it known that we have chosen that course of action because we don't believe in degrading women (which should be the bigger concern for us). That could be a powerful alternative. If the world wants to degrade women in that way, that is their choice, but we will have no part in it. And I'm not talking about just turning off halftime. What if Christians stopped watching sporting events, movies, and television shows that degraded women without forcing our morality on anyone else?

We must recognize that our instinct has become to police the culture rather than offer it an alternative. We have lost our purpose in many respects and have correspondingly lost most of our effectiveness as salt and light.

There were certainly exceptions, but if we look at the typical evangelical Christian response to the homosexual and transgender communities, what was mostly on display to the world? Was it judgment or mercy? Was it condemnation or sacrificial love? Was it rejection or compassion? I think the collective impression was, without a doubt, the first of each of those options. The prophetic voice isn't just criticism and calling out sin. It is the example of an utterly different way to live. This is what Jesus taught in Matthew 5:38–43. Rather than shouting down the ones who slap others in the face, sue for their coat, or force them to carry their pack, and rather than condemning them as unjust, sacrificial love showed another option. That is the challenge for the kingdom people in the face of complex social issues like these.

Being the Light

Christian theologian Miroslav Volf and coauthor Ryan McAnnally-Linz posit that there are four potential approaches that Christians could take when it comes to the issue of gay marriage:

> Negative/negative.—The church should discourage same-sex unions and call for government to give them no legal standing.
>
> Positive/negative.—The church should bless same-sex unions but call for government to treat same-sex and different-sex unions as different entities.
>
> Negative/positive.—The church should not bless same-sex unions, but government should treat them with equal protection under the law.
>
> Positive/positive.—The church should bless same-sex unions, and governments should treat them with equal protection under the law.[76]

While we can and should argue that things like rape or murder are universally unjust and create victims apart from Christian morality, it is impossible to put same-sex unions or homosexuality in that same category. Since kingdom life cannot and should not be legislated, pushing for laws based primarily or exclusively on kingdom morals should be avoided.

Instead, we are called to show love and compassion and demonstrate the life of the kingdom even to those whose lifestyle we disagree with. Those who live in ways that we believe are not compatible with the kingdom of God already know of that disagreement. They don't need constant judgment. What they need to see is the sacrificial love of the kingdom of God in action. They need to feel welcomed and loved in our gatherings and see our constant and caring presence in their lives and communities.

On the other hand, we don't want to swing the pendulum so far that we accept societal standards for the kingdom and become fuzzy on the biblical standard for sexuality and denial of self that is necessary to truly follow Jesus.

We must keep in mind that Jesus was always accused of hanging around with the wrong kind of people and tacitly approving their behavior by doing so. Could the same be said of us? He always began his interactions with those who were lost with love and compassion. Only after they tasted of the kingdom would he call them to follow him and leave their life of sin. That is a pattern that we should follow.

The Chapter in Review

- The response of the church to issues surrounding LGBTQ people has often been judgmental, inconsistent, intrusive, and unloving.

- To fully follow Jesus, we must all learn to reject the mantra of being true to ourselves and learn to deny ourselves. That is true for all humans.

- Mistreatment and oppression of people for their personal choices should concern and anger us every bit as much as sexual sins that are not part of the idea of the kingdom.

- We should only back laws that align with kingdom values and not laws that take away individual freedoms or choice or impose personal morality values.

- Our first response should be to adjust our behavior if something offends us rather than demanding that others change their behavior.

- We are called to show love and compassion and demonstrate the life of the kingdom even to those whose lifestyle we disagree with.

The Big Idea

❖ Christians should seek fair treatment under the law for all, including LGBTQ people, and consistently show all people the sacrificial love of the kingdom of God.

DISCUSSION QUESTIONS

1. Are you more prone to exhibit mercy or judgment when it comes to LGBTQ people and the legal issues that surround those lifestyles?

2. How do you think Jesus would respond to the LGBTQ community today? Would he denounce their behavior? Would he endorse their behavior? Would he show them life-changing love? How and when might he express a call to deny self?

3. How do you feel about the idea that we might, at times, find ourselves fighting against laws that are unjust but that prohibit behaviors that we do not accept as legitimate for a fully allegiant follower of Jesus?

Chapter 22

Engaging in Public Justice Issues

In the opening paragraph of Dallas Willard's Christian classic, *The Divine Conspiracy,* he tells of a pilot practicing high-speed aerial maneuvers in a jet fighter. She decided that she was ready for a steep climb and turned the controls to start her ascent. But before she knew what had happened, she flew straight into the ground, presumably dying in the ensuing crash. "She was unaware," says Willard, "that she had been flying upside down."[77] He utilizes that as a parable of human existence in which society has no clue to whether they are flying right-side up or upside down.

But it's not just citizens of the nations that can be guilty of that mistake. Christians can be just as prone to it. We can be cruising along, thinking that we are right-side up, turning the controls for a steep ascent, only to discover that we were upside down and are screaming toward the ground at an alarming speed. Willard argues that it is Jesus that helps us turn our direction right-side up, and I agree with him. Jesus' kingdom does allow us to recognize that we have been flying upside down all along, and only through his life can we right our course. But if we only see Jesus as death insurance or offering us escape from the consequences of our sin, we can miss the immensity of the kingdom. And when we do that, we can look at the complex issues of the world, grab the controls to respond and fly straight into the ground.

In this chapter, we will consider three areas of justice and how we might approach them in the public square. They are economic justice, racial justice, and immigration. These are not small issues in today's political climate, so it is vital that we think through each of these from a kingdom perspective.

Kingdom Mindset – Economic Justice

Jesus did not demonize wealth, nor did he baptize poverty as a positive state for human existence. When he proclaimed, "blessed are you who are poor" (Luke 6:20), he wasn't declaring that poverty was something to be sought after or idealized. He goes on to say, "for yours is the kingdom of God." We must not forget that Jesus said, "blessed are the poor in spirit" (Matthew 5:3), and "blessed are you who are poor." Both are true. But both are true in the kingdom of God, not in the empires.

From the nation of Israel to the kingdom, God consistently calls his people to care for the needy as one of their most central values. Ignoring the needy and focusing on self is characteristic of the nations, not of God's people.

Yet many Christians will grow passionate about the biblical calls to economic justice and care for those in need and then attempt to apply that vision to the public square. Should Christians force economic values on secular governments?

Wealth is the enjoyment of all aspects of creation, and Christians should affirm the dignity of each person to flourish in an adequate portion of that. The creation of wealth in a society is a good thing but is something that all should be allowed to participate in and not something reserved for a few. The kingdom of God should consistently call the nations to a view of wealth that recognizes that all people should partake in what Volf and McAnnally-Linz refer to as "created abundance."[78] We should ask the questions, say Volf and McAnnally-Linz, of whether the wealth that a society is creating is true wealth or a trick of the economy; if it is wealth that does not rely on the exploitation of others; if it is environmentally sustainable; and if it is accessible to all members of the society. Economies that judge their wealth creation primarily on the conditions of the richest are economies that are prone to economic inequity and injustice.

[In a world where more than two billion people live on less than $2 per day, there is plenty of opportunity for the kingdom of God to be good news for the poor (Luke 4:18).]

Kingdom Compassion – Economic Justice

Christians are to have compassion and mercy toward those who are poor. Pure and faultless religion, says James, is that which looks after the most vulnerable and prone to poverty in the community (James 1:27). Simply put, the greedy will not inherit the kingdom of God (1 Corinthians 6:10). Over and over, Scripture confirms that our loyalty should be aimed at those in need (Matthew 25:31–46, for example).

The kingdom itself is to be the embodiment of economic justice. It reflects the age to come, which will be without surplus or lack. The response of the Christians to the coming of the kingdom at Pentecost was to sell their surplus so that none among them had need (Acts 2:45). This ethic is continued throughout New Testament instructions. God's people should not show favoritism to the rich (James 2:1–13) and should not simply say to a brother or sister, or anyone else, to "keep warm and well fed" but do nothing to address their lack (James 2:16). They regularly took up collections for brothers and sisters in other parts of the world to address their needs, with the goal of economic equality within the kingdom (2 Corinthians 8:14).

Poverty and greed should elicit righteous anger among God's children. But often, in the modern religious world, it is the poor who are demonized and shunned. The rich and middle class are favored while the poor are neglected on a day-to-day basis, but then all guilt is assuaged because we give a couple of dollars to support a few people in the church who run a ministry to help the poor. Many in the religious community spend more time criticizing the poor and analyzing why they are in that condition than they do addressing the systems of exploitation and greed that contribute to the conditions.

Even a cursory reading of the Scriptures should lead kingdom people to feel solidarity with the poor and a desire to help. But this is where we must take seriously the biblical call that the kingdom is good news for the poor. What happens if we call people into the kingdom and they do not find that good news, or as Paul envisioned it, a community with equality as its hallmark and a place where "the one who gathered much did not have too much, and the one who gathered little did not have too little" (2 Corinthians 8:13–15)?[79] Could we then blame these brothers and sisters for turning to those in the world that will show solidarity with them and seek to help?

Communities or population groups that have been locked into the short end of economic disparity for generations need to experience the fullness of the kingdom of God. Let us not forget that Jesus warned that "the people of this world are more shrewd in dealing with their own kind than are the people of light" (Luke 16:8). He goes on to urge his followers to use their worldly wealth for the benefit of others (v. 9), just as he alerted those who followed him that they should be prepared to utilize their wealth to help those in need (vv. 19–30).

Kingdom Action – Economic Justice

What is often missed is that virtually all New Testament passages on care for the poor focus on creating a new reality within the church community. From Pentecost on, the church was to participate in the kingdom, where there is no surplus and lack. This was good news for the poor who were invited to join in with this new way of living, as most of the church's collections were utilized to provide equity for the poor among them.

Did the church ignore the poor in the society around them? No. They took care of one another first and then, in typical fashion, helped the poor in the nations, offering them samples of the kingdom life. The primary economic activity of the early church was collecting from those among them who had surplus and sharing with those who lacked. They were creating a new economic reality in which the purpose of money was no longer to provide security for oneself, but the value of wealth was now in how much one could give away to provide for others in need.

Above all, the posture of the early church to help the poor was self-sacrificial. They gave to those in need even when they didn't have much, although Jesus made it clear that to follow him would mean that the rich too must be willing to share what they had with those in need (Luke 18:22) and use their worldly wealth to help others (Luke 16:9).

What is often neglected by Christian communities when it comes to economic and other types of justice is being the prophetic kingdom that is living by the values of the coming age. The use of wealth to create a world where there is no surplus and no lack but equity for all does not make sense in the present age. It will not get us ahead in the world. It will not look wise by the world's standards. It's not meant to. Living the life of the future age will always be out of sync. If our life looks too normal or makes sense to the world around us, that should be a warning sign.

Economic justice starts within the kingdom. If Christians do not embrace a radically different approach to wealth within their own community, any calls to care for the poor in the world will fall flat. Most churches today spend most of their resources on buildings and staff salaries with very little of their budget going to those in need within their own church. Often, the little that is given to help the poor goes to those outside the community, which is not in line with the biblical emphasis. The kingdom must first become the economic alternative that it was intended to be. Again, in the kingdom, the value of wealth is in the ability to share it with those in need rather than storing it up to provide security for ourselves.

Once that is addressed, the kingdom can turn to the world and call for policies that encourage economic justice, and reject methods of wealth creation that favor the rich or further exploitation. The challenge here is that Christians should not support public policies that force people to care for the poor. We should strive for it, call for it, even fight for it. But forced wealth distribution is not a reflection of the kingdom. In Wilberforce's quest for justice, he always refused the temptation to visit injustice on even those who gained through injustice of their own. Shockingly, he attempted to treat perpetrators of injustice, namely slave traders, as fairly as possible. This challenges many of us to the core, but is it not a stunning example of Jesus' ethics in Matthew 5:38–48? We are to overcome evil with good (Romans 12:21).

Many well-meaning Christians want to apply Christian morals to care for the poor to the governing authorities and implement care for the poor by force through heavy taxation. This puts the burden on the government to correct economic injustice or imbalance but encourages or allows the church to abdicate its call to be the alternative society and sacrificial people. Why worry about it ourselves when we can get the government to do it for us through taxation?

Author and pastor John Perkins advocates that Christians need to affirm the dignity of people, motivate them, and help them take responsibility for what they can.[80] He argues that the most effective, and I would add, the most sacrificially kingdom-type response, is relocation. Members of the body of Christ who want to be like Jesus should live among the poor. "The Word became flesh," says the Gospel of John, "and made his dwelling among us" (John 1:14). To really impact the lives of people and make change, the most effective way is to dwell among them and take their condition and reality as our own. Perkins notes that Jesus did not commute back and forth to heaven.

Relocating offers a much stronger possibility of bringing reconciliation between those we now live among and God, which fosters further reconciliation between people and breaks down any economic, racial, tribal, or any other barriers that exist. This then leads to redistribution, says Perkins, not to take away from the rich to give to the poor. "Rather, it is when God's people with resources are living in the poor community and are a part of it, applying skills and resources to the problems of that community, thereby allowing a natural redistribution to occur. Redistribution is putting our lives, our skills, our education, and our resources to work to empower people in a community of need."[81]

Being the Light

What this means is that the lion's share of the church's efforts to help the poor should start with creating a new economic reality within the kingdom itself. This will take creativity and new thinking in many respects. What might it look like to have a community where the church helps send the children of poorer members to college, helps pay the debts of new members, helps to purchase necessities for those in need, or provides transportation for those who don't have it? This should go beyond just providing classes on personal financial responsibility. Although those can be beneficial, they often rest on the economic principles of the nations with a little Christian generosity sprinkled in rather than calling for the radical kingdom transformation of the purpose of wealth. Acts 2:45 (and other passages) describes the beginning of a whole new reality that had broken into the world. What would that look like in the twenty-first century? Remember, the economic system that the church should be employing is very different from what will work among the nations. Those are two entirely different realms.

We need to avoid extremes here. There are many modern Christians who engage politically in the realm of economics for their own self-interest. That does not mean that it is wrong to be a wise steward. The approach of many to economics, though, is more about security and trust in wealth than it is aimed at reflecting the kingdom. However, some Christians who have experienced generational poverty their whole lives will need to work toward creating a reasonable legacy of financial stability for their family. Those who have been given a legacy of generational wealth may emphasize the call to give up everything, but that call goes out to them from the pages of Scripture more than it does to the poor. The financially well off are to give as much as they can. The poor are to get to a level of sustainability so that they can, in turn, assist others. Creating a new economic reality in the kingdom means everyone has enough, not that no one has anything.

On the other end, there are Christians who are passionate about advocating for the poor in the world. That is good, but we should be careful about advocating this solely through the government. While I understand why that can be tempting and might be beneficial to re-dress ongoing and historic economic inequities, our first and biggest concern as the prophetic community should not be to try to fix the economic disparity in the world but to create an entirely new model, the one offered in the New Testament. This means that we must ad-dress often the biblical standards concerning greed, materialism, and generosity within the church.

Outside the church, we should call for economic equality and fight against exploitation. There will be different theories among Christians as to what type of economic system among the nations might be best, whether it be capitalism, socialism, etc. While eco-nomic prosperity and abundance that is not at the expense of others is good and something we can encourage, that should never become the focal point for kingdom people.

We should seek to demonstrate sacrificial love to help the poor as our starting point and primary focus of economic engagement. Jesus said that we would always have the poor among us (Matthew 26:11), and that is important to remember. We should stand up for the ex-ploited and poor but never fall into the trap of thinking that we can solve poverty in the realm of empire. There is no solution to poverty in the present age. The kingdom, however, should be a sample of what will one day be. We should serve as an alternative economic option that is radically different from the world, all the while constantly hold-ing the world up to a mirror to show them the ugliness of greed and exploitation and urging them toward generosity and benevolence.

Kingdom Mindset – Racial Justice

The kingdom of God is the gathering of the nations (Isaiah 2:2–4; Matthew 28:19). To fully reflect the call of the king to gather the na-tions necessitates that the kingdom will be diverse ethnically, tribally, and nationally. In God's new creation there are no statuses that bring advantage or superiority (Colossians 3:11; Galatians 3:28). We all have a new identity in Christ as part of God's people and holy nation.

But the world that we live in is full of prejudice, privilege, advan-tage, oppression, racism, tribalism, hate, division, and many other sins that separate us. Even with new identities in Christ, we must all experience how the world treats us individually each day, whether that brings privilege or disadvantage. And although we seek to eradi-cate these forms of prejudice and division in the body of Christ, they don't automatically disappear from our hearts the moment we enter Christ, any more than lust or pride do. Giving our allegiance to Jesus as King demands that we continue to do the hard work of transforming our minds so that we do not conform to the patterns of the world. Sadly, some disciples who still exhibit forms of prejudice or lack of love for others in their thinking believe that they are the least prejudiced of all. Humility and learning from others are keys to overcoming the taint of the world in these areas.

There is still a staggering amount of tribalism, racism, and racial injustice in the world. Denying that is almost as realistic as denying that sin still exists in the human heart. In the United States, racial injustice is not just a problem of the past, although it has improved in many ways. I am married to an amazing African American woman, and I have had a front row seat to many instances of her being discriminated against in the world even though she is a disciple of Jesus. From being denied renting a house that we were promised—that is, until the owner saw my wife—to constant unequal treatment at work, these problems still exist.

That creates a challenge for the disciple. On the one hand, Jesus made it clear that when it comes to personal mistreatment, we are not to retaliate but are to love those who treat us unjustly (Matthew 5:38–48). On the other hand, we are to stand up for the oppressed (Proverbs 31:8–9; Luke 4:18–19). This means, I believe, that we must be aware of and sensitive to racial or tribal injustice in our society, and willing to stand up for equality and fairness and defend the cause of those who are treated unjustly.

Kingdom Compassion – Racial Justice

The story of Jesus encountering a woman about to be stoned for adultery (John 7:53–8:11) has had a controversial past as to where it belongs and its location in the Gospels, but I do believe it to be an authentic account from Jesus' life.[82] When Jesus finds this woman about to be punished, he intervenes. It must have occurred to him that the man who was involved in this act was evidently not being punished. But notice that Jesus steps in to stop the crowds. His mercy triumphs over judgment. This was a pattern in Jesus' life. He sided with the poor, the outcasts, the oppressed, and those labeled as sinners. He was constantly derided for being with them, loving them, and taking up their cause. He called his followers to not judge others but be more concerned about their own sin (Matthew 7:1–5).

A kingdom that is called to gather people from every tribe, language, people group, and nation (Revelation 5:9) must be actively aware of the uneven ground that people are forced to stand on in this world. Injustice and oppression should elicit righteous anger in the hearts of the people of God. We must avoid two extremes, though, that I have seen often in churches in my country. Some disciples have a difficult time letting their racial identity go. The United States has a long and checkered past when it comes to the treatment that people of color have received from the white majority. On one side, there are some white disciples who have trouble letting their racial identity disappear in Christ. They will be the most vocal about race not mattering, but they are often extremely defensive about the notion that there are many advantages that come along with being white in this country, both historically and in the present. They will simply dismiss any notion of there being racial injustice and will fight against any suggestion that the church speak out or act in favor of those who have received the short end of the stick in our society.

On the other side, there are those who become obsessed with racial justice in the present age and lose sight of the purpose and power of the kingdom of God. Fighting for justice in the present age becomes all they practically care about, and they spend little energy imagining how these issues can be addressed by the kingdom to create a new reality. They forget that Paul's primary aim was not to end slavery in Rome but to ensure that it couldn't operate in the kingdom the way it did in the world. If you were a slave, your identity in Christ eliminated that within this new sphere; you were Christ's freed person and vice-versa—the free person was Christ's slave (1 Corinthians 7:21–22). If slaves could gain freedom in the world, they should, but it was not to be their focus. Representing the kingdom to those around them was their focus. In the kingdom, slave and free were called to treat one another as brothers, effectively ending slavery in the prophetic community (Philemon 1:16).

Kingdom Action – Racial Justice

The primary means that Christians have for destroying racial barriers and injustice, as well as similar forms of injustice, is by continuing to create within the kingdom a new way to experience community. That must go beyond just saying that we accept all people or even having racially diverse churches. It means putting in the work to become aware of issues and how people from groups other than our own are treated in the world. It means humbly listening to their accounts of how they are subtly and overtly treated with prejudice in the world. Only then will God's people learn how to truly implement God's victory over prejudice and oppression in the kingdom community. If we insist on not talking about these issues or ignoring them, we will usher these inequities right into the church. We cannot transform and avoid conforming to the world's patterns if we refuse to renew our minds.

Self-sacrifice is the key. Becoming all things to all people (1 Corinthians 9:22) demands that each of us be willing to learn about the culture and experiences of the other and to sacrifice our own preferences and comfort zones to make them feel truly loved and welcomed within the life of the community.

But creating a society of radical inclusion will prove hollow if that is all we do. If I told you that I love dogs and would prove it to you by treating well the two that I have in my house, you might believe me. But if you noticed that each day I walked by several dogs that were being severely abused and kept outside during harsh winter nights and did absolutely nothing, your faith in my love for dogs would rightly falter. To claim that we are the gathering of the nations and love all people but not be willing to stand up for all people when they cry out for relief from oppression and continuing inequity will rightly seem disingenuous to others.

The challenge is to not rush to the weapons of the world and immediately engage in politics to bring about change. There may be times when laws of protection need to be passed. Martin Luther King Jr. once quipped that the law could not make a man love him, but it could keep him from lynching him, and that was pretty important too. William Wilberforce found that to also be true of bringing slavery to an end in England. King utilized Jesus' methods of nonviolence and nonretaliation to bring shame upon the powerful and prejudiced, but he also put pressure on politicians to pass laws to ensure equal rights and protection for black people and other people of color. In those instances, laws were needed. It is possible for the church to engage in the world of politics to bring about protections for others without getting embroiled in partisanship or becoming emotionally attached to one political party. Great discernment must be shown. But complete inaction on behalf of the oppressed is not an option.

Being the Light

The primary means by which the kingdom must dismantle racism, racial inequity, and racial discrimination is by working to create a kingdom community that truly deals with these issues. This must go beyond just being diverse to becoming a group of people that is willing to humbly listen to and learn from one another and accept the word of those who have felt oppression in the present age. We should believe them, work to show them a different reality in the kingdom, and continue to work at it. This should be our biggest concern. God has provided the means to do what the world has not done and cannot do—bring the nations together in one family. We should embrace what God has made available to us and proclaim it to the nations. Churches that do not value this gathering of the nations and do not demonstrate radical diversity in their congregations fail to be the light to the world that they could and should be.

In the story *The Lord of the Rings,* the head-turning element of the fellowship of the ring was that an elf, a hobbit, a human, and a dwarf were traveling together. What were they doing together when there was so much that should keep them apart? They had something bigger than those identities that drew them together. In a world where there is so much that keeps us apart culturally, ethnically, and racially, to see a people who have exalted Christ above their ethnic and cultural identities will stand out. Christ must remain at the center or we risk creating idols of our cultural, ethnic, and racial identities. We can and must be the light in this area.

But we must also be willing to demonstrate our solidarity with those who have been marginalized and treated unjustly. This too must transcend our own ethnic or cultural identity. Telling people that they should be grateful because they're better off now than they used to be is unhelpful if they are still treated far worse than equal. If I punch someone in the face ten times a day, and then cut that down to twice, should I then tell them that they should be grateful for each of the eight times that I no longer punch them? Or might they still take issue over the twice daily smacks in the face?

One area that elicits a great deal of emotional responses is the alleged mistreatment of black Americans and other Americans of color at the hands of some police officers. This seems like a perfect area for the church to step in and speak to both sides. Abuse of power is wrong and should be called out and opposed. Calling for action against police officers that act inappropriately is no more hatred of all police officers than calling for action against teachers who sexually abuse students is hatred toward teachers and the profession of teaching. The church should actively call for fairness and justice from police forces, which should include cultural diversity training and independent investigations of allegations of abuse. On the other hand, demonization of all police officers or behavior demeaning toward them should be spoken against as well. They have a difficult job, and it should be appreciated. [Christians who are partial toward one of these groups should actively work to love and understand on a personal level those whom they feel negatively toward.]

The question arises, then, should Christians be members of police forces? I cannot answer that definitively, but I would encourage anyone in that position to carefully consider the call to be people of the coming age who demonstrate a different reality to the world. How would the potential call to enact violent and potentially deadly force, for example, serve as a sample of the kingdom where there will be no enemies and no violence? We will consider this a bit further in Chapter 25.

These are complex issues, without a doubt. What about a topic like reparations for slavery or the ongoing fight for equal protection under the law? When we look at issues like these, we must carefully apply our principles to stand up for justice wherever we can but with unwavering allegiance to Jesus, a firm refusal to utilize weapons of the world such as vengeance, retribution, coercion, and an instinct to put pain on the perpetrators of injustice, or even on the descendants of those perpetrators. We must also maintain a conviction that the true answer to these issues is the kingdom of God. Legal and political systems will never be able to eradicate racism or truly bring the nations together, though they can provide some protection from oppression. We should support those measures to provide freedom from oppression and freedom to thrive for all as a sample of the true meal of the kingdom of God. Finally, we must keep in mind that many proposals and responses that seem just and seem like good solutions in the present age simply do not meet the standards of demonstrating the life of the age to come.

Kingdom Mindset – Immigration

Nations and empires are concerned with economic interests, cultural preservation, and political integrity. The kingdom of God is worried by none of those, in the same way as it is not rooted in the present age. Allegiance to the way of the King is to imitate him as the one who has created a holy nation out of persons who were once not his people (1 Peter 2:9–10). Volf and McAnnally-Linz point to Jesus as the ultimate "welcomer" to the stranger and argue that Christians are called to imitate Jesus the welcomer.[83] If that is our primary ethic, then kingdom people will approach issues surrounding immigration vastly differently than will the nations.

Volf and McAnnally-Linz take it one step further than just welcoming. They argue cogently that "to respond faithfully to migration today, we have to consider what historical injustices have pushed people from their homes and then discern what justice requires of countries that contributed to those injustices."[84] This is no small task. It requires a great deal of spiritual maturity and the ability to separate oneself from a natural defensiveness about the actions of their own nation, viewing the past and the present as a kingdom citizen that has no favored nation.

Kingdom Compassion – Immigration

Nations must create legitimate limits to immigration. It is their right to administer security and reasonable preservation of their society's way of life, and Christians must respect that. But justice and a welcoming embrace are to be the driving motivations of the kingdom community.

There are two primary types of migration. Pull migration is when a country seeks to attract immigrants, usually the best of the best, to come for greater opportunities and to contribute to their new society. Push immigrants are those who are driven from their land due to violence, the threat of violence, or poverty. At times, crises happen that force many migrants from an area en masse, creating an immigration crisis.

Kingdom Action – Immigration

From the Christian perspective, argue Volf and McAnnally-Linz, immigration should largely focus on push immigrants, those who are refugees from dire situations. The first response is to welcome them.

The second is to call for an examination of how to address the roots of the problems that caused the migration crisis.

Being the Light

The sacrificial approach is not to be overlooked here. It might necessitate that Christians assemble resources to welcome refugees during a crisis or take part in ministries that facilitate their integration into the society once they have arrived. This is mercy over judgment. In some cases, however, the country in which we live might refuse immigrants fleeing from a crisis. How the kingdom responds to that will take discernment. Could it involve leaving the comfortable confines of our country and going to a place where we can serve the needs of those refugees? It might.

Welcoming the refugee is not just something that can happen within our own churches or communities. By definition, refugees will be strangers. We must welcome them into our world or, in some cases, go to places where they have been detained. Let Jesus' words echo in our ears as we consider what attitude and steps to take in response to immigration issues that arise:

> "Then the King will say to those on his right, 'Come, you who are blessed by my Father; take your inheritance, the kingdom prepared for you since the creation of the world. For I was hungry and you gave me something to eat, I was thirsty and you gave me something to drink, I was a stranger and you invited me in, I needed clothes and you clothed me, I was sick and you looked after me, I was in prison and you came to visit me.'
>
> "The King will reply, 'Truly I tell you, whatever you did for one of the least of these brothers and sisters of mine, you did for me.'" (Matthew 25:34–36, 40)

The Chapter in Review

- Christian economic values should not be mandated for others, but we should call for and fight for economic justice.

- This must start with becoming an economic alternative and example of the age to come where there is no surplus or lack.

- Once that new economy is established, we can bring to bear the surplus and sacrifice of our community for those in need outside the kingdom.

- The kingdom must serve as a sample economically of what one day will be.

- The church should and must care about mistreatment or oppression of people on racial grounds.

- We must start by being the example of the gathering of the nations.

- But we must also show solidarity and compassion for those who are oppressed or mistreated, sometimes to the point of advocating for legal protection.

- Christians must carefully separate the rights that nations have to define their borders from the responsibilities that we have to welcome strangers.

The Big Idea

❖ Christians should seek to establish an alternative society in the areas of economics, racial inclusion, and welcoming the stranger and then call the world to justice in these areas.

DISCUSSION QUESTIONS

1. What is the biggest area of needed change when it comes to the church and economics?

2. What is the biggest area of needed change when it comes to the church and racial justice?

3. What is the biggest area of needed change when it comes to the church and immigration?

Chapter 23

Engaging in Sanctity of Life Issues

When an influential Pharisee named Simon invited Jesus to his home for dinner, Jesus was more than happy to go. Simon was well known in his area and well respected. He was a theological leader and likely very influential. He would have been perceived as one of the more spiritual and godly men of his day. He took God very seriously and took the concept of sin seriously. Nothing, after all, offends God more than sin. The Pharisees believed wholeheartedly in the promise of God's coming age. In fact, they taught that it was sin that kept this age from becoming manifest. God would send his Messiah when the people of Israel shaped up morally. If all Israel would refrain from sin for even one day, the Pharisees claimed, God would do all that he promised. It was their love for God that drove them to do their best to help their nation drive out sin and deal with the sinners who were standing in God's way.

Jesus, on the other hand, was a problem. Yes, there were rumors of him being able to do wonders and miracles, and yes, he had the crowds on his side as he mesmerized them with his revolutionary words about God's future age being at hand. But there was one huge question. Why was he always allowing, and maybe even encouraging, sinners to hang around? People were beginning to think he didn't take sin seriously and, worse yet, even approved of sinful behavior.

As they were having dinner, another of those sinners came in. She had heard about Jesus and just wanted to see him. As was the custom of the day, Jesus would have been lying on his side, propped on an elbow with his feet pointing away from the table. When the woman approached with a jar of perfume, she knew just what she would do. But then she was overcome with emotion, weeping to the point that her tears wet Jesus' feet. That would have been embarrassing to Simon and the others at the table. But what she did next was downright scandalous. She revealed her hair and dried his feet with it. Had she no shame? This was extremely inappropriate. She then poured perfume on his feet, doing her best to honor Jesus.

But all Simon could see was her sin. It had to be confronted, and if Jesus were any kind of God-fearing man, especially a great one as the crowds were claiming, he would not approve of this kind of behavior. Simon was full of righteous indignation. This woman was shaming his guests and defaming God. And Jesus did nothing. How would she ever know to do better? How would she ever learn to obey God if she were not confronted and challenged on her sin?

Surprisingly, though, Jesus turns his attention to Simon, not this sinner. He tells a story of a moneylender who forgives one person a very tiny debt and another who forgives a rather substantial debt. Jesus asked pointedly, "Which of them will love him more?" (Luke 7:42). Simon rightly answers that it is the one with the bigger debt forgiven.

Jesus then teaches Simon a lesson that Christians have continued to overlook many times since the words left his lips. This woman understood that she was a sinner and undeserving, and her gratitude and love for Jesus were immense. But Simon didn't see himself as a sinner. He was moral and godly. Of course, he would have said that he was a sinner. But in his heart, he knew that he had left that life behind. He was righteous. He was not one of the active sinners. He was better than this woman. Jesus responds to the woman's humility by telling her that her sin has been forgiven. He never says that to Simon.

Simon's righteousness and defense of all that is holy and good did nothing for this woman. His convictions toward her behavior and his desire to see sin properly dealt with and repented of did nothing for her. What drew her in was the love that Jesus showed. Simon exuded judgment. Jesus exuded mercy. Which one changed this woman's life?

As I read this story in Luke 7:36–50 again, I am cut to the heart. Because far too often in life, I am Simon. I can easily become so devoted to God and to becoming like Jesus that I hate my own sin. I want to be righteous and holy, at least as much as I can be. But then something very ugly happens. I subtly shift from judging sin in my own life to judging others based on their sin. My sin is not good, but their sin? Ugh. I left that life, and I don't want to be dragged down back into the pit. I don't want to give the impression to others that I approve of their behavior. They must be told how much they are disappointing God. They need to know how far they are from him. They must become aware of how much of a sinner they are, because that is the only thing that will help them come to God and partake in his refreshment and renewal. Right?

Without ever intending to or realizing it, Christians can act far more like Simon toward the world than like Jesus. For that reason, I felt that it was an appropriate thought to frame our approach to life issues by focusing on two of the most contentious such issues, abortion and the death penalty.

Kingdom Mindset – Abortion

Since 1973 there has arguably been no other single issue that has pulled followers of Jesus in my country, the United States, into the political fray than has abortion. Most Christians are staunchly pro-life, and it is hard to imagine many things that are more clear-cut than someone taking the life of an unborn child. The unborn are the ultimate example of a defenseless person who is experiencing the worst kind of oppression and unjust treatment. They are completely and utterly innocent and are being murdered in my country and around the world, by the millions. Since abortion became legal in the US in 1973, there have been over 50 million abortions in this country. Worldwide, it has been estimated that more than 56 million abortions take place yearly.[85]

Heartbroken and outraged by this, Christians took action, and understandably so. The Republican Party, more than any other, promised to do something about this atrocity, and this pledge lured evangelical Christians into the world of partisan politics in droves. With such an obvious issue on the platform, many sincere Christians felt they had no choice but to vote for and support politicians who vowed to work against this scourge. Many Christians have become single-issue voters, meaning that the only item that matters to them when it comes time to cast their vote is where a politician stands on abortion.

Since 1973, lawmakers have slugged it out, with the Republican Party fighting to restrict or remove abortion rights, and the Democratic party fighting to preserve them. As part of that fight, many Christians took to the streets. They protested abortion wherever they could. They picketed around abortion clinics, shamed the doctors, and tried to persuade women from going into these abortion clinics, which many evangelicals labeled "death mills."

I understand the instinct. In many respects I agree. Abortion is not just the removal of some unwanted tissue. It is a human life, and there is a sanctity to life that should be respected. I understand that there are complexities that develop when we get into issues like embryonic stem cells and similar topics, but those go beyond the scope of this book. When it comes to the abortion of a growing unborn child, the position of a child of God should be clear.

I am pro-life. Most Christians I know would affirm the same thing. I believe that being loyal to Jesus as King means that we are pro-life. But it must be a consistent pro-life stance. It becomes problematic when Christians scream at the top of their lungs that they are pro-life but then adamantly support the death penalty and war. It is inconsistent to insist that young mothers have their children and are not allowed what seems like a viable option to them to end an unwanted pregnancy, but then turn around in the political arena and support anything that would restrict their access to healthcare and continued help throughout the life of that same child.

I stand with those who believe staunchly that they must oppose abortion. But the methods employed in that opposition have been controversial, to say the least. In a sincere outpouring of zeal, Christians labeled abortion doctors as doctors of death. They did anything they could to shut down abortion clinics and demonize those involved in the industry. They often shamed women who were attempting to have an abortion. And they refused to listen to or negotiate with anyone involved in supporting abortion.

Don't get me wrong. I am not in support of life-ending policies like abortion in any way, shape, or form. But to put it bluntly, the tactics have often looked more like Simon and less like Jesus. That's certainly not true of all Christians, but it has been true of enough that this has become the common perception of Christianity on this issue. We are now perceived as being radical, judgmental, inconsistent, and unloving toward women. Can we always let critics define us? No. But should we listen to what they are saying and see if they have a point? I believe so.

The big question, though, is whether politics was the right weapon to use in this battle. If our allegiance is to Jesus, then I do believe without a doubt that we will want to see as few abortions as possible. But we must be realistic about the fact that we live in a world where it is mostly legal. Keeping in mind that the kingdom way must be a choice, we need to balance that with the necessity of standing up for those who cannot fight for justice for themselves. That was never truer than with the unborn.

Kingdom Compassion – Abortion

In many respects, the typical Christian response to abortion has smacked of judgment over mercy much more than the reverse. Abortion providers have become the embodiment of evil as we quickly forgot that our battle is not against flesh and blood (Ephesians 6:12). In our passion to end this practice, we have often neglected to show compassion and lovingkindness to women who were considering abortions and those who had already had one. I once met a young a lady on a college campus, while inviting students out to a Bible study, who insisted that we wouldn't want her to come because she had had an abortion the previous year. What gave her that impression? She had walked by an abortion clinic months after her own procedure and heard Christian groups there chanting something about baby-killers, and she believed in that moment that she would never be welcomed by anyone with those beliefs.

Yes, Christians should show empathy with the unborn and protect them wherever we can, but never at the expense of loving those who engage in abortions. We are, after all, supposed to love our enemies as well as those whom we protect.

Abortion should incite righteous anger. But anger is the emotion designed by God to provoke us to action against injustice. It doesn't give us license to mistreat those whom we deem unrighteous. It doesn't give us free rein to unleash holy terror on all who disagree with us on important issues. Anger should incite us to unleash love toward everyone involved and wrestle with what that looks like.

Would a woman who has had several abortions and still thinks abortion is a good thing, but who also believes that she needs something else in her life that has been missing, feel permitted to come visit a group of Christians? Would she know that she would be loved and shown understanding? Would an abortion doctor feel that she would be embraced if she visited a church of kingdom citizens? Would a staunch pro-abortion activist ever feel like he could walk into a church if God began to work on his heart and show him his need for the life of the kingdom?

Even more gentleness and compassion need to be present when we address situations in which young women who seek an abortion have been victims of rape and incest. Even though these situations are statistically rare, that doesn't mean we should dismiss them as statistics. We must seek to offer free care and counseling for these young women, even more sensitively than in other situations. We also need to be extremely careful with our rhetoric so that we do not make these victims of terrible situations feel demonized or further victimized if they do choose an abortion. Christians can work fervently toward promoting life while not painting those who get an abortion and need mercy the most, as evil or having committed an unforgiveable sin.

Kingdom Action – Abortion

"For though we live in the world, we do not wage war as the world does. The weapons we fight with are not the weapons of the world. On the contrary, they have the divine power to demolish strongholds" (2 Corinthians 10:3–4). Here's what we often miss about this important passage: if the weapons of the kingdom have the power to demolish strongholds, then the implication is that the weapons of the world do not. The world is powerless to change the human heart through the means of political power, warfare, coercion, or any other of the usual methods. The weapons of the world may seem enticing, but they will never bring about the big and lasting changes.

That is not to say that there is never a time and place where it becomes necessary to step in and encourage the passage of laws or the establishment of measures to defend the helpless and oppressed in the present age, but those can never become our primary goal and hope.

In the fight against abortion, the element that has been most often neglected is the kingdom weapon of self-sacrifice. In Chapter 20, I briefly described the Roman practice of exposure for unwanted infants. The early church did not respond by demanding legal change. At great expense and risk to themselves, they took as many of these children in as they could.

What if that was the kind of response to abortion the kingdom was most known for? I agree that I would love to see a world where abortion was not a reality, but that wishful thinking does next to nothing for a young girl who suddenly feels trapped by a pregnancy that she doesn't feel equipped to handle. Yes, I could chide her that her real choice took place when she decided to have sex, and it would be true. But would that be merciful or helpful in that moment?

What if we spent the bulk of our energy setting up programs that offered to pay the expenses of women who were pregnant until they gave birth and then gave them the option of keeping the baby and getting more support to help with that, or they could give the baby up for adoption and we would be willing to take in that baby? What might that demand of us? Would that open the door for those who might take advantage of the situation? Possibly. But would the benefits not be worth being taken advantage of by a few? There are programs like this, but not enough.

Supporting politicians and political parties that do not uphold the sanctity of life is a position that is, in my opinion, untenable for a follower of Jesus. That includes abortion but would also apply to other issues involving life. As kingdom citizens, we would do well to consider positions that support whole life rather than just reducing our concern to pro-life in the abortion debate.

Being the Light

How can we be light in the face of such a contentious and divisive issue? Remaining silent is not the answer. Relativizing the importance of abortion and yoking together with politicians that support abortion is not the answer. Utilizing worldly weapons of intimidation, violence, or raw political power may seem attractive but cannot be the way.

Any response to abortion must start with and continue to be characterized by sacrificial love and mercy. Those are the things that change people's hearts and win converts. Judgment and law simply don't yield the results that we would want. I have alluded to this before, but the early church was often criticized by opponents for their ridiculous love for others. They were not criticized for their judgmentalism or lack of mercy. It was their love and mercy that drew so many people to them. They didn't have to go advertise or engage in blitz evangelism. Their radically different lives spoke volumes.

Should we get involved in abortion issues on the political front? I don't think it helps much. Keith Giles, in *Jesus Untangled,* says that "the truth is, the abortion issue is the 'shiny red button' that the Republican Party loves to hold out to us as a way to manipulate us to vote for their candidate. But once that person is elected, the issue of abortion is never a priority for that politician."[86] Does that mean we should avoid rallies and marches? Like many of the questions that will arise around these matters, I don't think there is a definitive answer. But the question must be asked, does that activity truly demonstrate the light of the kingdom or is it employing tactics of the world?

In his book *One Nation Under God: How Corporate America Invented Christian America,* historian Kevin Kruse describes how wealthy businessmen, beginning in the 1950s, worked to link together conservative Christianity, Republican politics, and libertarian economics to create a powerful new force with all three seeing "Big Government" as their common enemy. This was the movement that spawned novel sentiments like "In God We Trust" (adopted as the national motto in 1956) and "One nation under God" (inserted into the Pledge of Allegiance in 1954).

Giles describes how this propaganda worked on him and he grew to be a diehard Republican, believing that it was his duty as a Christian to engage politically and vote for such a God-focused agenda. But he eventually came to realize that it was all a lie. Pure and simple manipulation. "We are all victims" he writes, "of a well-funded, decades-long campaign to twist our faith into an easy-to-control voting bloc. This is why it is so imperative for us to open our eyes, throw off the chains and return to Jesus—and Jesus alone—as our Lord and King."[87]

I was kept in line for a long time on the strength of the argument that to do anything other than vote for a pro-life candidate was to promote murder. Giles speaks to that, pointing out that "if this is true, then those who vote for a pro-war candidate are also guilty of bloodshed when innocent women and children are bombed in a foreign land. I can't think of a better reason why Christians should not vote at all."[88]

I personally have great sympathies for Giles' position here. But there is a different perspective, of course.

My good friend and biblical teacher, James Becknell, says that the nonvoting perspective is "often a luxury that people from the majority culture tend to promote." We are mostly safe, well fed, and have no major concerns for our personal security, so it is easy to say that we will refrain from voting because we don't want to be yoked with non-kingdom entities. But for the poor and marginalized, he argues, there are other reasons to vote or not vote. Poor, minority, and marginalized communities are often "the primary and immediate victims of powermongers, tyrants, and those promoting extreme forms of capitalism once they are in power." Voting, says James, can be a faithful activity in some circumstances.

My friend makes a good point. My instinct on this is, I believe, kingdom focused but it is also colored by the privileged status I was born into. It's easy to say, "It's your duty to vote, so you must." It's easy to say, "Christians shouldn't vote." But what is needed is for people to carefully think through these positions from a kingdom perspective and come to decisions based on that alone (perhaps utilizing the principles I proposed in Chapter 20). It is good to ask questions about if, when, and how we should vote, and to realize that as situations shift, so might the answers.

Abortions have been reduced as judges have been appointed and laws passed by the pro-life political pressure, but at what cost? Supporting legislation for a specific cause is a different thing from getting married to a political party. And while one party may support a kingdom cause, in this case the Republican Party of the United States, becoming yoked together with everything that party stands for is a steep price to pay. We should not, in my opinion, be yoked with any political party or candidate in any country or context. Any political group or party will never and cannot ever truly represent kingdom people, because they are steeped in the values of the present age. There will always be a disconnect. When the kingdom is firmly connected with a partisan political group, the kingdom will always lose its identity. Every. Single. Time.

I think it is important not to completely demonize the Republican Party on the abortion issue. While I do believe it was a mistake for many Christians to accept the Republican platform hook, line, and sinker based on their position for abortion, I will concede that there are many who are sincere on this issue and have done much to combat this evil. When we can align with them on this issue, I would encourage that, but without giving full allegiance to one political party. I would also add that the Democratic Party has consistently taken a position in favor of protecting abortion, so they certainly should not escape criticism here. Please don't mistake the amount of ink given to the Republican position as favoring one ideology over the other.

An Historical Precedent

There is a precedent for us to look at. Estimates are that at least 20 percent of pregnancies ended in abortion during the period from 1840 to 1880. Nineteenth-century writer Edmund Hale cited evidence that up to two-thirds of pregnancies during that period ended in abortion. But by 1910, "that abortion rate had been cut in half by a movement of Christians who provided women with positive alternatives to abortion."[89] Christians focused on helping those in poor communities, especially young pregnant women and prostitutes. They helped them carry their children until birth and then helped them find adoptive homes or assisted them in substantial ways if they decided to raise the babies themselves. Their love and insistence on finding alternatives to abortion worked and eventually inspired laws to be changed to restrict abortions. But these were laws that people wanted because their hearts had been changed. They weren't partisan laws, nor were these Christians beholden to any one party. When these efforts faded, so did the desire to keep such laws. These women were lovingly engaged on one issue utilizing kingdom methods, and great change was brought about. This serves as a powerful model for us who face similar issues today.

Kingdom Mindset – Death Penalty

There are many other issues involving the sanctity of life, but as I seek to offer only a few examples in this portion of the book as a means of guiding future thought and discussion, I will focus the rest of the chapter on the death penalty.

It is perhaps ironic that those who are most adamant about speaking out in favor of life on the abortion issue are often most supportive of the death penalty for convicted criminals. The argument is that one group is innocent and the other is not. We must agree that according to Romans 13, the nations have the authority to enact the death penalty if they so choose.

However, the death penalty is fraught with difficulty in modern society. Despite one of the main arguments for capital punishment being that it is a powerful deterrent to future crime, "scientists agree, by an overwhelming majority, that the death penalty has no deterrent effect."[90] Additionally, there are multiple studies that reveal that approximately one in twenty-five people sentenced to death in the United States are later shown to be innocent, some after they have been executed.

For kingdom citizens, however, the death penalty is not our realm. Taking life is not a kingdom value and is problematic if we lustily support it in any form. We can concede that governing authorities have been given the sword by God to use if they must. Our role should not be to support or encourage that but to call for it to be used justly and sparingly.

Kingdom Compassion – Death Penalty

Jesus was crystal clear about loving enemies. The world might tell us that we should love our neighbor and hate our enemies, but if we are going to be children of our Father in heaven and imitate him, then we will love even our enemies (Matthew 5:43–46). God is perfect or complete, says Jesus, in loving even the unrighteous, and so too we should embrace that kind of completeness (vv. 47–48). In other words, there should be no one who falls outside the grip of our loving mercy.

That doesn't mean we can be unwise and advocate for murderers and violent criminals to be forgiven and let run free. But I do think it means that we seek for them to be treated justly and with dignity regardless of what they have done and for them to be provided the means whereby they might seek repentance and redemption one day. If they are killed, that opportunity is lost. And the reasonable possibility that one in twenty-five may be innocent should give us great pause.

There is a way to show compassion and kindness to victims of crime but also demonstrate empathy toward perpetrators. Should we be angry about violent crimes? Of course. But we should also be angry at the right thing, which is sin and the powers of evil behind it. We can remain realistic and savvy while insisting on showing empathy and kindness toward prisoners and guilty criminals.

[No matter how we might want to spin it, it is virtually impossible for kingdom people not to look hypocritical when we scream for life at abortion rallies and then rail for death in any other setting.]It's just not consistent with the reflection of the values of the coming age. There are certain realities that we need to concede to in this period of overlap between the present age and the age to come, but advocating for death is not one of them.

Kingdom Action – Death Penalty

Death is simply not a weapon available to kingdom citizens. Little more should need to be said. Certainly, advocating for the death penalty or the death of enemies in any context is not the sacrificial way of Christ, who could have easily killed all his enemies. Sacrifice may entail supporting criminals in prison even though we may feel that they have forfeited the right to life due to their actions. There have been many men and women, though, who have turned to the kingdom because of the loving and sacrificial actions of Christians in forgiving them for what they have done or by ministering to them while in jail. The death penalty takes away any of those possibilities.

Becoming an advocate for the humane and kind treatment of prisoners and for doing away with the death penalty does not equate to being "soft on crime," approving of the actions of the perpetrators, or dishonoring victims. It is to take seriously the reminder of Jesus that those who show kindness to the prisoner do so to him (Matthew 25:36).

Being the Light

True justice belongs to God's future age. We would do well to remember that. The idea of garnering justice in the present age is illusory at best. That does not mean that we simply jettison any notion of justice and ignore it. One of the marks of the kingdom, one of the samples that we give and fight for, is justice for the weak, marginalized, and oppressed.[Temporary justice is still a good thing, but it is not the ultimate good. The kingdom of God points to the ultimate good, which is God's restored creation.]

We never want to be in the position of excusing crime but should be the display of mercy and God's grace at every possible opportunity. Therefore, it would seem that the kingdom community would err on the side of life and not support turning to or expanding the death penalty.

When it comes to prisoners, many Christians have worked tirelessly to show them mercy, kindness, and the love of God. But far too many of us have shamefully been willing to let them be put out of sight and out of mind, and to embrace vengeance against the "guilty" more than anything else. Many Christian churches are more known for their stance of being "tough on crime" than anything else. Stances that support victims are wonderful, but we must also show love toward perpetrators and not just victims. This should include an interest in addressing societal issues in support of school-to-prison pipelines, removing inequities in prison sentences that mean people of color are statistically given longer sentences for equal crimes, and rectifying laws and programs that target crime in lower-income neighborhoods in comparison to the same crimes committed in more affluent areas.

We must also be realistic that in many countries, and certainly in the United States, people of color and poor people are much more likely to be charged with crimes that others commit at the same rates; are more likely to be imprisoned for those crimes at much higher rates; and receive significantly higher sentence times for similar crimes. Surely the gospel that was good news for the prisoner and the oppressed includes working for justice in these areas (Luke 4:18).

Might the role of the prophetic community be to allow the state to do their work of limiting evil through the use of force, all the while holding them to justice and fairness, but then have a concurrent role of showing lovingkindness to the prisoner? Thus, a balance is struck that neither endangers public safety nor ignores the call to show solidarity with and love to the people who need it most.

The Chapter in Review

- When engaging with the world on any issues, we must always ensure that we are starting with mercy rather than judgment.

- Christians are right to oppose life-ending actions like abortion but must fight using kingdom weapons.

- We must show empathy for and protect the unborn, but never at the expense of loving those who engage in or believe in abortions. We must protect the innocent but still find a way to love our "enemies."

- Great change was made in the nineteenth century to reduce abortions and turn the hearts of the people against abortion through kingdom methods rather than political might.

- Death is not the realm of the kingdom, especially the death penalty. That is the realm of the nations.

- Christians should show compassion and stand up for both victims and perpetrators. Thus, we might advocate for just laws, but also for humane prison conditions and fair sentencing practices.

The Big Idea

- ❖ Christians should seek to be truly pro-life consistently and in all areas.

DISCUSSION QUESTIONS

1. How has the Christian response to abortion in the last fifty years often not demonstrated the kingdom to the world?

2. How might we fight for the innocent while still showing love and mercy to those we deem as perpetrators?

3. Are there any situations where Christians might advocate for death and still be holding to kingdom principles?

Chapter 24

Engaging in Environmental Issues

Do we look forward to a new heaven and earth or a renewed heaven and earth? You may have never thought about the difference, but there is one and it does matter.

When we enter Christ, we are renewed. The old has passed away, says Paul in 2 Corinthians 5:17, and the new has come. There are two main Greek words for "new." Paul could have used *neo*, which refers to something that is new in time that has not previously existed. Or he could have used *kainos,* which describes something that has new qualities or has been renewed. In this passage, Paul used *kainos.*

This is the same word that Peter uses in 2 Peter 3:13 when he speaks of looking forward to the return of the Lord and the new heaven and new earth. It is also the word that John uses in Revelation when he anticipates the coming of the new heaven and new earth (Revelation 21:1) and the time when God makes everything new (v. 5).

The apostles are not referring to the earth being destroyed and thrown away and then something entirely new taking its place. Nor do they teach that one day the earth will be destroyed and only a heavenly realm will remain. Rather, they look to the time when heaven and earth will be renewed and brought together as one (Ephesians 1:10).

Jesus alluded to this period of renewal when the entire creation will be restored to an Edenic state when he spoke of the time of "the renewal of all things" (Matthew 19:28). There, he used the term *paliggenesia,* which means regeneration, or quite literally, the return to the genesis or beginning state. Peter refers to this same reality for the future of the cosmos, preaching that "heaven must receive him until the time comes for God to restore everything, as he promised long ago" (Acts 3:21).

One of my main premises of this book is that as kingdom people, we have been called to demonstrate to the world what the age to come will look like. Our main aims are not rooted in this present age, and that means that often our behavior will make no sense or will even look crazy or dangerous to those who do not grasp that we no longer live for ourselves.

Once we embrace that, it changes everything. No longer do we have to try to water down or contextualize Jesus' teachings in places like the Sermon on the Mount. No longer do we have to futilely attempt to mash together Paul's directives in Romans 12 with those in Romans 13, as though the behaviors and strategies apply equally to kingdom people rather than describing our realm (Romans 12, 13:8–10) and our interactions with the realm of the empires (Romans 13:1–7).

This vocation we have as followers of Jesus will become particularly relevant when it comes to consideration of how we might approach issues that are related to our environment. It hasn't always been this way, but the environment and our treatment of the planet has become one of the most contentious and passion-inducing topics in all of politics and in our world in general. This is no longer a subject that we can ignore or not think through well. For many people, especially younger people, the state of the climate and of our environment are now the primary topics of concern in the world today.

The challenge is that these issues are incredibly complex. Chances are very high that as you read this book right now, you are not a climate scientist or an expert on air pollution, water pollution, or any of the other areas that concern the environment and issues like climate change.

In Alexander Pope's epic poem, "An Essay on Criticism," he penned the now-famous line, "A little learning is a dangerous thing." Indeed it is. And we live in a world that is full of so-called experts and information that is readily accessible to anyone with an internet connection. Suddenly, everyone thinks they are an expert on almost any topic because they have read a few internet articles or watched a couple of convincing videos on YouTube. The access to information that is not peer reviewed or subject to challenge by those with knowledge in the area under discussion is staggering.

The result is a growing number of people, for example, who are convinced that the earth is flat, even though no experts in the field who can fully understand the topic hold to that position or think it is anything other than laughable. There is a small army of people who have become quite hostile toward vaccinations, despite the fact that every reliable study has shown that there is no observable link between vaccines and certain conditions such as autism, and the vast majority of medical experts confirm that there is no link.

Experts certainly make mistakes. There is no doubt about that. Sometimes the consensus of science is wrong. But we live in an era when experts in a field are easily dismissed as having an agenda or being in the pocket of some grand conspiratorial puppeteers, handing out money to anyone who will dance to their tune. We dismiss those who have spent their whole lives learning about a topic, and embrace as our gurus hobbyists who do not have a full grasp of the complex issues of which they speak.

This same phenomenon may be happening when it comes to the issue of climate change. Let me be honest here. I don't know anything about how to scientifically prove whether the earth is flat or a globe. But I have studied the issue and find no rational reason to reject all the experts in that field. I don't know the first thing about vaccines, but I have looked into it enough to believe that there is no reasonable justification to reject the major scientific studies that show no link, as well as the overwhelming position of the experts in the field. And I don't know much of anything about climate science. It's a safe bet to say that you don't either. That leaves us in a bind.

Who should we believe on the subject of climate change? The majority of experts say it is happening and a potential threat, although the common claim that 97 percent of scientists agree on that is fairly easy to research and discover to be an exaggerated claim.[91] Some reputable scientists don't believe it is a threat. Interestingly, several new studies have demonstrated that what we believe about climate change is not related to our level of education, our religion, or any similar factors. Beliefs about climate change are most directly related to one's political position. What they are largely not rooted in, for most of us, is deep scientific understanding of the issues at play.

Adding to the difficulty in wading through much of the hysteria regarding climate change is that much of the concern for the future is based on computer models and the worst-case scenarios of what might happen if all of the assumptions plugged into the computers about the present are correct. Yet predictive models from ten years ago or twenty years ago have proven to be inflated. That doesn't mean there is not a problem now or that there will not be one, but usually the consequences predicted are the worst of worse-case scenarios.

Where the environment is concerned, there are the ongoing issues of pollution and creation care, and then there is the relatively recent concern over global climate change that if not addressed, could cause irreversible cataclysms and change life as we know it for the worse. [There are three general Christian responses to climate change.] There are those who are deeply concerned about it and feel that human-caused climate change is one of the most important, if not the most important, political issues at hand today. They feel that to do anything other than take urgent action is to invite global disaster.

Then there are those who do not believe climate change is an issue or believe that it is a natural phenomenon. They are convinced that it is an invention of powerful political forces that wish to control governments and economies around the world by ringing a false alarm about climate change events that have taken place naturally throughout the history of the world. They believe that it is a liberal plot and needs to be opposed or it will destroy freedom and the economies of developed nations around the world.

Finally, there are those who don't think much about it and would prefer not to get involved either way.

One final word before we move on. I believe that all kingdom citizens should be passionately opposed to being involved with the taking of life, and in Chapter 23, I advanced the concept that Christians have often been used by one political party by wooing them in on the abortion issue. I think the same is true for many when it comes to the Democratic Party on the issue of environmentalism. There are many who are sincere on this topic. But there are also forces that have seized on this issue to advance their own power and greed and shown a great deal of hypocrisy in their own lives, mandating that others live in environmentally responsible ways while failing to do so themselves. Many sincere Christians have been lured into political partisanship because of their passion for this issue. As much caution is necessary here as I advocated for in Chapter 23.

How can we possibly respond in a way that maintains the integrity of the kingdom, retains allegiance to our King, and addresses the issues of the world regarding climate change and environmental care in a way that is relevant to the world to whom we are called to minister and demonstrate God's rule?

Kingdom Mindset

There are three basic views of nature. Anthropocentrism views the world in terms of how it can provide for human needs. The role of the government is to remove unnecessary regulation and allow for economic prosperity as much as possible. Human dominion over nature is virtually unlimited, and it can be used for pleasure and profit. Traditionally, this view has also held to the understanding that God would one day destroy the earth, so there is little need to be overly concerned about its long-term outlook.

Biocentrism says that nature itself is the center and biggest priority, and human needs are just another component in a complex web. Because nature is the chief priority and human needs or continued human thriving are secondary to the balance of nature, nature must take precedence.

Theocentrism recognizes God at the center of creation. Humans have been entrusted with specific responsibilities and obligations that are unique to their created vocation as image bearers of God. Human dominion over creation remains under God's authority. In this view, God has created his good world and though it currently is not in its ideal state, God will one day restore and renew it to its intended glory.

I contend that the theocentric view is the biblical view. Humans are the pinnacle of God's creation but have been given the role to be stewards and care for it. As people who are being renewed in God's image (Colossians 3:10), we certainly are to take part in care for all aspects of God's creation. That has been one of the primary aspects of image bearers since the very beginning (Genesis 1:28).

Many well-meaning people who hold to the biocentric view work passionately toward green initiatives that will restore and heal what is broken on the planet to bring about a harmony with nature. It can become tempting to mock that passion because quite often, nature itself becomes a deity for those people. But we should not be so quick to dismiss their concerns. God has promised to restore and renew the earth to a perfect condition, which means he is "green" as well. Rather than dismissing the instincts of these people, they can be shown a God who does love and care for his creation, even more than they do.

Most scientists do agree that consumptive human behavior has played at least some part in current negative climate trends. According to the World Wildlife Fund, humanity has been the chief factor in wiping out approximately 60 percent of species of mammals, birds, fish, and reptiles since 1970, and this annihilation, if left unchecked, could have grave consequences for human life.[92]

It is not good policy to simply dismiss any reports on the state of the environment as "fake news" or something "bought and paid for" by some shadowy conspiracy group. That is not to suggest that we should sound the alarm at the direst of predictions either. For the kingdom community, this is not merely a political or economic issue. We have an obligation as God's people to carefully steward his creation and point the way forward to his promised renewal of all things. Our behavior now should serve as the anticipation of that time, which means that we very much need to be concerned about the environment and should be wary of approaches that solely focus on economic utilitarianism.

In complex situations, or when we are unsure of what the right answer is, shouldn't God's people err on the side of care for the environment, as that is one of our chief roles in God's creation? We certainly do not want to move into the realm of worshiping the creation. Nor do we want to support extreme environmental measures that stifle the ability for humans to survive or thrive. But care for creation we must.

We must also recognize that it is very seductive to react so strongly against excesses in pro-environmentalist positions that we drift into positions that are so pro-economy and short-term utilitarian that, for all intents and purposes, we become antienvironment and in favor of whatever makes life more convenient, comfortable, and profitable at the moment.

Kingdom Compassion

If we are to remain focused on our purpose of demonstrating the life of the kingdom and the new creation, then caring for God's creation and being good stewards of that will be one of our highest priorities.

Creation is merited by God as being good without the mediating presence of humans (Genesis 1:10, 12, 18, 21, 25), which means that it is valuable in itself and not strictly for how it can be utilized by humans. We have a role, then, in doing what we can to preserve the goodness of creation both for our good and the good of creation itself. We have been given dominion but not sovereignty over God's good creation as agents that "work it and take care of it" (Genesis 2:15), or in other words, both utilize it and preserve it carefully.

Human thriving is a good thing that we should care about, but it cannot come at the expense of the environment. A delicate balance must be struck. Volf and McAnnally-Linz rightly point out that "since the nonhuman creation is valuable in its own right, prudent self-interest cannot be the main reason to care for the planet. True extreme environmental degradation threatens the well-being and survival of humanity." They continue, asserting that "there *are* good prudential reasons to adopt creation-friendly environmental policies and sustainable ways of life.... We have a responsibility to preserve the world that we have received, regardless of whether that is necessary for human survival."[93]

This level of solidarity with the creation not only fulfills our proper role as stewards but points ahead to God's ultimate restoration of the entire creation.

Kingdom Action

Far too many Christians base their philosophy on the environment on their political or economic interests rather than rooting them in God's role for humanity and its relationship to his creation, which matters to him a great deal. Or they take no active interest in the environment at all. The website www.footprintcalculator.org calculates how many planets would be needed to sustain life if everyone on earth used resources at the same rate that you do. I recently went to the site and was dismayed to learn that if everyone lived like I do we would need seven planets. That is convicting. Who am I and how entitled must I be to think that I have the right to use up that amount of resources?

Christians should recognize that the creation is groaning and awaiting liberation from the curse under which it now suffers as a result of human behavior (Romans 8:20–24). We have the firstfruits of the Spirit and can anticipate that liberation both in our lives and in how we treat the creation.

There are challenges when considering what action Christians can or should take when it comes to responsible creation care.

The first is that living a life that reduces consumption and contributions to pollution of the planet is difficult if you live in a consumptive country like the United States. Dismissing the amount of resources we use personally because it is normal in our country is not good enough. We should have people in each church, ideally, who develop an expertise in how to guide us as a body and also as individuals to reduce our consumption and waste.

The second is that the case I have made in this book is for kingdom citizens to trend toward utilizing kingdom weapons, which do not rely on forcing individuals to act in a certain way, and to be judicious in supporting laws that restrict or mandate behavior. But in this case, if there is an impending crisis, then failing to mandate radical change now will do nothing to resolve the issue.

The third is finding the balance between creation care and supporting the ability for humanity to thrive. Those who value the environment are often pitted against those on the opposite end of the spectrum, who emphasize economic freedom and opportunity and consuming resources toward that end. Christians need to carefully find the balance, not simply dismissing the majority of scientists who warn of impending disaster, but also avoid extreme alarmism.

The fourth is that most of us simply do not understand the scientific debate on climate change. Many have formed opinions about it that are based more on which news sources they have decided to distrust or trust than on their ability to discern what is causing the current problems, how bad they are, and what the impact will be in the future.

Given these challenges, we will arrive at different conclusions within the body of Christ, but again, I believe that we should err toward creation care. Taking action in favor of protecting the environment may be necessary and limit some economic freedom, but the possible consequences of not taking action if the majority of scientists are correct are far worse.

Volf and McAnnally-Linz suggest five reasonable steps forward for Christians:

- We must make good use of the resources of creation and avoid wastefulness and excess consumption.

- We must live simply and contentedly and reject the trend toward materialism and the pressure to constantly buy more and newer goods.

- We must be faithful in our care for the rest of creation regardless of whether our actions will make a significant impact.

- We should encourage governments to encourage individuals and businesses to adopt environmentally friendly practices and prohibit behaviors that seriously damage creation.

- We should encourage countries to coordinate a just distribution of the economic costs that address climate change and other major global environmental problems.

Being the Light

At the very least, Christians can be respectful in our tone and language to those who are radical in their desire to care for creation. Some virtually worship the planet or "Mother Nature" as a divine entity in a way that we think distorts their priorities and values. That does not mean that we need to be dismissive or act in a derogatory manner toward them. Our behavior should start with self-sacrifice as we reduce our own waste and consumption. We can then continue in respect to listen to the concerns that people have and model responsible creation care whenever and wherever we can.

The Chapter in Review

- The priority for kingdom people is to demonstrate the life of the coming age.

- Issues surrounding a topic like climate change are multifaceted, and few of us understand the complexity of the science behind it, so we must wisely choose whom we are to believe.

- Christians want to support the ability for people to thrive economically and in all manners, but should err on the side of caring for the creation if there is a question.

- We have a responsibility to preserve and care for the world.

- Churches should have members who develop an expertise to guide the body in reducing consumption and waste.

The Big Idea

- ❖ Kingdom communities need to find the balance between creation care and supporting the ability for humanity to thrive.

DISCUSSION QUESTIONS

1. Have you ever found yourself becoming hostile or verbally abusive toward people with whom you disagree on political topics?

2. Use the footprint calculator to determine the resources you consume. What are your thoughts about your rating?

3. How can the Christian community utilize concerns that people have over global climate change to be a light for the kingdom?

Chapter 25

Engaging in Enforcement Issues

On July 6, 2016, thirty-two-year-old Philando Castile, a long-time employee of the St. Paul School District, was pulled over by a police officer not more than three miles from my home and on the same street that my then twenty-one-year-old son drove down every day to go to work. Accompanying Castile in the vehicle were his girlfriend and their four-year-old daughter. They were returning from grocery shopping.

Officer Jeronimo Yanez, whose dashcam was recording the incident, radioed in that he was going to pull Castile's car over and check his ID because his "wide-set nose" fit the description of a robbery suspect in the area. Once he had pulled them over, Yanez asked Castile for his license and registration. While reaching for his identification, Philando did what the law required of him, informing the officer that he had a legally registered firearm in the car. Officer Yanez began to shout at Castile, telling him, "Don't reach for it, then," with Castile responding that "I'm, I, I was reaching for…" Yanez shouted again, "Don't pull it out," and Castile replied with, "I'm not pulling it out." His girlfriend said, "He's not…" Yanez repeated, "Don't pull it out" and then shot at Philando in close range seven times, five of those striking him, two piercing his heart. Then Philando's girlfriend uttered, "You just killed my boyfriend." Philando forced out, "I wasn't reaching…" She confirmed his last words, "He wasn't reaching…"[94]

This incident hit home for many people around the United States and the world that had grown weary of increasing militarization of the police and a perceived penchant for shooting first and asking questions later, especially when it comes to young men of color. Before grief and outrage could really set in around the country, another tragedy struck.

Former Afghan War army vet Micah Johnson, enraged over police shootings of black men, sought revenge. On July 7, 2016 he fired on a group of police officers in Dallas, Texas, wounding nine and taking the lives of five police officers, Lorne Ahrens, Michael Krol, Michael Smith, Brent Thompson, and Patricio Zamarripa. Johnson stated that he wanted to kill white people, especially white police officers. After the shooting, Johnson fled into a building on the campus of El Centro College, and following a three-hour standoff was killed by police with a bomb attached to a remote-control bomb disposal unit.[95]

The reaction to this horrific event was swift by many around the country, especially those who feel that police are heroic defenders of the public good who are much maligned and misrepresented as targeting certain groups of people.

The divide between those two perspectives is often deep, real, and emotional. The perception is that the two camps of those who are critical of police tactics and inappropriate police action and those who wholeheartedly support the police are divided along racial lines. While there may be some statistical truth in that, the divide is often more cultural and political than strictly racial. Those from cultural backgrounds that experienced governing and policing forces that terrorized black people, for example, still tend to fear and mistrust the police. Those from cultural and economic backgrounds that experienced the police as a positive and consistently safe force for good in their lives tend to support the police when any controversial issue breaks into the news. There is also truth in the assertion that the politically conservative tend to take the side of the authorities, while those who are politically liberal tend to take the side of the marginalized and those without power.

Both events are tragic. That is true whenever lives are lost. The divide that quickly erupted once again into my own country after these two incidents on consecutive July days seeped its way into many churches. How could Christians possibly respond? Those who spoke out against the seeming injustice of July 6 and the need for police accountability were quickly shouted down on July 7 by those who felt that policemen who were unappreciated and unfairly cast were now under assault, and it was the critics' fault. The same serious lines of division that appear in the world potentially run right down the middle of any culturally, economically, and ethnically diverse church.

It's not just issues over policing that can divide us. Church members can develop very divergent attitudes toward war and the military. In my own country, the current majority response is to support both police and military with an almost religious devotion. It has become an accepted tenet that protecting innocent human life is the greatest possible good, and so those who undertake that mission, risking their own lives at times, have become the greatest heroes. Certainly, it is not wrong to respect and support these institutions to a degree, but what should be the role of kingdom people when it comes to these enforcement forces?

I am from a military family and have profound gratitude for the sacrifices that the men and women who serve in the military and in police forces have made. That is not, however, the issue when it comes to the Christian response and participation with these forces.

My proposed position here will be easily misunderstood if we do not keep firmly in mind our calling to be people of the new creation. There are two ages at work in the world today. The present age has its weapons and approaches that it must take. And those who have entered the age to come through Christ have our own. If we forget that, we can easily come to differing conclusions from what I am about to suggest.

Kingdom Mindset

We would do well here to keep in mind that one of the primary criticisms leveled against Christians of the first three centuries, in addition to their hesitancy to participate in public offices and political matters, was that they would not join the Roman military, which served as both their police force and their armed forces. There were apparently a number of Roman soldiers who had converted to Christianity while in service. There was no option for them to simply opt out of their twenty-five-year commitment in the Roman army, but once they became Christian they were expected to request a role that would not cause them to take a life, a conviction about life that was virtually synonymous with becoming a Christian. And they got out of the Roman army as soon as they could. Those who willingly joined the military after becoming a Christian, though, were removed from fellowship within the church.

The Christians were not hostile to the military. They did not preach that failure to immediately leave the military was a sin or that the ideal state was for the nation to lay down its arms. They recognized that these were necessary functions of the nations. This was a reality of the present age. But they also were clear that this was not the realm in which Christians could function. To do so would be a complete loss of understanding of what it meant to be a citizen of the kingdom. There could be no primary national allegiance outside of the kingdom. There could be no inclusion of taking life in the life of the age to come. There could be no enemies, no hate, and no vengeance. They were a people who would overcome evil with good alone, not using the weapons of the world. Their primary role was to pray for peace, and they took that responsibility very seriously, believing it to be of great impact.

They were trying to be good citizens of their empire, but that was not their highest priority. Their greatest concern was showing the world what it will look like to live under God's reign in the renewed creation. Anything that betrays that takes us off mission.

Our allegiance must be to God and his kingdom alone. But one of the things that gets us off track the quickest is the subtle lie that protecting human life is the highest good. It is important. We should do so whenever we can. We should be prepared to do so at our own risk. But it is not the highest good. Peace that comes through the sword may preserve some lives (while taking others), but it does not point to the kingdom of God.

That's the strange dichotomy of the kingdom. Life in the present age is important, but not the most important. Christian Volf and McAnnally-Linz perfectly describe the balance that we seek. "Our biological lives are a precious gift from God, and intentionally terminating lives is an evil." But they continue, "Our biological lives are not our highest good, so death is not the greatest evil."[96]

We cannot simply throw out the mission to display and spread the kingdom of God to the world in the false pursuit of preserving biological life. It is good, but not the greatest good.

But what if everyone in an entire country became a kingdom citizen? How would that country function? Those are not simple questions, but Jesus was clear about the road of those truly following him and that it would be quite narrow and sparsely populated (Matthew 7:14), which keeps an entirely Christian citizenry a remote possibility. Many, says Jesus, will claim the name of Christ, but few will do the will of the Father (v. 21).

Can our position be to simply refuse service in military and police forces, though? We are also called to stand for justice. But this is a stand that should not be biased by our economic or racial identity or a national loyalty. To be a blessing to all is our goal. On the other hand, earthly justice is a good priority but will become an idol if we allow it to become the greatest good in our mind.

Kingdom Compassion

The kingdom is good news for all, but especially for the marginalized and oppressed. That reminds me that our greatest work for justice will be focused on the poor, the homeless, the prisoner, the refugee, and the defeated. It can be easy to draw the line of good and bad so that it separates us and the other "good" people from the "bad guys." Anyone then dealing with the "bad guys," regardless of the methods they use, becomes a hero for us. I can appreciate the work that these men and women do to bring order to the society, but that cannot blind me to working for justice and fair treatment for all. That doesn't mean we demonize those who are "keeping the peace," but we must find a balance.

In the 2010s, for example, 69 percent of professing evangelicals approved of the actions of the American CIA and their treatment of suspected terrorists in detention. I find that mind-numbingly shocking. That is a higher percentage of approval than by non-Christians. Evangelicals were also the group most likely to deny that the behavior amounted to torture.[97] If the only purpose in life for the follower of Jesus is to demonstrate and display his kingdom, what do these sentiments tell the world about the kingdom of God?

In Matthew 25, Jesus chides those who claim to follow him but fail to share samples of the kingdom with those in need. And in so doing, we are limited to the weapons of the kingdom. But what if we applied Jesus' logic to other areas? What would be our response if he said, "I was tortured, and you approved it because I was not a citizen of your country"? Or, "I was beaten by policemen, but you turned a blind eye because I was deemed a criminal"? Just because someone commits a crime does not mean that we are not to love them and work for fair and just treatment for them. That is the whole point of what Jesus says in Matthew 5:43–48.

Anyone could support their police officers and military heroes. And that's not a bad thing. But no one will naturally show love for the criminals that those police officers are arresting, or for the terrorists that those soldiers are hunting down. I am not suggesting that we stand in the way and not allow the police and military to do their jobs, but our role remains to cry out for force to be as limited and controlled as possible, justice to be applied equally for all, and treatment to be as fair and humane as it possibly can be. What we cannot do is simply label someone a "bad guy" and then write them off. We must wrestle with what it would look like to radically love even the worst sinner with God's kingdom love.

Kingdom Action

There is no call for kingdom people to utilize violence, ever. The closest thing to an argument that can be mustered is when Jesus remanded his disciples to sell their cloak and buy one sword if they didn't have one. They quickly scrambled and found two (Luke 22:38), hardly enough for twelve men to mount a defense if that was the intention. But Jesus made it clear that this was solely to fulfill the prophecy that the Messiah would be found among "the transgressors" (v. 37). When they later used one of the swords in a violent manner, Jesus rebuked them unequivocally. "Put your sword back in its place," he said, "for all who draw the sword will die by the sword" (Matthew 26:52). Jesus made clear that he could call on a vast army of angels if that were his play, but that is not what the kingdom is about. Early church leader Tertullian famously quipped that in disarming Peter, Jesus disarmed every soldier. He also asserted that it was only without the sword that the Christian can "wage war," because the Lord has abolished the sword from the arsenal of the kingdom.

Some might also point to the fact that soldiers were not called to leave their positions, for example, in their conversation with John the Baptist (Luke 3:10–14). Examples like this that come during Jesus' life and before the opening of the kingdom fall into the same realm as arguments that baptism is not necessary because the thief on the cross was not baptized, which ignores the fact that he couldn't be baptized into Jesus' death because Jesus had not yet died and been resurrected. Additionally, John tells these soldiers, "Don't extort money," but that is a poor rendering of the term he uses. The word, *diaseio,* is used only here in the entire New Testament, and it means to shake violently by intimidation or force. This term could easily, and I believe should have been, translated in its full meaning, which would have John saying something like "Do not inflict violence or intimidation on anyone."

Police and military have the authority among the nations of the present age as the governing forces to use the sword. But, again, that is not our realm. That is not our mission. That is not one of our weapons. Knowing this should radically change how we think about and engage in these areas. We must demonstrate a love for all and a desire to see justice done even for those who might be the least worthy of it. Representing what was the standard teaching of the early church, Tertullian reasons,

> But now the inquiry is made about this point, whether a believer may turn himself unto military service, and whether the military may be admitted unto the faith, even the rank and file, or each inferior grade, to whom there is no necessity for taking part in sacrifices or capital punishments. There is no agreement between the divine and the human sacrament, the standard of Christ and the standard of the devil, the camp of light and the camp of darkness. One soul cannot be due to two masters—God and Caesar. [98]

Tertullian then goes on to list several objections that critics might raise regarding all the figures from the old covenant who engaged in war. He draws a sharp line of distinction between that time and those who are now citizens of the kingdom:

> But how will a Christian man war, nay, how will he serve even in peace without a sword, which the Lord has taken away? For albeit soldiers had come unto John and had received the formula of their rule; albeit, likewise, a centurion had believed; still the Lord afterward, in disarming Peter, unbelted every soldier. No dress is lawful among us, if assigned to any unlawful action. [99]

The early Christians were accused of profiting from the work of the soldier while refusing to take part in it. They were accused of benefiting from Rome but showing no loyalty to her. They countered that by saying that it was not cowardice that kept them from such endeavors. In fact, they argued, they would make the best soldiers because they proved regularly that they were not afraid to die. They were not soldiers because it was not part of the realm of the kingdom. Tertullian writes:

> For what wars should we not be fit, not eager, even with unequal forces, we who so willingly yield ourselves to the sword, if in our religion it were not counted better to be slain to slay? [100]

He goes on to point out that because of this refusal to join in their policing and military actions, the Romans deemed the Christians as enemies, but they should be grateful for this. Because, he says, if any other group were truly opposed to the Romans as their enemies and living among them as the Christians did, they could raise insurrection and cause major problems. But the Christians did no such thing. They lived in peace and they prayed for the Romans. Thus, even though the Romans called them enemies, the more Christians there were, the fewer enemies Rome had.

Utilizing the positions of these early Christians is not so that we may establish doctrine based on their practices. Rather, we look to the examples of these disciples who were closest to the teaching of the apostles, and in some cases knew people who had learned directly from apostles. To see how they implemented and lived out the Scriptures can be very instructive as we seek to be led by the Word as well.

At this point, many Christians in the modern era might point to World War II. Isn't this a shining example of good coming through military and political might? Many innocent lives were saved. How can that be anything but good? I would never argue that it is not positive to save human lives. But if war is the only response we can think of to stop violence of that nature, I would urge us to think more deeply.

First, citing Romans 13:1–7, nations may deem it necessary to engage in war at times. This is where historic Christian arguments of just war might be quite applicable as we seek to ensure that our nations engage in just and limited war. Second, merely because it limits evil, which is the role of governing authorities, that does not necessitate that killing others or involvement in that war with the possibility of killing another is a viable option for a kingdom citizen. Third, was World War II the best option or the only option? For the nations, maybe. But the results have been complicated to say the least. Yes, millions of innocent lives were saved, but at the cost of 75–80 million lives during the war itself. And the war set in motion political events that have resulted in the deaths of countless millions more around the world.

The early church faced the constant pull to support Rome's military and wars to provide stability and peace around the world, and consistently argued that their role was as a kingdom of priests who prayed for peace, not a people that picked up the sword. They were criticized and called traitors, but they remained solid on that point for nearly 300 years.

Being the Light

[We can acknowledge the right of the governing authorities to limit evil while recognizing that this is not our role. We can respect and appreciate that role without participating in it. It would not be hypocrisy, then, to call a police officer, for example, if we were being threatened by a criminal. That is their role in the present age. But we have a kingdom agenda.]

We promote life and justice without either of those becoming exaggerated to the role of the highest good. We cannot abandon our kingdom principles in the name of preserving biological life or temporary justice. Nor can we limit justice to certain portions of the population by reducing it to throwing the bad guys in jail or bombing evil nations.

When looking to the coming of the Messiah, Isaiah described his kingdom, prophesying that "Nation will not take up sword against nation, nor will they train for war anymore" (Isaiah 2:2–4). This limitation to our proper role will not be popular among the nations, but it will be a light if we hold firm to our convictions and calling.

We should never look down upon those who have taken up these dangerous vocations. It is a monumentally difficult role. But before kingdom citizens decide to go down these paths, or continue in them, they should carefully wrestle with what our role in the world is to be and if they can reflect the light of that role while in that position. Can Christians be police officers or soldiers? I don't think it is possible to make a definitive statement and answer for all people everywhere in every situation, as much as I am tempted to do so based on my own convictions. There are even some countries where people do not have a choice but to enter the armed forces.

The question is: Could I serve in this way and remain loyal to Jesus and all that he taught? Since the fourth century, we have a record of sincere Christians who have engaged this topic, and they have not often found agreement. As with other areas of dispute, it is important for each individual and spiritual community to wrestle with kingdom values and make the decision that they feel is the most faithful, without passing judgment on others who have come to a different conclusion (although we can keep trying to lovingly convince each other of our position). But before a Christian willingly undertakes one of those vocations, I would encourage them to carefully study out the New Testament, with special emphasis on the Sermon on the Mount, to determine whether they could live by every word of Jesus in that sermon while serving in that role.

I would apply this line of thinking to any related vocation, whether it be lawyer, judge, county official, or the like. I would never presume to make a blanket statement that Christians should not be involved in those professions. I would encourage anyone considering them, though, to consider how they might engage in those fields without compromising any kingdom standards. If they cannot find a way to do that, then would I counsel them to consider engaging with society in a different field.

We haven't covered every possible topic when it comes to our engagement in the political world. We haven't even come close. Hopefully, we have sampled enough areas to demonstrate how we might think about and work through challenging complexities as God's kingdom people. There is one last aspect we will consider in the final chapter, where I will not examine another specific political topic, but rather how we engage in discourse in general.

The Chapter in Review

- We must examine what the role of the kingdom should be when it comes to enforcement forces like the military or police.

- The early Christians were consistent in their standard of not participating in the Roman military, which served as both army and police forces around the empire.

- Our role is to provide samples of the kingdom to a world that desperately needs an alternative way of living.

- Christians should promote life and justice while not exaggerating the importance or place of either one. Kingdom principles cannot be abandoned in the name of preserving life or attaining temporary justice.

The Big Idea

- ❖ Kingdom communities need to carefully consider what their relationship with the military and police forces of the nations will look like.

DISCUSSION QUESTIONS

1. Utilizing the scriptures that direct life in the kingdom, how should Christians approach the topic of using or not using violence as a weapon available to us?

2. What are some things Christian communities can do to call for justice for all in the realms of military and police enforcement?

3. What are some things that churches could do to support soldiers and police officers without participating in those roles?

Chapter 26

Coddling and Critique

As a child growing up in the 1970s and early 1980s, one of the things that I heard over and over was to never talk to strangers. Some bad things had happened to children in the 1970s that had become news around the country, and even the globe in some cases, and the reaction from society was to encourage children to never interact with someone that they did not already know. "Stranger danger" was the motto, and we embraced it.

The problem that is just now being identified is that while this seemingly avoided one problem, it created another. A whole generation of kids around my age grew up having no clue of how to engage with people that we didn't know. Where it was exposed as a real dilemma was when we were involved in a crisis in which we might need to reach out to someone for help. We did not know how to talk to strangers and didn't have any skills developed to discern who would be helpful and whom to avoid. Because we simply avoided any interaction with strangers, my entire generation became more vulnerable and easily fooled by people with nefarious intentions. It seems that encouraging us to not talk to strangers made us more susceptible to stranger danger than if we had learned how to do it and developed skills in that area to protect us from harm.

Similarly, we have found ourselves today in a culture that is unprepared and incapable of having anything resembling productive conversation when it comes to controversial issues like politics. That is true in the world in general and in the church.

Most of us have grown up in a culture that has pounded into our heads the idea that it is impolite to talk about religion or politics. So, being the good-mannered guys and gals that we are, we have dutifully avoided such talk, with the result that we have no idea how to engage in conversation about difficult and complex issues about which we might have very different perspectives and views.

And then came social media. In the last ten years the universe of social media has completely revolutionized the world. Nearly 3 billion worldwide now utilize social media regularly, and that number is es-timated to go over 3.1 billion by 2021. Social media adds a whole other element into the mix, because now people can say whatever is on their mind with the illusion of anonymity. This has developed what can be called internet courage, whereby people are quite bold and even cruel online because they have no fear of direct confrontation, so they say things online that they would never say to someone's face. A genera-tion of people who have no skills in difficult political discourse have suddenly been thrown into the middle of the Pacific Ocean with no boat in sight.

Then we need to factor in how fragmented a world we are. The di-visions between us are exacerbated by the modern era of customized newsfeeds and information sources that cater to specific worldviews. This results in many of us existing in an echo chamber of ideas where our beliefs are constantly touted as correct while other perspectives are caricatured and then knocked down as ridiculous or dangerous. We hear constant criticism of the other side and nothing but praise for our own ideologies without ever really interacting with the fleshed-out and authentic vantage point of opposing views. Because of this sheltered fantasy, more and more people are increasingly sensitive to any real critique or opposition of their own beliefs and have been rendered incapable of having productive dialogue in which their po-sitions are seriously examined or challenged.

Finally, there has been a dramatic shift in world culture related to what causes offense, which has become a factor in our inability to have productive discourse. When I was a young man, the primary de-termining factor in offending another person was the intent of the speaker. If I said something that caused you to feel offended or angry, my response might be, "Oh, that's not what I intended. What I meant to communicate was..." And that would be the end of it. If my intent was good, then the impact that those words or actions had was largely rendered meaningless. This is no longer the case. Now it is impact that determines the level of offense. If I say or do something that hurts or offends another person, the important element is how they felt about it and the impact it had on them. I can counter with what my intent was until I am blue in the face. It doesn't matter. My intent is irrele-vant. That is a big shift.

Take a culture that has not learned how to have difficult

conversations and interactions with opposing views. Add in a cup of universal access through social media, two scoops of the echo chamber, a teaspoon of hypersensitivity to other perspectives, and a gallon of change in what causes offense, and you have a world rife with poor and unproductive interactions.

Political discourse in our world today is broken. We demonize those who think differently from us and are virtually unable to communicate with others in a rational and productive manner. And when others do listen to us, unless they immediately "repent" and come to see things as we do, we cry out that we were never listened to and that they refused to hear our side of things. So we retreat back to our echo chambers of customization where everyone agrees with us and the news we hear always affirms our suspicions, and we become increasingly incapable of understanding how a rational human being could ever hold such beliefs as do those maniacs on the other side.

How might we approach dialogue and discourse in a way that will benefit the kingdom rather than distracting from it, tearing it down in the eyes of the world, or virtually ignoring it?

Finding Balance

One of the theories that is growing in popularity to explain the rise of politicians like Donald Trump in the United States and Boris Johnson in the UK is that it is part of a backlash against political correctness. Political correctness is the ideology that people should avoid expressions or actions that insult groups of people who are socially discriminated against or disadvantaged in some way. That doesn't sound bad, but in the eyes of many it has been carried to extreme levels of ridiculousness where it becomes almost impossible to say anything without offending someone. So the backlash begins, and those who will say almost anything and speak their mind without worry of the potential consequences are hailed as heroes by some.

Should Christians embrace political correctness? It depends on what we mean by that. I think that we absolutely should show respect to all people and honor the dignity of each person. Being empathetic toward other people is not something that Christians should have a hard time doing. That should become our default. Kingdom communities should have the expectation that we speak kindly and gracefully about everyone, especially those who might consider themselves our enemies. This includes those whose lifestyles we may not agree with or embrace, those with whom we disagree politically, and even famous people. None of them are outside the parameters of people we are called to show love to (Matthew 5:43–48).

Antifragile

There is a balance to that, however. In their book, *The Coddling of the American Mind*, Greg Lukianoff and Jonathan Haidt suggest that there are three bad ideas currently being embraced in Western culture (and quickly spreading to other cultures as well) that fuel extreme versions of political correctness and make dialoguing with those who think and believe differently than we do an almost impossible endeavor these days.[101]

The first bad idea, say Lukianoff and Haidt, is that what doesn't kill you makes you weaker. We have become a culture obsessed with safety and have accepted the untruth that people, especially young people, must be protected at every turn, both in their physical environment and in their psychological environment. Thus, anything that might challenge them or disagree with them has come to be viewed as unsafe and an act of violence, even if it is just words of disagreement.

Citing the work of Nassim Nicholas Taleb, they point out that some things are fragile and break easily and other things are resilient in that they can withstand trauma and are not easily broken. Children are antifragile, which means that they are like an immune system or a muscle, which requires "stressors and challenges in order to learn, adapt, and grow."[102] When deprived of stressors, antifragile systems will become weaker.

The second bad idea is that we should always trust our feelings. Feelings may be quite compelling, say Lukianoff and Haidt, but they are often unreliable and distort reality, which deprives us of insight and can damage relationships. We live in a culture that idolizes the self and exalts the idea of being true to yourself. This, of course, is the exact opposite of how God designed us, which is why one of the central tenets of Jesus' teaching was to deny self. Trusting completely in self and our feelings leaves us in a reactive state and largely unwilling to investigate what is true.

Following our feelings induces us to overgeneralize and label others, both of which make it difficult to understand other perspectives and have productive conversations with others, let alone to find compromise. It is this exaltation of emotion that has led to the world of microaggressions, because we start with our feelings and justify those feelings by concluding that someone has acted aggressively toward them. This is often fueled by assuming the worst about others right off the bat and reading their actions as negatively as possible. This will make them feel further marginalized, oppressed, or assaulted and make discourse nearly impossible.

The third bad idea, according to *The Coddling of the American Mind*, is that life is a battle between good people and evil people. It is here that judging others on the impact of their actions and refusing to consider their intent deprives us of the opportunity to show charity or empathy toward an offender and paints them into the bichromatic world of good and evil where you are either with me or against me, friend or foe. In that world, there are often only two options, victim and oppressor, and everyone is placed into one category or the other. The authors point out that part of the genius of Dr. Martin Luther King Jr. was the ability to find commonalities and shared morals across the divide and, rather than demonizing their opposition, King and his adherents humanized them and consistently and relentlessly appealed to their humanity. Rather than painting them as evil, they reasoned with them.

Cancel Culture

When we put these three bad ideas together we are left with a call-out-and-cancel culture where anything can put us in the crosshairs of being publicly shamed if we say or do something that makes someone else feel the slightest bit uncomfortable. We are shamed, shouted down, and removed from whatever job, role, or position we might hold that would allow us to continue to air our opinions that others find disagreeable. These are not healthy trends.

But what can Christians do about it? The road is not easy. When we mix partisan political fervor into the church community with the creep of the call-out-and-cancel culture, it makes it nearly impossible to be prophetic, not just in the world, but in our own church. Ministers must walk on eggshells, knowing that if they critique the actions of a politician or party, they risk being eviscerated by some within their own church community. They may very well have a valid kingdom critique in that situation and regularly critique all spectrums of political thought when they act unjustly or in a manner that is not in line with God's kingdom, but political idolatries within the body of Christ will cause their words to be perceived as biased, political, evil, and worthy of being silenced. And in my experience, both conservative and liberal-minded Christians are equally guilty of this type of behavior.

We must plot our course in a culture that is extremely sensitive to any perceived criticism. Those are difficult waters to navigate for a people called to be an alternative and a prophetic voice.

Kingdom Strategies for Communication in a Fragile World

It is not easy to effectively communicate in the world in which we live. The challenge for Christians is that we want to have a presence across the spectrum, so we cannot just preach to the choir, so to speak. We will have to engage at times with those who might not be immediately friendly to our message. I will offer six strategies that I believe will help us navigate these choppy waters.

First is that we must be prophetic. This means being a true alternative to the world's ideologies. The kingdom agenda may occasionally overlap with those of the world, especially in pointing out problems or oppression, but those overlaps will be infrequent and our response to them will rarely, if ever, look like the world's. That is, if it is a truly kingdom response. If our solutions look very much like a political party that one can find in the world, then what is the point of the kingdom of God? The prophetic community must remain committed to God's will on earth as though we were in heaven. That will call us constantly to offer people a new choice and a new way, but it will be sacrificial and often make little sense from an earthly perspective.

Being truly prophetic demands that we don't ally our passions with the politics of the world because it would rob us of the ability to critique systems that don't offer the opportunities and solutions that God's kingdom does. When we yoke ourselves with one of the philosophies of the present age, we lose the ability to distinguish ourselves from the world, and the prophetic voice is silenced as we are shouted down by those within our own ranks who accuse us of being what they actually are, which is partisan and beholden to the weapons of the world.

Second, we must be empathetic. Empathy is the ability to share in and understand the feelings of others. A prophetic spirit without empathy quickly becomes judgmentalism. Being judgmental is ugly and does not advance the kingdom. Yes, it might be easy to look down on someone for swearing in public or smoking, for having the wrong perspective on what is best for our society when it comes to economics or healthcare, or for having an abortion or engaging in homosexuality. Some things we look down upon are just behaviors that we don't prefer. Some are legitimately destructive sin.

But Jesus never looked down on people. He loved them. When he confronted the Samaritan woman at the well (John 4), he first talked with her about her needs and showed empathy before revealing truth to her. He also criticized those who jumped to looking down on others without first being painfully aware of their own failings (Luke 18:9–14; Matthew 7:3–6). There is great fruit for the Christian in first considering why someone might be doing what they are doing and then how we can address their need with love while reserving judgment. Not judging (Matthew 7:1) doesn't mean that we have no discernment about what is right and wrong for those who will follow Jesus. It means that we focus both ourselves and others on Jesus rather than on judging their behavior. When we experience and embrace the love and kingship of Jesus, those behaviors will lose their appeal.

Third, we must remain kingdom focused. That means that we orient our solutions and positions toward bringing the life of the age to come. We may offer samples of that life and show how it applies to the present age, but bringing complete justice and peace to the present age can never be our goal. Political issues will seem far more complicated and puzzling for kingdom people if we take our eyes off the coming age and settle for a good life in the present age.

This will greatly influence how we interact and speak with others. I once had a wonderful friend who was trying to teach his ministry about living as people of the coming age, but he quickly grew frustrated as they failed to grasp the depth of what he was teaching and continued to embrace present-age living. He called me for advice and expressed that some in his ministry had commented on his state of frustration. What I talked to him about was the utter impossibility of calling people to the transcendent peace and love of the kingdom without modeling it himself. By allowing himself to grow frustrated with their slowness, he was no longer taking hold of the eternal life himself. Our speech and actions should always be aimed at reflecting the light of the kingdom.

Fourth, we must show loving hospitality. Hospitality in the biblical sense is living with an open hand. It is sharing our resources, homes, and lives with strangers, especially those in need. Hospitality is not just an action, it is a state of mind. When we approach the world with a heart focused on being hospitable and generous in everything, we will stand out as salt and light to them. Too often we approach the world as a scolding and disapproving parent rather than a loving, hospitable host.

Fifth, we must model antifragility. Antifragile systems need stress and opposition to reach their full potential. They are not broken easily but get stronger as they are put in hostile environments. Yet some Christians seem to be convinced that the opposite is true. Far too many of us don't want the stress or discomfort of difficult conversations on politics, social issues, or race. We don't want to be around sinners or sin. We want to remove our children from any potential exposure to the world and its way of thinking.

There certainly are limitations and boundaries, and we must be wise about that, but kingdom people must lead the way in being willing to wade into difficult situations. Jesus was constantly criticized for being around the sinners and less desirable people. Surely, he must have heard a few inappropriate words or attitudes, and he ran the risk of others thinking he approved of sinful behavior. Jesus was decidedly antifragile, and so must we be. We must demonstrate grace with those who live and think differently, patience with those who mock, criticize, or wish to argue, and love to those who curse us and hate us. When we model fragility and want to get rid of everything we don't like, we do not show the world the kingdom. But by modeling antifragility, those who need it so desperately will be able to catch a glimpse of the strength of the indomitable kingdom.

Sixth, we must speak carefully. "Be wise," warned Paul, "in the way you act toward outsiders; make the most of every opportunity. Let your conversation be always full of grace, seasoned with salt, so that you may know how to answer everyone" (Colossians 4:5–6). Take time to think before you act or speak, whether it be in person or online. We can easily break Paul's advice here into five separate principles that serve as guidelines for any spoken or written conversation:

1. Be wise toward outsiders.
2. Make the most of every interaction.
3. Be graceful in your words.
4. Demonstrate the uniqueness of the kingdom wisely.
5. Learn how to interact with others in a way that demonstrates the kingdom of God.

If you have a penchant for posting things on social media, for instance, that do not build up the kingdom of God, I suggest you type up these verses and/or the principles from above and put them near your computer screen or somewhere you will see them often.

The Backfire Effect

Usually the kingdom is best displayed through action rather than words, but there will be times when we find ourselves engaged in dialogue with others. During those times, we must be wary of thinking that we can persuade others simply by presenting facts and truth. Normally, we think that presenting someone better or more complete information will help them change their mind and see our way of thinking, but studies have shown that the opposite is more often the case. Disproving misconceptions can strengthen a person's belief in those misconceptions. This is what Tru TV's *Adam Ruins Everything*, hosted by Adam Conover, calls the backfire effect.[103]

The more we prove someone wrong through fact and argument, the more they tend to hold to their original thinking and beliefs and reject what we are sharing with them. When we try to change the minds of others, their first instinct is to feel attacked and hunker down and defend their position regardless of truth or fact. According to Conover's cohost, Emily, being proven wrong activates the same area of the brain as physical pain. She goes on to point out that when fact contradicts our belief, we tend to hide behind emotional arguments that cannot be disproved. The irony here is that I have found that both sides of the political divide in my country are inclined to accuse the other of hiding behind emotionalism while only they stick to the facts. Emotionalism is so prevalent because, as research shows, our emotions are faster than logical thought, so our brains respond to the perceived attack rather than to the new information. That means that all of us are prone to jumping to emotions before reason.

It is difficult for us to separate fact from our own biased beliefs. It is important in respectful dialogue to calmly and humbly repeat facts several times so that they have time to sink in. Providing people with an alternative narrative, according Conover's expert guest, Dr. Stephan Lewandowsky, Professor of Cognitive Science, is more effective than simply telling somebody that what they believe is not true. Finding common ground before launching into reorienting truth is also an invaluable and effective strategy.

Fake News

A book about politics written in 2020 would not be complete without a mention of the phenomenon of fake news. A few years ago, the phrase was unheard of, but today it represents one of the most significant developments in the global community in the last one hundred years or more. Fake news is now everywhere. It has become a cottage industry. Not a day goes by that I can't go on social media and see that one of my friends has posted a news story that takes just one or two clicks to fact check and prove to be a fake story.

When I refer to fake news, I am not referring to stories whose conclusions we may not like, or whose author we feel has a political bias hostile to our own bias. Fake news and bias are different animals. I refer to the intentional creation of news that is not rooted in fact and is deliberately misleading or outright untrue.

A recent Pew study suggests an alarming response to fake news. The more people recognize it as a reality, the more they limit their news sources to ones they like, which tends to drive them toward more designer and polarizing sources, driving a wider gap between groups and causing people to consume less information overall and even reduce social relationships.[104]

Jesus says, as he sends his disciples out like sheep among the wolves, that we should be as "shrewd as snakes and as innocent as doves" (Matthew 10:16). Simply put, be on your guard. Reserve the moniker "fake news" for things that really are false rather than just slants or takes that you don't agree with or don't like. Don't fall for politicians who decry anything that is remotely critical of them as fake news. And don't post things without fact-checking them through credible fact-checking sources. Here are eight websites that function as fact-checking outposts:

1. Mediabiasfactcheck.com
2. Snopes.com
3. Politifact.com
4. Factcheck.org
5. Truthorfiction.com
6. Leadstories.com
7. Hoax-slayer.com
8. Fullfact.org

Social Media

There is a lot of good that can be done through social media. But there is also a lot of damage that can be done with a careless comment or post. When it comes to politics and disciples, social media is fraught with temptations and dangers. In Colossians 4:5, Paul urges, "Be wise in the way you act toward outsiders." We often forget that every conversation we have on social media is like standing in front of a picture window that the whole world can look into.

Disciples of Jesus should be very wary of having political conversations and posting on politics at all. Have these conversations offline, where we have to look one another in the eye. There is just a different dynamic that kicks in when we are posting online. We get internet courage and post things that we would be far less likely to say to a person's face. Jesus spoke with the Pharisees and teachers of the law face to face. Paul challenged Peter in person. Having these discussions in person is far more likely to bring us together than arguing with another disciple about politics for the world to see will ever have.

A Final Thought

In the church, we are divided by political beliefs and opinions, and because we are equally unable to carry on conversations, we often settle on a "don't ask, don't tell" policy, which means the best we can hope for is that everyone keeps their political opinions to themselves. But this will only work in churches that are not diverse, something a true reflection of the gospel will not afford, or if we are shallow in our connections and relationships. This is a problem.

I recently watched a short video advertising a video course on 1 Corinthians from New Testament scholar and prolific writer, N.T. Wright. He said that he is asked frequently what the Apostle Paul might say to the church today. Wright says that, in his mind, the answer is unquestionably clear. Paul's biggest shock, he says, wouldn't just be that we are disunited, but that we don't care that we are disunited. He refers to the current state of much of Christianity as a collusion with radical disunity. I can't disagree. We have shrunk the kingdom down to bite size and have missed the immensity of what it demands of us and calls us to. If we truly gave our full allegiance to Jesus and his kingdom, I believe firmly that the political gaps between believers would shrink down to very manageable distances that could be worked through and appreciated. But without that, we remain hopelessly far apart.

We have a calling to be a light to the world and a city on a hill. Let us not be caught up by the divisions of the world. As Paul reminds us in Galatians 6:15–16, the categories and divisions of the world don't mean anything. "What counts is the new creation. Peace and mercy to all who follow this rule."

The Chapter in Review

- Due to factors of not learning how to engage in controversial discourse, the explosion of social media, customized news and information, oversensitivity to other perspectives, and other shifts, the world is not adept at dialogue with those with opposing viewpoints.

- As kingdom people, we must learn how to interact well with those who think and believe differently from us.

- Christians need to be kind and empathetic without giving in to some of the excesses of political correctness.

- Humans are antifragile, which means that we must be stressed and challenged in order to grow.

- We must be a prophetic community.

- We must be an empathetic community.

- We must remain a kingdom-focused community.

- We must be a community of loving hospitality.

- We must be an antifragile community.

- We must be a community that speaks carefully.

- Christians need to be aware of the backfire effect and learn how to navigate through that to help people come to understand and embrace truth that is new to them.

- Kingdom people must be aware of and not become victims or pawns of the fake news phenomenon.

The Big Idea

❖ We must learn how to navigate a world that is full of dangers and obstacles in communication.

DISCUSSION QUESTIONS

1. How does understanding that humans are antifragile help us as Christians to be better prepared for our role in the world?

2. How do we find a balance between being prophetic and empathetic?

3. What is your biggest takeaway from this book

Epilogue

COVID-19 in the United States and the Kingdom

Upon completing any book there is a period between the author saving the file and closing their computer, so to speak, and the general audience reading the finished work. It frequently spans several months as the manuscript goes through the necessary process of finalization. Often, feedback is sought from experts and knowledgeable people who can confirm that what the author has written is valid or push back on a few points, causing rewrites, clarifications, and tightening up of ideas and arguments. When that stage is finished, the manuscript goes off for proofreading, fact-checking, and editing. This is a monumentally vital task, as any author will tell you that a good book is just a bad book that has been well edited. After that comes the work of laying out the book, designing a cover, and many other odds and ends before it is ready for publishing and eventual release.

I have talked to many other authors about this period to find out if it is as relieving and simultaneously torturous for them as it is for me. For most it is, I'm happy to report. Or should I be sad to report that? Either way, it is a unique time. I find myself relieved that after two years of reading, research, planning, and writing (in the case of this book), I am finally done. I can relax.

But then the torture starts. Did I add that thought somewhere or did I forget? Did I say that well enough? Should I have been sharper on that point? Should I have been softer? Then comes the slow trickle of new ideas, new thoughts, new ways of explaining things that come after I send the manuscript off. Should I stop the proofreading and add this in? Oh, I wish I had made that point. It can become maddening if you let it.

I have become more proficient with each passing book at managing that voice. When I'm done, I'm done, and I try to leave it at that. I haven't always succeeded, but that is the goal.

The Pandemic Arrives and Divides

I finished this book in the opening days of March 2020. Just a few days after that, COVID-19 hit the United States. Suddenly, we were following shelter-in-place guidelines and trying to adjust to a whole new reality. As the world tries to react to an event that is unprecedented in our lifetime, our unity, along with many other aspects of our society, has been strained.

The question that has peppered my mind for the last several weeks is this: is this an important enough event that I would be neglectful to not at least say something about it in a book that will be released while we are still dealing with this pandemic globally? My first thought was that this is a public health issue, and while we have touched on such matters in this book, that is certainly not its focus, nor is it my expertise. But then the ugly monster of politics reared its head in the midst of the response to the pandemic, and it has reached a point where I feel that I need to address it, at least briefly.

For the first few days it seemed as though this might bring us together. The whole world had a common enemy, this novel coronavirus, and like the humans in all the alien movies in which the world is threatened by an intergalactic foe and joins forces to defeat them as a united people, this might prove to be our time to find that we have much more in common than what our differences are.

But that illusion was soon shattered, in the United States at least. Some countries have been able to put aside their differences and unite against this threat to public health. But my country quickly divided politically, along the same general lines that seem to separate us on most things these days. Within weeks, the lines had been drawn. There are always exceptions, of course, but as an archetype, the liberal portion of the country claims that the president acted too slowly and that conservatives were too hesitant to lock down the country and too quick to dial back social distancing and other preventive measures once they were in place.

Many on the conservative side of the political aisle have railed against the impingement on their freedoms, and large protests have even been staged against such measures. Some have even claimed that the virus is a plot by world governments to increase their power and control over the masses. Many conservatives claim that media hysteria has hyped this virus into a much bigger thing than it is and that most of the preventive steps are an overreach and unnecessary. Additionally, social distancing and shutting down the economy, they argue, could have far-reaching and cataclysmic effects on the national and world economy, which could usher in a global depression that sets off a global pandemic of starvation and poverty that could potentially kill far more people than the virus itself.

At the other end of the spectrum, the liberal position has come to assert that this virus is extremely dangerous, especially to the most vulnerable portions of our society, like the elderly and those with pre-existing conditions that weaken their immune or respiratory system. The weak must be protected, and anything other than fully accepting social distancing and all other safety measures is horrific, selfish, and endangering the lives of others. The conservatives, claim the liberals, care more about profit and the economy than they do about people's lives. They believe that the so-called "pro-life" people are being exposed as nothing of the sort. No one likes social distancing and shutting down the economy, concedes the liberal position, but nothing takes precedence over human life and safety.

And so, the lines have been drawn and now even a global viral pandemic has become a divisive political issue.

Differing Values

As with this book in general, my goal is not to wade into this debate and pick a side or expose which group is right and which is wrong. I am not an expert on zoonotic viruses and how they are transmitted from the original animal host to humans. I am not an epidemiologist or a pandemic specialist. I don't know the best ways for the population to respond to such a threat. Chances are, you are not one of those things either. That right there should give us pause about becoming too dogmatic on the issue. I'm amazed at how quickly we can become convinced and unbending about an opinion when the truth is that we don't know the science behind things and are simply trusting what someone else, who may or may not have expertise themselves, says.

My concern is that, once again, I see the political divides of our society inserting themselves into an issue and dividing our nation, and then that same dynamic being played out in God's kingdom. Some disciples are very anxious about this virus and the impact that it could have on the health of others. They embrace the necessity of social distancing and wholly support the politicians and scientists who are championing it. They have given full throat to their criticism of politicians and others who remain skeptical or think that these measures are doing more harm than good. Other Christians have embraced a more conservative perspective and are beginning to voice their distaste for the measures. They violate our freedoms as American citizens and are unjust. Each person has the right to decide for themselves what they can or will not do, and the government should not be limiting those rights.

I have already seen intense clashes over this between followers of Jesus, and it will likely worsen when restrictions ease or become voluntary and the divide becomes more obvious and visible.

The rhetoric between these two worldviews has reached a sharp tone, and I fear that it could become quite ugly in the not-too-distant future as I write this in April 2020. Each side thinks the other is unreasonable, irrational, and monstrous, and there is little headway to be made in discussions because conservatives think liberals are fascist tyrants who want to take away their freedom and destroy the country, and liberals think conservatives are uncaring maniacs who value profits over life and would happily risk the lives of other people if it meant another dollar in their pocket. Each side has demonized the other in a way that tends to rally their supporters against the enemy.

How can any common ground be found in a debate in which the positions seem so irreconcilable?

There does not appear to be a high percentage of either side that is seeking compromise. Does that mean that the church will be in danger of these same cracks of division appearing in our foundations? I think the first step forward is for Christians to understand the rationale behind each position and not simply dismiss either one as stupid, uncaring, or inexplicable.

From the conservative perspective, values like freedom, autonomy, self-determination, and self-responsibility are of the highest order. They are more important than life. These are people who have seen the evils that can result when governmental power becomes unchecked and there is no force of the public left to stop its absolute authority. For the good of everyone, they believe they must stand up against tyranny when it first encroaches and keep it at bay, or the results could be devastating for the world. Most folks in that camp would be willing to risk their lives for freedom. They have come to believe that it is the greatest virtue both in the world and as a Christian and that they must act for their own liberty and that of others. They value life a great deal, but not more than liberty for all, because without freedom, the right to life will quickly vanish. And they put their money where their mouth is by being willing to sacrifice their own life and liberty for the freedom of all people.

From the liberal perspective, values like safety, survival, and equality are of the highest order. Nothing is more important than safety. Liberals value rights and freedom, but not above survival and preserving life for those who have been born. Freedom is important and wonderful, but what is the point if you don't have your health, your security, and your life itself? Those who favor this worldview see it as an absolute Christian value and cannot fathom that anyone would place anything above life. If put in a difficult spot, they will sacrifice certain freedoms for safety and security. They believe that no one should have an advantage over others, so the most vulnerable must not be put at risk at any cost. And they put their money where their mouth is by being willing to give up their own rights, comfort, and freedoms for the survival of all people.

I admit that when we make broad sketches like those above it will not apply or perfectly describe everyone, but I do think that they capture the two most prevalent worldviews that are currently pitted against one another, at least in my country.

It is easy to see why a person holding the other position is seen as such an enemy. They are willing to give up the greatest value of my group, and that is perceived as nothing less than an attack on everything that is good and right in the world. How could they be anything but a monster? Each side will see the rationality of their own position and will either not consider that the other side has a valid concern or color them as terrible people for choosing one value over the other.

Of course, not everyone falls into these two extremes. Many find themselves somewhere along the spectrum and leaning one way or the other, and some will understand both perspectives and land right in the middle. But those people are often viewed negatively by people on both sides and painted as an enemy for not fully embracing their value system.

What Can a Christian Do?

How can Christians move forward in unity when a situation arises that goes right to the jugular vein of our value systems? Those who value life will feel strong affinity for one political perspective and view the other as outright sinful. Those who prize liberty will feel strong affinity for one political perspective and view the other as opposed to our God-given rights. And because the other position is so obviously wrong and sinful, people feel justified in giving full vent on social media and anywhere else to expose such injustice and criticize everything about that position and its proponents.

As with the other positions that I have attempted to consider in this book, the key is to start with a kingdom perspective. God values life, but biological life is not the greatest good for the citizen of the kingdom. God values freedom, but it is not the greatest good for the citizen of the kingdom. God values loving others and putting their benefit above our own, but that is difficult to do when there are competing values at play. For instance, we might put all our energy into social distancing because we value life above the economy, but what happens if that leads to a global depression that causes millions upon millions to die of starvation?

There is simply no easy answer or position to take here. I don't believe there is a clear-cut path for the Christian community. We must do the best we can to find the balance between caring for others, preserving life, being willing to sacrifice, not causing worse damage down the road, and so much more. What does it even look like to love others in this situation? On a grand scale, it is not as clear as we might like.

For God's people there will be times when we don't really know what loving others looks like, but we must try to love anyway. But unity among God's people is so important that Jesus spent a large portion of his last night in the flesh praying for it (John 17).

Before we can even begin to cut our way through such a complicated bramble, we must be unified with our own brothers and sisters. We need to start by recognizing that justice and life are wonderful gifts that we can and should pursue, but they are only temporary and cannot become the greatest good in our minds. We cannot value them at the expense of unity and love.

And it carries beyond just our relationships within the body of Christ. If I become so passionate about issues of temporary justice, convincing myself that this is the only way that a godly and rational person could possibly view this issue, and then free myself to unload on those with differing views, I may very well be cutting my field of evangelism in half. We become so vocal in our passions and criticisms of others that we show no love, no concern, and no grace, and we also leave ourselves with no chance of bringing that person to the kingdom of God because we have made them our enemy.

The Danger of 'Othering'

We must avoid the temptation to consign people to an "other" category where we can safely label them, dismiss them, and continue to see the world only from our own perspective.

In Luke 18:9–14 Jesus tells a parable about a pharisee and a tax collector. This story is bigger than being about two individuals. I believe Jesus intentionally uses the labels that people in the first century would have used to categorize these individuals into their social groups. Once I know someone's label, I know everything they are about, and I know their worth. The pharisee didn't know this tax collector from a hole in the ground. But he knows what tax collectors value, and so he knows that he is not a good person. That's all there is to it. He doesn't need to know him in order to know him.

The tax collector, however, doesn't do that. In humility, he doesn't look any farther than God. He refuses to label the other man or categorize him. He knows that he himself needs God's mercy. That is all.

And he receives God's mercy.

There is not much in the Bible about exactly how we should respond to such situations. In the third century when facing a terrible plague that was killing thousands by the day, and when most people who had the means to escape the large population centers and isolate themselves were doing so, the Christians decided to stay and take care of one another and those outside their group who were stricken with the illness. They knew that many would die in doing so, and some did. But they were more concerned with unity with one another, living like others, and loving those in need, even if it meant risking their own biological lives.

That was their response, and it was effective from the kingdom point of view. That doesn't mean that their actions give us a clear way forward in our current situation or any other. But it does call us to view pandemics like this from a heavenly perspective rather than an earthly one.

I have no idea how deadly or dangerous the coronavirus will turn out to be. I don't think there is one right response that Christians can have. What is clear to me, however, is that the attitudes we have toward one another and our fellow humans must be kingdom-minded and earthly loving, not earthly minded.

We will face complicated situations like COVID-19 and its aftermath again. We must gain perspective and realize that it is easy to accept as our greatest values things that are important but are not the greatest value in the kingdom of God. And when the way forward isn't as simple and clear as we might like it to be, we must avoid putting others into the category of enemy or deciding that they do not need to be shown love and kindness.

When complex issues arise, we must view things not just from our own vantage point but also from the perspective of the other person. I believe this was Jesus' primary point with the parable of the rich young man in Luke 18:18–30. He challenged the young man, who wanted to know how he could find the life of the age to come, to sell everything he had and give it to the poor. There is no indication in the text that Jesus meant this call for just this individual. Matthew, Mark, and Luke all include this account, and they all seem to have thought that there was something important for followers of Jesus to hear and be challenged by.

Yet nowhere in the New Testament is this command ever given as a must for all Christians. I think what Jesus was doing was challenging the rich young man to love others by entering their situation. In giving everything he had, he would become poor and experience the world from that position. Only then would he know how to love them. That is the principle of what Jesus was teaching here and that we can and must take away. It's not that we must give all our possessions to be part of the kingdom. We must be willing to take up the position of others and love them wholeheartedly.

The kingdom of God cannot allow itself to become divided over the coronavirus or any other situation that will arise in the future. Put the kingdom first. Love others. Try to view their actions from their perspective. Only then will we be able to appreciate and love them fully and start to move forward as a unifying force in our culture rather than becoming part of the division. It will be a challenge to do that with everyone, but that is the call for those who follow Jesus.

Appendix

One important key to discerning how and when Christians should engage in political matters involves recognizing that not all issues are of equal weight. This appendix is a slightly edited version of a section that I wrote in a 2013 work of mine, C.O.R.E. Curriculum, Volume 1: *The Word of God*. In this work, I speak of classifying beliefs and teachings into three categories of descending importance. I will leave it up to believing communities to work together to determine where each of the political topics I have highlighted in this book, and other similar issues, lies on this spectrum.

In 1964 the case of *Jacobellis v. Ohio* came before the Supreme Court of the United States. The case concerned the issue of obscenity. In the ruling on that case, Supreme Court Justice Potter Stewart famously quipped that pornography was hard to define but "I know it when I see it." The truth is that there are some things that you can know and identify, but they become problematic when you seek to define them specifically or put them in a list.

Biblical doctrine is a bit like that. The fact is that not all biblical doctrines are the same; Jesus confirmed that when he criticized the Pharisees in Matthew 23. They were so zealous to follow every minute detail of the law that they tithed their spices and carefully covered their cups with mesh during meals so as not to accidentally drink in gnats, which were considered unclean according to the Law. Jesus rebuked them not for being so painstaking in their efforts, but for doing so while ignoring the more important aspects of the law such as justice, mercy, and faithfulness. "You blind guides!" he charged, "You strain out a gnat but swallow a camel" (Matthew 23:24).

Doctrine is important in our life in Christ. But there are equal and opposite errors when it comes to doctrine. On one end, some stress every point of doctrine and virtually make correct doctrine the sole test of whether you are a Christian. On the other end are those who relegate doctrine to a position of being something that need not be worried about at all. The first group stresses doctrine and pays little attention to how one lives. The second group only cares about how one lives and pays no attention to doctrine.

The truth is that both are important, as Paul stressed in 1 Timothy 4:16. But that doesn't mean that they are the same. Many times you see large, beautiful houses surrounded by a fence. What you never see is people paying more attention to the fence than the house. Have you ever seen a property where more money was spent on the fence than the house or where the fence was more ornate than the house? The fence serves the purpose of protection. It keeps the good things in and the bad things out. The fence is indispensable, but the focus of the property should always be the house. For us, that is a good picture of life and doctrine. Our life in Christ or loving others and sacrificing for them (as most clearly depicted, perhaps, in Matthew 5–7) is like that house. It should be the focus of the property. It is the jewel in the crown. But doctrine is like that fence. You can't neglect it, or the house comes to be in great danger.

But as Jesus made clear, not every doctrine is equal. There are certain core doctrines that simply must be defended. Yet we would be foolish to claim that the doctrine of the resurrection of Jesus or the nature of salvation is on an equal scale with whether instrumental music should be used in worship, for instance. As we read Scripture, we will do well to have a way to think of Scripture and doctrine so that we can stress the right things and keep doctrine in its proper role.

We must find a way to distinguish between doctrines that affect salvation, doctrines that are important but do not appear to be salvation issues, and doctrines that fall into the realm of opinion. To do so, we will consider categories that we will label "blood," "ink," and "pencil." We will simply and briefly describe each category while recognizing that we cannot try to comprehensively make a list of or thoroughly define each category. We get into trouble when we try to make comprehensive lists of core doctrines, but we can get to a point where we know them when we see them.

The first category of biblical doctrine is that of blood. These are the doctrines that are, so to speak, written with the blood of Christ. They cannot be changed, ignored, or discarded without changing the very nature of Christianity or the gospel message. A good example of these types of core issues comes in Ephesians 4:4–6, where Paul describes the importance of one body, one Spirit, one hope, one Lord, one faith, one baptism, and one God and Father. If you mess around with those core doctrines, you wind up with a different faith and a different gospel.

These are the types of core doctrines that Jude referred to when he urged the saints to "contend for the faith that was once for all entrusted to God's holy people" (Jude 3). When we speak specifically of false teachings and false doctrines and the need to part company over such things, it is these categories to which we should be referring. We need to watch out for these types of false doctrines so that we will not "be carried away" by error and "fall from [our] secure position" (2 Peter 3:17–18).

Examples of blood doctrines would include things like the deity and humanity of Jesus; the crucifixion and resurrection of Jesus and the resurrection of believers; the nature of salvation; baptism into Christ; the nature of the Bible; the Father as God, the Son as God, and the Spirit as God; being part of the body of Christ, and so on.

The next category of biblical doctrine is that of ink. These are important doctrines that need to be defended but that do not completely change the nature of the gospel or necessitate a break in fellowship. These are the types of issues that can become quite emotional that Paul addresses in Romans 14 and 15. As important as these issues can be, Paul still calls them "disputable matters" (Romans 14:1) and urges the disciples to accept one another despite these differences. He encourages them to strive for unity without ever telling them that they must come to agreement in every area.

Three things are important to note when it comes to ink issues. First, there is the tendency to elevate these matters and treat them as if they were blood issues. It is true that many of these issues accompany blood issues and so, in our minds, they go together, but that is not always the case. For instance, we might not agree with certain tenets of predestination or Calvinist teaching, but that does not automatically make these salvation issues. Quite often, though, these teachings do accompany false teachings on salvation, so they become associated in our minds. We must be careful, then, to focus on the important issues and not elevate ink issues into the blood category.

The second is that if not watched carefully, ink issues can become blood issues. One example of this was the respect shown for martyrs in the early church. This quickly turned into an ink issue where some engaged in special treatment of these martyrs, such as eating special meals at their graves, kissing their bones, and burying them under altars. This wasn't guarded against, however, and it soon turned into full-blown veneration of the saints, and eventually Christians were praying to saints and appealing to them to mediate to God on their behalf. What was once an ink issue ballooned into a blood issue, so we must be careful with these issues.

The third is that we must avoid the temptation to say, "These aren't blood issues, so I can go ahead and do whatever I want, and no one had better tell me otherwise." This is not the spirit behind Romans 14 and 15, where Paul calls believers to be willing to sacrifice their rights to put the interests of one another first. We must be willing to seek unity by emphasizing love for others over our own freedoms and rights, which will demand that we accept convictions that differ from our own.

The final category of biblical doctrine is that of pencil. These are areas of complete opinion, but that does not mean that we have been given a blank check to do whatever we wish. These opinions come in areas where the Bible is not completely clear, but we should still seek to be guided by scriptural principles (we just have to be aware that Scripture confirms that we will have different opinions and convictions in these disputable matters, and we must respect and accept that). These issues include getting tattoos, musical preferences in worship, drinking alcohol in moderate amounts, going to movies, what time of day to have a quiet time, and many more.

The danger in this category is like that in the ink category. We must be careful not to expand these issues into ink or even blood issues and get into fights or even break fellowship over these matters. It is vital to strike a careful balance between defending the faith and loving others, never forgetting that as Christians we are called to love all people, even our enemies or those who disagree with us.

Finally, we must say that the real challenge is to apply biblical and godly discernment in determining what category an issue belongs in. This will be the biggest and most important challenge as we read and study the Bible.

Bibliography

Beckwith, Francis J. 2010. *Politics for Christians: Statecraft as Soulcraft.* Downers Grove, IL: InterVarsity Press.

Block, Peter, Brueggemann, Walter and McKnight, John. 2016. *An Other Kingdom: Departing the Consumer Culture.* Hoboken, NJ: John Wiley & Sons.

Boer, Roland, and Petterson, Christina. 2014. *Idols of Nations: Biblical Myth and the Origins of Capitalism.* Minneapolis, MN: Fortress Press.

Boesak, Allan A. 1987. *Comfort and Protest: The Apocalypse of John from a South African Perspective.* Eugene, OR: Wipf and Stock.

Boesak, Allan A. and DeYoung, Curtiss Paul. 2012. *Radical Reconciliation: Beyond Political Pietism and Christian Quietism.* Maryknoll, NY: Orbis.

Boyd, Gregory A. 2007. *The Myth of a Christian Nation: How the Quest for Political Power Is Destroying the Church.* Grand Rapids, MI: Zondervan.

Brueggemann, Walter. 2001. *The Prophetic Imagination.* Minneapolis, MN: Augsburg Fortress.

Carter, Warren. 2006. *The Roman Empire and the New Testament: An Essential Guide.* Nashville, TN. Abingdon Press.

Catherwood, Catherine. 2003. *Whose Side Is God On? Nationalism and Christianity.* Great Britain: SPCK.

Christianity Today International Study Series. 2008. *Current Issues Bible Studies: Politics.* Nashville, TN: Thomas Nelson.

Claiborne, Shane and Haw, Chris. 2008. *Jesus for President: Politics for Ordinary Radicals.* Grand Rapids, MI: Zondervan.

Forster, Greg. 2008. *The Contested Public Square: The Crisis of Christianity and Politics.* Downers Grove, IL: InterVarsity Press.

Giles, Keith. 2017. *Jesus Untangled: Crucifying Our Politics to Pledge Allegiance to the Lamb*. Orange, CA: Quoir.

Goldberg, Michelle. 2007. *Kingdom Coming: The Rise of Christian Nationalism*. New York, NY: W.W. Norton & Co.

Gorman, Michael J. 2011. *Reading Revelation Responsibly*. Eugene, OR: Cascade.

Grudem, Wayne. 2010. *Politics According to the Bible: A Comprehensive Resource for Understanding Modern Political Issues in Light of Scripture*. Grand Rapids, MI: Zondervan.

Gundry, Stanley N. and Black, Amy E., eds. 2015. *Five Views on the Church and Politics*. Grand Rapids, MI: Zondervan.

Haselby, Sam. 2015. *The Origins of American Religious Nationalism*. New York, NY: Oxford Press.

Hauerwas, Stanley and Willimon, William H. 2014. *Resident Aliens: Life in the Christian Colony* (Expanded 25th Anniversary Edition). Nashville, TN: Abingdon Press.

Howard-Brook, Wes and Gwyther, Anthony. 1999. *Unveiling Empire: Reading Revelation Then and Now*. Maryknoll, NY: Orbis Books.

Huckins, Jon, and Swigart, Jer. 2017. *Mending the Divides: Creative Love in a Conflicted World*. Downers Grove, IL: InterVarsity Press.

Hughes, Richard T. 2009. *Christian America and the Kingdom of God*. Urbana and Chicago, IL: University of Illinois Press.

Hughes, Richard T. 2018. *Myths America Lives By: White Supremacy and the Stories That Give Us Meaning*. Urbana, Chicago, and Springfield, IL: University of Illinois Press.

Hurtado, Larry W. 2016. *Why on Earth Did Anyone Become a Christian in the First Three Centuries?* Milwaukee, WI: Marquette Press.

Jones, Tom A. and Brown, Steve D. 2010. *The Kingdom of God, Vol. 1: The Future Breaks In*. Spring Hill, TN: DPI.

Jones, Tom A. and Brown, Steve D. 2011. *The Kingdom of God, Vol. 2: The Sermon and the Life.* Spring Hill, TN: DPI.

Keesmaat, Sylvia C., Walsh, Brian J. 2019. *Romans Disarmed: Resisting Empire/Demanding Justice.* Grand Rapids, MI: Brazos Press.

Kenmeny, P.C. 2007. *Church, State and Public Justice: Five Views.* Downers Grove, IL: InterVarsity Press.

Kinnaman, David and Matlock, Mark. 2019. *Faith for Exiles: 5 Ways for a New Generation to Follow Jesus in Digital Babylon.* Grand Rapids, MI: Baker.

Koester, Craig R. "Revelation's Visionary Challenge to Ordinary Empire." 2009. *Faculty Publications.* 10. http://digitalcommons.lutheransem.edu/faculty_articles/10.

Koyzis, David T. 2019, 2nd ed. *Political Visions & Illusions: A Survey and Christian Critique of Contemporary Ideologies.* Downers Grove, IL: InterVarsity Press.

Kraybill, Nelson J. 2010. *Apocalypse and Allegiance: Worship, Politics, and Devotion in the Book of Revelation.* Grand Rapids, MI: Brazos.

Kreider, Alan. 2016. *The Patient Ferment of the Early Church: The Improbable Rise of Christianity in the Roman Empire.* Grand Rapids, MI: Baker Academic.

Lukianoff, Greg and Haidt, Jonathan. 2018. *The Coddling of the American Mind: How Good Intentions and Bad Ideas Are Setting Up a Generation for Failure.* New York, NY: Penguin Press.

McKenna, George. 2007. *The Puritan Origins of American Patriotism.* New Haven, CT and London: Yale University Press.

Monsma, Steve. 2008. *Healing for a Broken World: Christian Perspectives on Public Policy.* Wheaton, IL: Crossway.

Noble, Alan. 2018. *Disruptive Witness: Speaking Truth in a Distracted Age.* Downers Grove, IL: InterVarsity Press.

Noebel, David A. 1992. *Understanding the Times: The Religious Worldviews of Our Day and the Search for Truth.* Manitou Springs, CO: Summit Ministries.

Norris, Kristopher and Speers, Sam. 2015. *Kingdom Politics: In Search of a New Political Imagination for Today's Church*. Eugene, OR: Cascade Books.

Newbigin, Leslie. 1989. *The Gospel in a Pluralist Society*. Grand Rapids, MI: Eerdmans.

Rahner, Hugo. 1992. *Church and State in Early Christianity*. San Francisco, CA: Ignatius Press.

Rynne, Terrence J. 2014. *Jesus Christ, Peacemaker: A New Theology of Peace*. Maryknoll, NY: Orbis Books.

Salter McNeil, Brenda. 2015. *Roadmap to Reconciliation: Moving Communities into Unity, Wholeness, and Justice*. Downers Grove, IL: InterVarsity Press. 2.

Sider, Ronald J. 2019. *If Jesus Is Lord: Loving Our Enemies in an Age of Violence*. Grand Rapids, MI: Baker Academic.

Sider, Ronald J. 2012. *Just Politics: A Guide for Christian Engagement*. Grand Rapids, MI: Brazos Press.

Smith, James K.A. 2017. *Awaiting the King: Reforming Public Theology*. Grand Rapids, MI: Baker Academic.

Stassen, Glen H. 2008. *Just Peacemaking: The New Paradigm for the Ethics of Peace and War*. Cleveland, OH: The Pilgrim Press.

Taylor, Charles. 2007. *A Secular Age*. Cambridge, MA and London, England: The Belknap Press of Harvard University Press.

Tisby, Jemar. 2019. *The Color of Compromise: The Truth About the American Church's Complicity in Racism*. Grand Rapids, MI: Zondervan.

Tyson, Jon, and Grizzle, Heather. 2016. *Creative Minority: Influencing Culture Through Redemptive Participation*. San Bernardino, CA: Heather Grizzle.

VanDrunen, David. 2010. *Living in God's Two Kingdoms: A Biblical Vision for Christianity and Culture*. Wheaton, IL: Crossway.

Volf, Miroslav and Croasmun, Matthew. 2019. *For the Life of the World: Theology That Makes a Difference*. Grand Rapids, MI: Brazos.

Volf, Miroslav and McAnnally-Linz, Ryan. 2016. *Public Faith in Action: How to Think Carefully, Engage Wisely, and Vote with Integrity.* Grand Rapids, MI: Brazos Press.

Wallis, Jim. 2005. *God's Politics: Why the Right Gets It Wrong and the Left Doesn't Get It.* New York, NY: Harper Collins.

Watts, Craig M. 2017. *Bowing Toward Babylon: The Nationalistic Subversion of Christian Worship in America.* Eugene, OR: Cascade.

Zahl, David. 2019. *Seculosity: How Career, Parenting, Technology, Food, Politics, and Romance Became Our New Religion and What to Do About It.* Minneapolis, MN: Fortress Press.

Zahnd, Brian. 2019. *Postcards from Babylon: The Church in American Exile.* St. Joseph, MO: Spello Press.

Notes

1. Robert Alter's acclaimed translation of the Hebrew Bible renders Genesis 1:2, "and the earth then was welter and waste and darkness over the deep and God's breath hovering over the waters."
Alter, Robert. *The Hebrew Bible, A Translation with Commentary: The Five Books of Moses*. New York: W.W. Norton, 2019.

2. Brueggemann, Walter. *The Prophetic Imagination*. Minneapolis: Fortress Press, 2001.

3. Ibid, 103.

4. In the biblical languages, "the satan" simply means "the accuser." It is not a proper name, but a description or title. The biblical texts never give the satan a personal name. Even though it is standard in English to capitalize this phrase and drop the article, giving it the appearance of a personal name, I have chosen to go with "the satan" and to resist any capitalization so as not to give more credit than is due.

5. Bercot, David. *The Kingdom That Turned the World Upside Down*. Amberson, PA: Scroll.

6. Bates, Matthew. *Salvation by Allegiance Alone*. Grand Rapids, MI: Baker Academic.

7. Ibid, 80–82.

8. Ibid, 87.

9. Ibid, 92.

10. Wright, Tom. *Matthew for Everyone: Part One*. Louisville: Westminster John Knox, 2002, 52.

11. We cannot have certainty that Tychicus was the letter reader for Philemon. We do know, however, that he carried the letter to the Colossians along with Onesimus (Colossians 4:7-9) and that Philemon lived in Colosse, so it is likely that he was indeed the disciple who brought the letter to Philemon and would have read it, having carefully practiced and rehearsed the reading with Paul and Timothy.

12. "Turn Your Eyes Upon Jesus" (originally "The Heavenly Vision") by Helen Howarth Lemel.

13. YOLO is an acronym for "You only live once."

14. Koester, Craig, R. "Revelation's Visionary Challenge to Ordinary Empire." *Union Presbyterian Seminary* January 2009, 10.

15. Koester, 5.

16. Koester, 7.

17. Kraybill, J. Nelson. *Apocalypse and Allegiance: Worship, Politics, and Devotion in the Book of Revelation.* Grand Rapids, MI: Brazos, 54.

18. Ibid, 62.

19. Gorman, Michael J. *Reading Revelation Responsibly.* Eugene, OR: Cascade Books, 2011, 155. Eugene Peterson also presents this view of Revelation 19 in *Reversed Thunder: The Revelation of John and the Praying Imagination.* New York: HarperCollins, 1991.

20. The unanimous declaration of the thirteen united State of America, ratified July 2, 1776 and publicly announced on July 4, 1776.

21. Carter, Warren. *The Roman Empire and the New Testament: An Essential Guide.* Nashville, TN: Abingdon, 16–26.

22. Ibid. 18.

23. Zahnd, Brian. *Postcards from Babylon: The Church in American Exile.* St. Joseph, MO: Spello Press, 2019, 15.

24. Kreider, Alan. *The Patient Ferment of the Early Church.* Grand Rapids, MI: Baker Academic, 2016, 9–10.

25. Martyr, Justin. The First Apology of Justin, Volume 1, Chapter 16, 169.

26. Kreider, 26.

27. Kreider, 51.

28. Kreider, 61.

29. Kreider, 60.

30. 2 Clement 13. Early Church Volume 9, 254.

31. Dictionary of Early Christian Beliefs, 545.

32. Ibid.

33. If you have not already figured it out, there has been no such discovery. I have completely fabricated these letters to make a point.

34. Ibid.

35. Ibid.

36. Ibid.

37. Ibid.

38. Giles, Keith. *Jesus Untangled: Crucifying Our Politics to Pledge Allegiance to the Lamb.* Orange, CA: Quoir, 23.

39. Watts, Craig M. *Bowing Toward Babylon: The Nationalistic Subversion of Christian Worship in America.* Eugene OR: Cascade, 2017, 5.

40. Giles, 164.

41. Watts, 19.

42. Watts, 24.

43. Mather, Victor. "A Timeline of Colin Kaepernick vs. the NFL." nytimes.com/2019/02/15. February 15, 2019. Accessed 1/5/20.

44. Watts, 50.

45. Ibid, 51.

46. McKenna, George. *The Puritan Origins of American Patriotism.* New Haven, CT and London: Yale University Press, 2007, 49.

47. Watts, 54.

48. Watts, 60.

49. Ibid, 61.

50. Zahnd, 10.

51. Giles, 86.

52. My apologies if you're not familiar with North American football and find these details confusing, but just stick with it, and my point will make sense even if you understand nothing about football.

53. Keller, Tim. "How Do Christians Fit into the Two-Party System? They Don't: The historical Christian positions on social issues don't match up with contemporary political alignments." *The New York Times* Sept. 29, 2018. www.nytimes.com, accessed 1/10/20.

54. "Politics." *Oxford Dictionary,* 2020. lexico.com/en/definition/politics.

55. Origen Against Celsus, Ante-Nicene Fathers, Vol. 4, ed. Alexander Roberts and James Donaldson. Peabody, MA: Hendrickson, 2004, 668.

56. Ibid.

57. Zahl, David. *Seculosity: How Career, Parenting, Technology, Food, Politics, and Romance Became Our New Religion and What to Do About it.* Minneapolis:

Fortress Press, 2019, 142–143.

58. For more on the impact of culture in a diverse church, see: Burns, Michael. *All Things to All People: The Power of Cultural Humility.* Spring, TX: IPI, 2019.

59. Sider, Ronald J. *Just Politics: A Guide for Christian Engagement.* Grand Rapids, MI: Brazos, 2012, 5.

60. Ibid, 16–17.

61. Monsma, Steve. *Healing for a Broken World: Christian Perspectives on Public Policy.* Wheaton, IL: Crossway, 2008, 13–18.

62. Sider, 4.

63. Hauerwas, Stanley and Willimon, William H. *Resident Aliens.* Nashville: Abingdon Press, 2014, 39.

64. Ibid, 38.

65. Ibid, 41.

66. Ibid, 40.

67. Mammon was a catchall word that referred to wealth and material possessions, but also often encapsulated the concept of greed and materialism. Mars was a Roman god of war.

68. Zahnd, 59.

69. Ibid.

70. Woodberry, Robert D. "The Missionary Roots of Liberal Democracy." *American Political Science Review* Vol. 106, No. 2, May 2012, 244–274.

71. Palpant Dilley, Andrea. "The World the Missionaries Made." *Christianity Today* January/February 2014, 39.

72. Ibid, 40.

73. Katongole, Emmanuel, and Rice, Chris. *Reconciling All Things: A Christian Vision for Justice, Peace, and Healing.* Downers Grove, IL: InterVarsity, 2008, 46.

74. Lackey, Darrell. "Christian: You Are Upset About the Wrong Things." *Progressive Christian.* www.patheos.com/blogs/unfundamentalistchristians/2017/06/christian-upset-wrong-things/. Accessed 1/30/20.

75. Hafiz, Yasmine. "11 Bizarre Church Laws That Could Send You To Jail." www.huffpost.com/entry/weird-church-laws_n_5398732. Accessed 2/1/20.

76. Volf, Miroslav and McAnnally-Linz, Ryan. *Public Faith in Action: How to Think Carefully, Engage Wisely, and Vote with Integrity*. Grand Rapids, MI: Brazos, 88.

77. Willard, Dallas. *The Divine Conspiracy*. New York: HarperCollins, 1988, 1.

78. Volf and McAnnally-Linz, 34.

79. Some may cite Paul's words in 2 Thessalonians 3:10, "The one who is unwilling to work shall not eat," as an argument that people should not be supported within the Christian community or benevolence given to the poor. This is a misuse of what Paul says here. He presumes that those in need will be supported by the church and that, as a minister, he also would have the right to access a support share, just as a widow might receive. But the ones who did receive daily support from the church were expected to serve and work in the church (see 1 Timothy 5:9–10 for an allusion to the kind of work that widows performed within the church community). If people refused to serve and minister in the church, then they would not be part of the community and would not receive support.

80. Perkins, John M, ed. *Restoring At-Risk Communities: Doing It Together and Doing It Right*. Grand Rapids, MI: Baker, 1995, 21–23.

81. Ibid, 23.

82. Manuscript evidence is clear that the current location for this passage in John 7:53-8:11 is not its original location, having first appeared in this position around the fifth century. In earlier manuscripts it does appear elsewhere in John and even in Luke. The balance of the evidence seems to point to the fact that this was an authentic account regarding Jesus' life but that the proper location among the Gospels has been lost. It is even possible that it was an independent account that became so loved that it was included along with the Gospels and eventually became confused as part of them.

83. Volf and McAnnally-Linz, 127.

84. Ibid.

85. Sedgh, Gilda, SCD, Bearak, Jonathan, PhD., and Alkema, Leontin, PhD. "Abortion incidence between 1990 and 2014: global, regional, and subregional levels and trends." www.ncbi.nlm.nih.gov. Accessed 2/6/20.

86. Giles, 109.

87. Ibid, 116.

88. Ibid.

89. Ibid, 118.

90. Amnesty International. "A Clear Scientific Consensus That the Death Penalty Does Not Deter." https://www.amnestyusa.org/a-clear-scientific-consensus-that-the-death-penalty-does-not-deter/. Accessed 2/6/20.

91. Epstein, Alex. '97% Of Climate Scientists Agree' Is 100% Wrong. Forbes. https://www.forbes.com/sites/alexepstein/2015/01/06/97-of-climate-scientists-agree-is-100-wrong/#5e2466a73f9f. Accessed 2/7/20/.

92. Linney, Gordon. "Thinking Anew—A Christian Response to Climate Change." *The Irish Times* 12/1/2018. Accessed 2/7/20.

93. Volf and McAnnally-Linz, 43.

94. Exhibit 1a, Yanez Audio Squad 151 (PDF), July 6, 2016. www.ramseycounty.us. Accessed 2/12/20.

95. "2016 Shooting of Dallas Police Officers." Wikipedia. Accessed 2/12/20.

96. Volf and McAnnally-Linz, 118.

97. Posner, Sarah. "Christians More Supportive of Torture Than Non-Religious Americans." *Religion Dispatches* December 16, 2014. https://religiondispatches.org/christians-more-supportive-of-torture-than-non-religious-americans/. Accessed 2/13/20.

98. Ante-Nicene Fathers, Volume 3, 73.

99. Ibid.

100. Ibid, 45.

101. Lukianoff, Greg, and Haidt, Jonathan. *The Coddling of the American Mind: How Good Intentions and Bad Ideas Are Setting up a Generation for Failure.* New York: Penguin Press, 2018.

102. Ibid, 23.

103. *Adam Ruins Everything,* Season 2, Episode 8, "Emily Ruins Adam." Original Air Date: 8/29/17. TruTV.

104. Graham, David A. "Some Real News About Fake News." *The Atlantic* 6/7/19. https://www.theatlantic.com/ideas/archive/2019/06/fake-news-republicans-democrats/591211/. Accessed 2/14/20.

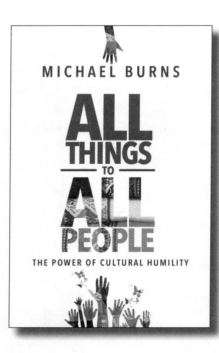
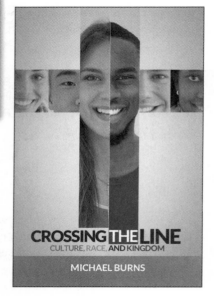

Keep up with the latest news, articles, schedule and work of the teaching ministry of Michael Burns at

www.MichaelBurnsTeachingMinistry.com

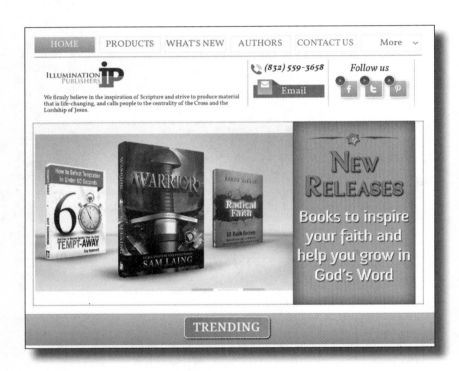

Illumination Publishers

www.ipibooks.com